PRAISE FOR *UP Is Not the O*

"This move to employee ownership of careers, coupled with the pressure to create and implement processes that provide flexible delivery options and rapid response to needs, make *Up Is Not the Only Way* a valuable tool for career development practitioners as well as HRD professionals."

Lindy Williams, Director, World Wide Career Development
American Express

"Beverly Kaye's innovative and sensitive approaches are assisting thousands of Marriott associates to plan successful careers in rapidly changing and uncertain economic and business environments. A classic, *Up Is Not the Only Way* is essential reading for influential organization and career development practitioners."

Michael Horne, Director, Organization Development
Marriott International

"Dr. Kaye's work is an essential guide to motivating employees when downsizing and delayering have reduced promotion prospects, and emphasis on team work means that people should be oriented to getting results rather than climbing the ladder."

Rosabeth Moss Kanter, author, *The Challenge of Organizational Change* and *When Giants Learn to Dance*

"Bev Kaye's book . . . is right on time and right on target for the tasks we all face now. Read it and keep it handy."

Robert J. Lee, Ph.D., President, Center for Creative Leadership

"*Up Is Not the Only Way* provides a roadmap of six viable career options that anyone can install in their career planning tool kit. These six options will work for anyone, pursuing any goal, in any profession or industry. This book is certain to become the new 'bible' in the field."

Marsha Boettger, Career Consultant, Chrysler Corporation

"Beverly Kaye's concept of career development can best be described as 'relevant.' She effectively marries individual development with organizational learning, career self-ownership with mentoring, and skills building with organizational savvy."

Tom Stafford, Director, Human Resources & Site Services
Hoechst Celanese Corporation

"This book is essential reading for managers and human resource professionals who care about helping employees succeed in this era of restructured workplaces and aging baby boomers."

Dave Jamieson, coauthor, *Managing Workforce 2000: Gaining the Diversity Advantage*

"In *Up Is Not the Only Way,* Bev Kaye has captured the fundamentals of career development in the most meaningful way for employees of the nineties. This book is a must read for individuals or companies with new or ongoing career development initiatives."

> Michael F. Werneke, Ph.D. , Manager
> Employee Resource Development, Cytec Industries Inc.

"Dr. Kaye has made a career of helping others to gain greater control of their own destiny and has done it with a combination of solid research, imagination, and a delightful touch of fun! This book is, like Bev herself, a combination of wisdom and hope."

> Warren H. Schmidt, coauthor, *A Peacock in the Land of Penguins:*
> *A Tale of Diversity and Discovery*

"Beverly Kaye was the first to come up with the concept *Up Is Not the Only Way* in the first edition of this book over a decade ago. . . . This book is right on the mark and even more relevant today than when it was first published."

> Richard L. Knowdell, author, *Building a Career Development Program*

"*Up Is Not the Only Way* is the career development practitioner's handbook of practical tools and approaches for sewing the requisite developmental norms, behaviors, and attitudes into the fabric of organization culture."

> Mike Stromes, MSHRD, Senior Consultant
> Human Resources Development, Ciba-Geigy Corporation

"Bev's ideas about developing high-potential employees are right on the mark! She applies the dynamics of individual and group, peer and mentor relationships to bolster employee learning, build self-confidence, and measure results. She guides the group to look at both sides."

> Betty Dickey, Manager, Human Resources
> Hoechst Celanese Corporation

"This book contains the perspective, the skills, and the mind-set that offers the potential to help. In fact . . . it's surround-sound help."

> Samuel Culbert, Professor
> Anderson Graduate School of Management, UCLA
> author, *Mind-Set Management*

"*Up Is Not the Only Way* will be a wonderful resource for all of us as we continue to respond to shifting organization priorities, changing technologies and the demands of 'remaining relevant' and continuing to grow into more useful and creative careers."

> Edith W. Seashore, Organization Consultant

UP
Is Not the Only Way

SECOND EDITION

UP
Is Not the Only Way

A GUIDE TO DEVELOPING WORKFORCE TALENT

SECOND EDITION

Beverly L. Kaye

Davies-Black
an imprint of Nicholas Brealey Publishing
Boston • London

Reprinted by Davies-Black, an imprint of Nicholas Brealey Publishing, in 2010:

20 Park Plaza, Suite 1115A	3-5 Spafield Street, Clerkenwell
Boston, MA 02116, USA	London, EC1R 4QB, UK
Tel: 617-523-3801	Tel: +44-(0)-207-239-0360
Fax: 617-523-3708	Fax: +44-(0)-207-239-0370

www.nicholasbrealey.com

Special discounts on bulk quantities of Davies-Black books are available to corporations, professional associations, and other organizations. For details, contact us at 888-273-2539.

14 13 12 11 10   11 10 9 8 7 6 5 4 3 2
Printed in the United States of America

Library of Congress Cataloging-in-Publication Data
Kaye, Beverly L.
   Up is not the only way : a guide to developing workforce talent / Beverly L. Kaye
       p. cm.
   Originally published : Englewood Cliffs, N.J. : Prentice Hall, c 1982.
   Includes bibliographical references and index.
   ISBN 0-89106-099-5 (cloth)   ISBN 0-89106-163-0 (paper)
   1. Personnel management.   2. Vocational guidance.
   3. Career development.   I. Title.
   HF5549.K32   1997
   658.3'124—dc21   96–40276

SECOND EDITION
First paperback printing 2001

To Lindsey
May you grow up knowing that up is not the only way . . .
but learning is!

Contents

Exercises

Cases

Foreword

Organizations are seeking their new meanings in the marketplace. They used to know who and what they were; they no longer do. The corporate, social, and political worlds have been dumped into the global blender and the switch has been thrown. We don't know where we are going, and we are moving there at an ever-increasing speed. Welcome to the excitement and anxiety, opportunity and apoplexy of life in the maelstrom of twenty-first-century organizations.

The corporate landscape is changing so quickly that no sooner do we map it than our map is out of date. And if we cannot rely on our maps, what are we to do? The same thing that explorers of the natural world did long before us: Navigate by the stars. In today's corporate world, while some of us are busy blaming our management for not following last year's map, others of us have put aside those old maps, are looking to the stars and reaching for our sextants. This involves us in quite different perspectives, other technologies, and new ways of getting around. It requires looking up into the heavens, in our case the marketplace, to see what is revealing itself, rather than down onto a map of what used to be happening. "No, that interstate doesn't go through here any-more. . . . That mountain's in the way and we don't have a map to get around it. . . ." Now what in the world does *that* have to do with career development?

I learned my organizational skills in post-World War II America. More predictable times. Times when maps and plans and policies meant something for years, not just weeks. I grew up in and around major companies that were moving toward their planned futures with a measured step and at a moderate pace. As I served those companies, I tried to serve their workers, helping them create jobs and careers that fed not just their families, but their lives. Recently I became clearer about how out of date this post-World War II perspective has become. Though not yet entirely irrelevant, it is becoming history. I am tempted to hold onto it because it is my history too; it is what I know. I am clearer about where organizations have been than where they are going. My holding onto the past has no impact on the emergence of the future—except to divert me from the reality that the future is here. I ought to be asking, What kind of a contribution will I make in this new organizational millennium?

I speak for myself, and I believe I am also speaking for career development. We grew up together, career development and I, in the corporate prosperity of the fifties, sixties, and seventies. We learned about and adapted to the organizations we were a part of. And as proud as we still are of the programs developed, the projects completed, and the people who benefited, career development and I are as out of date as a pair of polyester bell-bottoms! Holding onto our old pants and our old programs prevents us from seeing what is going on today.

Those of you who have been around career development a while: Imagine going through your bookshelves and files, pulling out and piling up everything written before 1982, and tossing it! Throwing it away today. . . . Notice your reaction to this thought; your reaction might offer clues to what you are holding onto. And what does clasping all these older notions to your chest prevent you from picking up? Hmm. . . .

It's time for career development to do a little career developing of its own. What is it we ask others to do when helping them consider their futures? Gather information? Be open to options? Create a vision? State values? All good advice for reflecting on career development's future. And that's what this book is about, career development's future in the organizations just now emerging.

After all is said and done, after all the process improvement, work redesign, quality initiatives, empowerment, and reengineering, people make the difference. They are the most mysterious and maddening and marvelous element of the organizational dynamic. The organization that can find, grow, tap, and hold these precious human resources will likely distinguish itself in the marketplace. That's an important half of the career development story. The other half is intriguing too.

Consider what kind of person you want to become. What kind of organization do you want to serve? And how will your work serve your life? That's the other half of what career development is about. Career development seeks to create a partnership in which the lives of the partners are fulfilled. "The lives of the partners. . . ." Not the job descriptions, not the mission statements, but the *lives* of the partners are fulfilled. The life of the company, the lives of its employees, the lives of suppliers, of owners, of customers, and the lives of the other communities served.

We are talking about much more than work here; we are talking about people and organizations working together for life purpose. Career development systems and programs that are narrowed to work purposes miss the point and will not succeed. To succeed, career development must reach beyond the plant gate and office parking lot to tap into the larger lives that people go home to.

Career development's potential lies in two directions: First, it can help work become positive and meaningful life experience for workers. And second, those workers can help deliver products and services valued in the marketplace. The more closely related these two directions are in the minds of the company and the people in it, the greater is the potential for synergy. The task of the career development professional is to maintain a constructive dynamic between the forces of the individual and the forces of the organization. This is usually a troublesome realm. Actually, I think it is supposed to be. Most of us have mixed feelings about being a part of an organization . . . and also about *not* being part of an organization. Career development, more consistently than any other profession, asks the organization and its members to consider what they see in and need from each other. Career development tries to broker a good marriage contract and to help all parties live up to their aspirations.

Beverly Kaye has been saying for years that individuals must take responsibility for their careers. She has protested against parental career development systems in which Big Daddy/Mommy Corporation were expected to be accountable for the futures of their "children." More of us should have listened to her earlier; that might have prepared us for the nineties, during which many of us are being put out of the house or up for adoption! These times emphasize the need for individuals to think, plan, feel, intend, intuit, and act for themselves. In the midst of all this corporate intermarriage, divorce, adoption, and confusion, it is not enough for us to continue to blame the parents. Our energy is better invested in sorting out what kind of adults we want to become and what we intend to do about getting there. This is the *big* opportunity for thoughtful, proactive people in the coming millennium.

For an organization to live and to attract people to it (customers, consultants, stockholders, contractors, communities, suppliers, partners, and employees), it had best let others know the direction it is committed to pursue. Notice that I did not say it must put together a mission, strategy, and plans. No, it must be honest about its intentions. Its intentions will hold longer than its plans, so that's where clarity is needed; organizations will navigate by their intentions. An organization needs to express this in words and ways understandable to all its supporters. Why? Not just because it's trying to be a good citizen or a corporate nice guy, but because the supporters are needed to make intentions become reality. Some of an organization's intentions have to do with the people it wants to attract, retain, and grow. What can and will it promise them? How will they be assured this will happen? And conversely, what will those people promise and assure? What will they take responsibility for doing?

The special value of this second edition is that you can look over the shoulder of one of career development's most influential consultants; you can watch Beverly Kaye apply her learning, shaping what career development is becoming. Her name is on all of our "top ten" lists of the most invested, knowledgeable, and practical people in this field. She grew up within the same organizational frameworks that I did; she has done a wonderful job of anticipating the future. She has seen career development in all its forms; she has participated in many of its experiments. Bev Kaye keeps returning to this career development work because she is invested in the lives of people and organizations. She knows that the dynamic between them is worth nurturing, worth sustaining, worth the hard work. She saw earlier than most of us that "up is not the only way"; she anticipated our needs for the eighties and nineties. And now she is anticipating what we will need for the twenty-first century. If we are smart, we will listen to her message.

Geoffrey Bellman
Seattle, Washington
April 1997

Preface

I think, no matter what I do or say, I will go down in career development history for the six words that form the title of this book. It's not bad, given other reasons one could go down in history. But I never dreamed, when I first wrote them, how they would grow in importance over the years, becoming more and more critical, and just as difficult to implement, inculcate, and live by. I often joke to my fellow practitioners that my biggest mistake was not popularizing the notion—printing mugs and tee shirts and writing a parable or two about it. Instead, the first book, as this edition, was written for the practitioner—the professional involved in supporting the implementation of a development effort inside an organization. It was a big and complex job then; it still is.

It is also interesting to me that both editions turned out, in hindsight, of course, to be unique and memorable self-development experiences. In different ways. So at least I'm learning.

The First Time Around

The first edition was the direct result of my own doctoral dissertation and the luck (where preparation *does* meet opportunity) of connecting with an editor at Prentice-Hall who was interested in and willing to support a new author. That first contract was not the development experience; the route to getting there was.

Getting there meant failing my doctoral orals three times. At UCLA, one defends his or her dissertation approach in an oral exam before an examining committee. I was so sure of myself that I brought along a tape recorder to record it for my folks! Little did I know that my committee would not let it happen so easily. My get-it-done-and-get-out approach was rejected, and I was told that the committee had spotted my "flat side." They announced that they felt I operated too much from my intuition and that I was not a good thinker or theory builder. They wanted me to address this "flaw" if I expected to leave UCLA with a doctorate!

First mistake: I said, "Don't do this to me . . . at the end of my education!" Can you imagine, I used the word *end*. Now, determined even more to show me that this was, in fact, far from the end, they asked me to look into phenomenological research, or grounded theory. I had no idea what it was—but I knew I would not like it.

I was right. It required that I build my own theory. Theories are built by looking at a phenomenon and collecting data about it. One interviewee leads you to the next, and eventually as you sit with your data, categories bubble up. When the categories hold all your data, you have a theory!

But nothing bubbled up at first. Then what bubbled didn't hang together—and I started again, and again. Finally I had an idea. I was finding the process excessively lonely. I am not a loner. So I found someone to listen to me talk about the data. Just someone to look interested, even look excited (though that was harder). Eventually, with another person to bounce ideas off of, I finally found those categories. And the categories held my data, and my committee said, by George, she's got it!

Those categories became the first edition of this book, and interestingly enough, they still ground me today. Those of you who know my recent work will see the current 5 P's (person, perspective, place, possibilities, and plan) embedded in the original language of profiling, targeting, strategizing, and so on, that form the chapters of this book. You will see that my belief is still that career development is not just an educational intervention, but instead demands an organization development or planned change approach.

I learned that as a practitioner, it is important to have a theory that guides you, one that is always being massaged, but one whose core you can depend on. To this day, my practice is built around these key ideas that now (and even then) seemed so obvious.

I also realized that my own best thinking style occurs in concert with others. My practice and my know-how have developed through the clients I have had the privilege of serving, and the colleagues with whom I have shared the pleasure and privilege of co-invention. I now move to collaborate quickly. Yes, I got smarter.

The Second Time Around

When the acquisitions editor at Davies-Black approached me with the idea, I was flattered but not very excited. The very thought of even reading this book again, after over fifteen years, was not enticing. And I was leading a hectic life. I had since become a late-in-life mom, had a consulting and a publishing practice, soccer games, Brownies, a travel schedule that took me everywhere but my own hometown, and a husband who, although very supportive, did want to see me once in a while.

But I agreed to reread the book. I found, at first glance, to my amazement, that much of it still held its ground. And the editor had asked for an update, not a total rewrite. I thought, this I can do. Then I read it again. After I signed the contract. Now I was in trouble. I found that while much of it was indeed still true, still helpful to the practitioner, it was "old hat" to me and I was doing new and different things. I saw the job as massive, and I got depressed.

This time, I didn't linger there for long. I acted on my past lessons. I found several colleagues whose opinions I trusted, who were quite experienced, but who hadn't been buried in just the study and practice of career development as I had been. We formed a learning team. Dave Logan, a consultant himself, doctoral candidate, and USC MBA professor, Sharon Jordan-Evans, a longtime consultant with a specialty in executive coaching and change management, and Thora Christiansen, also a doctoral student and instructor at USC, worked with me from start to finish. When I got frustrated with all I wanted to add (thus building a dictionary-sized book), they stopped me. When I wanted to start from scratch, they stopped me. Soon, we began to enjoy the process. We had some great philosophical debates and some good laughs about words (and companies) that had been obliterated since the first edition, and we came to consensus about what would be useful and what was, indeed, old hat.

I remunerated them (and will continue to do so) in what I like to think of as elegant currencies. Elegant currencies are those things only you can offer, that another person wants, and that are fairly easy for you to give. They are the ultimate quid pro quo, and if one is truly development-minded, these opportunities can easily be career driven and directed.

I might have started the book without them. I would never have finished the book if not for them. We hope you find it useful.

Acknowledgments

The Center for Creative Leadership (CCL), in its exquisite work on learning, suggests we gain most of our learning in three ways: from assignments, from other people, and from hardships. That message is one I truly believe in, one I teach and preach, and one that is the perfect construct for acknowledging some of the people who made the ideas in this book possible.

FROM ASSIGNMENTS

I think one of the major ways that I know what I know and do what I do, is that I have had some wonderful and tough stretch assignments in my own career. And I've learned to learn from each and every one. My client organizations have taught me the true art of listening, of being patient, of going outside the nine dots, of even doing it backwards! They've taught me that there is no one way to roll out a systemwide effort, no one way to train managers, no one way to train employees, and of course, no one way to train trainers. They've taught me that indeed internal practitioners do know as much as I do, but can't always say it, or get the attention they need to MAKE IT HEARD. So while sometimes we externals get the credit, we don't always deserve it. Internals pave the way, and lay the groundwork, and, quite often, could have said it just as well, if not better, if they had had the chance.

While there are many to thank, for all have taught me, there are a few in these last few years who have particularly stretched me. They include Tom Stafford and Betty Dickey from Hoechst Celenese, Lindy Williams and Gaby Giglio from American Express, Mike Stromes from Ciba Geigy, Steve Bauman and Mike Horne from Marriott, Marsha Boettger from Chrysler, Rey Froiren from Dun and Bradstreet, Lee Craig from Intermec, Judy Mason from Dow Corning, Lucy Visceglia from Kraft, Jane Michel and Chris Holt from Chevron, Donna Drake from the *New York Times*, Susan Weir and Mark Taylor from McKesson, Joe Arbanas from Pacificare,

Tracy Coon from Intel, and Jane Creech from Quantum, to name just a few. Thank you.

FROM OTHER PEOPLE

I have been rich in my relationships. I learned that I do my best work in concert with others, and I have been smart enough to play in a lot of concerts that have been held in a variety of concert halls.

The Career Systems Team in Scranton brings me wonderful support and amazing insight. I thank Kay Tomasko, Nanci Hendrickson, and Sherri Volkert. My own BKA team in California supports me like no other: Thank you Janet Schatzman, Lynne Merenstein, and Rosalind Sago, for truly being there.

My marketing and sales team in Pittsburgh and Fairfield makes it possible for me to be in many places at one time, and truly helps me grow in my business. I could not do it without Yolanda Perusse, Jerry Pavlof, Marilyn Greist, and Mark Olevin. In addition to his marketing savvy, Mark brings graphics savvy as well.

The BKA Associates themselves are too numerous to mention here. Without them, though, there would be no business. They have taught me that "cloning" is NOT the way to go; instead, they bring their own special expertise, their own way of expanding on ideas, their own unique personalities, and their own remarkable additions that strengthen our team and our program.

I do need to mention my own kitchen cabinet. I have received support, friendship, brilliant ideas, and unending devotion from two particular individuals who have been in my corner almost all of my professional years. Bev Berstein and Betsy Jacobson have "been there" and "done that" without hesitation during the ups and downs of my personal and professional life. It is through my collaboration with each of them that I have tapped into the best of my creativity and utilized the depths of my own talents.

I have also had the good fortune to develop professionally through several partnerships. One was with Caela Farren and the late Zandy Leibowitz, with whom I partnered in the founding of Career Systems, and with whom I developed many of the products that organizations still use. Both have contributed a great deal to the field and to my own thinking. Kim Barnes, Alan Vengel, Judy Lash, and I partnered in the Influence Alliance. From them I learned the importance of being able to gain commitment, not just compliance.

There are also several colleagues who have become partners-in-kind in a variety of ways. Each has influenced me greatly. I appreciate all I have learned from Katherine Reynolds, Julie Savinar-Moseley, Gary Schuman, Sharon Jordan-Evans, Ranny Riley, and Pat Thorton.

My two mentors succumbed to cancer during the last years. Consultant and author Alice Sargent connected me to important people, supported my early efforts, and served as a "working mom" role model. Pam Jones did similarly. Pam was my first client when she was at GE in the seventies. She was the first to say . . . be creative, do something different, try it here! She remained my client at all the successive organizations that she moved to, and she became a very special friend.

This secton simply would not be complete without mention of my family. My folks, Mollie, Abe, and Ruth, siblings Alan, Jeff, and Marilyn, and their families all listened patiently, supported quietly, and celebrated loudly. My husband, Barry, and daughter, Lindsey, make my life complete. Somehow they both put up with the workaholic mom, the traveling mom, the just-one-more-phone-call mom, and the oldest-in-the-whole-school mom. They have been my security blanket, my inspiration, my joy.

FROM HARDSHIPS

CCL suggests that we also learn from hardships. These stories I shall save for the next book. Trust me, though, there have been some. Each has taught me, challenged me, and delivered me to the next place. Each was not fun in the moment, and each seemed unending. Thankfully, I had friends to walk with and talk with on each journey. Those people know who they are and that they are deeply appreciated.

| 1 |

The Process and the Payoff

"The significant problems we face today
cannot be solved at the same level of thinking
we were at when we created them."
−ALBERT EINSTEIN

I t all used to be so simple. American workers selected a career area, educated themselves to pursue it, settled into an organization that could use their talents, worked to achieve higher rungs on the corporate ladder, and collected a gold watch at the mandatory sixty-five-year retirement age.

Myriad social, economic, and legal changes of the past decades have radically disrupted this long-standing pattern. Individuals and organizations seem at a loss for means to anticipate and cope with the turbulence and rapid evolution of their environments. Rather than direct their own progress, individuals and organizations are instead controlled by their environments, with a subsequent loss of power and productivity. It is important that both the organization and the individual develop the ability to manage and direct such change to their own benefit.

Organizations are forced to deal with a rapidly changing environment, increased competitive pressure, pressures of globalization, swift and drastic economic shifts, as well as an exponential growth in the area of technology. How do organizations come to terms with these environmental conditions? The literature abounds with different strategies. Some advise being proactive, taking action *before* the environment forces the organization to react. Others tout reengineering, overhauling the structures and processes for quality and flexibility. Still others advocate self-design, building in the mechanisms for the organization to strategically and continually change itself. And there are also those who think the solution lies in the learning organization, a dynamic organization that constantly seeks and responds to feedback.

The individual operates in this same turbulent environment. To remain relevant and competitive, the individual must take action. Just as businesses face fiercer competition, employees must also compete. Career planning and development activities are to the individual what reengineering is to the firm. The individuals in today's business environment must be dynamic and ready to take charge; they must take a business approach to planning their careers.

Career development is ideally a joint effort between the individual, the manager or leader, and the organization. While the individual has the primary responsibility for his or her own career, the leader is a supportive coach, and the organization provides the necessary systems and information. Career development involves looking realistically at the present conditions and at the career environments of today and tomorrow in order to regain the control necessary to ensure future productivity and job satisfaction.

And career development is more than this. Not only does it aid the individual in confronting and coping with a rapidly evolving working world, but it can also be a vital link between individual and organizational goals and objectives. It can become the vehicle for implementing the human resource aspects of a company's strategic plan (for such a plan must also look closely at this resource and formulate a framework for its development and use). Career development in this sense, therefore, is not simply another human resource activity; instead it is an integrating concept that systematically ties together and builds upon human resource programs that already exist, so that they simultaneously support individual and organizational growth.

This book addresses the rationale and design of such career development efforts and is directed to those individuals who are charged with initiating and implementing those efforts within the organization.

The Employee Stimulus

The rising interest in career development has been stimulated by heightened (or at least more vociferously articulated) employee desires, such as:

- Increased personal responsibility for their careers
- Increased career opportunities
- Increased participation in decision making
- More meaningful work leading to a feeling of contribution to society
- Increased job challenge and satisfaction
- More opportunities for self-actualization
- More on-the-job learning experiences
- More flexible work schedules
- More openness and trust from management
- More opportunity to enhance their employability

Employees who are dissatisfied with any of the above areas or with the "old" motivators of money, status, or other tangible rewards are not hesitating to leave the firm at the first sign of a better offer. And they will leave the second job if conditions are not much better. Job changing, especially among the younger workers who are needed to prime the future management pump, is becoming a common phenomenon. And it is costing management a bundle, especially when it is unintended or occurs just at the point where the employee is beginning to return some of the initial investment made in training and development. Besides moving from firm to firm, employees of all ages and persuasions are beginning to see "dropping out" as a viable alternative to job stress and dissatisfaction. Men and women, young and old alike, are dropping out, returning to school, touring the country, or changing careers in midstream with increasing frequency.

In addition, employees are prepared to back up their demands for a new lease on working life. The spectacular sales records of self-insight, self-help books, such as *What Color Is Your Parachute?*, point to a population that is ready to assume responsibility for its own career decisions. Today's workers do not show the blind faith or undying loyalty to their employers that those of the last generation demonstrated. Their first loyalty seems to be to themselves.

But what was it that changed the mind-set of employees in such a major way? Obviously loyalty is a two-way street. After more than a decade of massive layoffs, downsizings, streamlinings, and rightsizings, organizations face a workforce that no longer can rely on a lifelong commitment from the organization. Sharon Jordan-Evans, leadership consultant, related to me one of countless examples of this new reality of vanishing loyalty: "The CEO of an aerospace subcontracting firm pointed me to his firm's empty parking lot. 'This parking lot used to be full at 6 P.M. Now, as you can see, it's empty at 5 P.M. And many of those people used to log a very productive hour between 5 and 6 P.M. We're losing about 200 hours of productivity per day.' This is a very telling indicator of the diminishing loyalty and commitment."

Employers and employees thus must forge a new relationship, based not so much on mutual loyalty as on mutual benefits. As Waterman and Associates (1994) put it, in return for their employees' productivity and commitment to the work at hand, employers offer an opportunity for individuals to develop their abilities and enhance their employability.

Changes in the workforce also affect how organizations manage their human resources. The baby boomers are middle-aged, causing a congestion at the middle- and upper-management level. There is also evidence that the younger generation has not received the quality education needed to shoulder increased responsibilities. And most important, the workforce is becoming increasingly diverse. Women have entered the business world in full force, minorities have more open access to opportunities, and the globalization of business means more organizations are managing a multicultural workforce. While difficult to manage effectively, a diverse workforce offers an opportunity for quality and flexibility.

To further confuse current corporation-employee relations, there are the increasing pressures and expense of keeping up with technological change. Our knowledge base is growing so quickly that individuals will no longer be able to think in terms of career education, but rather of a lifetime of multiple careers. It is the job of the organization to assist its employees in coping with this rapid change. The firm must be prepared to help its employees avoid the erosion of their skills and the onset of individual obsolescence.

Rapid changes in business technology require flexible employees and employers who are receptive to change. Those who cannot meet this demand become difficult to utilize. Management is then faced with a difficult decision: how to maintain productivity levels without having to terminate employees who contributed years of effective performance before reaching obsolescence. Complicating this issue, of course, is the implication of possible age discrimination. It is not an easy decision to make.

The Organizational Response

During the days of a rapidly growing economy, organizations could better bear the burden of retaining some marginal performers. Total revenue was growing fast enough to allow many companies to relax their vigilance on cost control. Under such conditions it was possible to avoid or postpone the ultimate blow to the employee's self-esteem by moving obsolescent employees out of the mainstream of activity and into a less vital position where they could be carried until retirement. Today this option has virtually disappeared.

Economic growth has greatly slowed and inflationary costs are eroding profits. Efficiency, profitability, corporate growth, and perhaps even survival of the firm depend upon maximum utilization and development of all corporate resources, including the individual employee. With legal and regulatory actions, capital costs, and governmental procurement shifts largely beyond the control of individual companies, management has turned to areas within its direct influence and control to improve profitability and assure sustained growth. One of these areas is human resource management. Companies are, more than ever, coming to see that an investment in developing people, whether they are men or women, minority or majority, old or young, managerial or administrative, is an investment in the future of the organization.

Considerable attention is being directed toward getting maximum benefit from human resources. A company cannot succeed in meeting its corporate goals if it is plagued by high turnover rates and low productivity, or if it has an inadequate base from which to draw fresh management talent. How to attract, keep, and fully use talented and innovative employees who have their own personal concerns has become a basic corporate need.

To meet this need, a variety of human resource–related techniques have evolved. Recruitment programs, performance management systems, training programs, management development seminars, and a variety of learning forums are among the key tools of any human resource department. These tools were all designed to better use the talent that a corporation possesses in its employees. Unfortunately, many of these programs are less effective than they might be because they are not integrated closely with (or may even be working at odds with) one another, and because they do not take into account the actual career interests of the individual.

A carefully planned and thoughtfully implemented career development program can provide the means to help an organization combat this lack of integration. Such a program pulls the assortment of human resource development activities together into a coherent unit and provides links with the organization's bottom line. A well-designed career development effort can (1) help identify individual talents and desires and place employees in work situations that are personally meaningful because of relevance to those talents and desires, (2) assist employees to view the organization as one that respects their unique abilities and encourages their utilization and growth, (3) involve employees in communicating their needs and aspirations at all levels of the organization, and (4) enable individuals to continually develop their potential and to be challenged by future learning possibilities. In short, a full range of human resource problems, evidenced by symptoms such as frequent turnover, skill deficiencies, low morale, or decreased productivity, can be addressed by a career development effort.

Career development supports the recognition that different individuals are motivated to on-the-job effectiveness by different organizational endeavors. For example, while the security of continually demonstrating talents on the same job may stimulate one person, new experiences or a perceived chance for growth and change may stimulate another. While some employees may be inspired by a sense of organizational "caring" about their well-being, others may want more specific rewards and incentives for continued growth. Career development, with its emphasis on ongoing diagnosis of individuals' unique needs and capacities, allows organizations to discover and direct appropriate means of satisfying a variety of employee preferences, while at the same time meeting organizational needs in the most efficient manner—filling jobs with people best suited to them.

A Framework for Action

There is a need today to define a new relationship between the employee and the corporation, to develop a relationship that blends the individual's career objectives into overall corporate goals. When it is effective in this, career development cuts across traditional organizational boundaries. It cannot be constrained by arbitrary functional designations.

Human resource practitioners who restrict career development to the role of a single event (such as a goal-setting workshop or an annual career discussion) force it to become an isolated event with no particular influence over the organization or any of its units. Integration of the different aspects of career development and human resource development becomes virtually impossible under these conditions, and the potential effectiveness of the program is lost.

To be effective, then, a new system is in order—one that realigns these boundaries and allows the career development practitioner access to people and information throughout the organization. This can be accomplished by shifting our perspective to focus upon the career development effort as our system of interest, and by looking at other human resource development activities as they might relate to that effort.

THE PLAYERS

Every career development effort requires the participation of several distinct groups: the organization as a whole, represented by senior decision makers; the leadership, represented by traditional supervisors, managers, and other leaders with informal power; and the individual, represented by those employees who elect (or are selected) to participate in the process. The practitioner is usually either part of a professional staff with the overall responsibility for the career development effort, or an outside consultant. A useful metaphor to fully understand the role of the practitioner in the process is that of the practitioner as an orchestra conductor. The practitioner should not be the one *making* the music, but rather should *lead* and *guide* the different players in making their own music. (In those organizations that may not have professional career development practitioners, the leader will sometimes inherit the practitioner's role. In other situations, the leaders may have a follow-on role that is involved in the later implementation of career development efforts.) These players interact with one another within a common environment containing all the political, legal, social, economic, cultural, and natural forces that influence the program in different ways.

The world of career development, then, can be shown to embrace a larger and more complex environment than that of the organization alone, or of a single individual's attempts at development. It is important to understand the interaction and interdependence between the individuals, their leaders, and the organization, and the impact of programmatic intervention on each, in order to manage an effective career development effort.

This book is addressed to persons termed *practitioners*. These practitioners might be full-time consultants or career development professionals; they may be human resource staff who are charged with the development and implementation of a career development effort; they might be training and development professionals who find themselves working in the career development field as a result of organizational needs or diversity requirements; or they may be line managers, team leaders, or supervisors involved part-time in career development programs for their subordinates. No matter what the case, this book is aimed at and meant to serve as a guide for whoever is fulfilling the practitioner role at any particular time in the career development process.

The Six-Stage Process

A complete career development effort moves sequentially through six stages and involves separate as well as interactive participation by the practitioner and each of the three players described above. Each of these stages constitutes a vital step in a complete career development effort, yet each has substantial payoff of its own. Although the greatest return on investment comes at the completion of all six stages, there are distinct contributions to both the individual and the organization at the conclusion of each stage. The relative emphasis, discreteness, and interconnectedness of these stages, though, can vary greatly among organizations.

This six-stage career development model can provide the framework by which the practitioner can link the frequently disconnected activities of the human resource department. The same stages also serve as the guiding framework for the design of workshops and individually directed career counseling sessions. The stages become a checklist to facilitate evaluation—by comparing an existing program with the stages in the model, one can identify areas that have been neglected or areas that have been overemphasized. Practitioners can also use the model to identify stages within their influence, as well as to understand the broader picture of organizational career development. A clear understanding of the processes involved in each of the six stages will provide a guide to determining which steps must be undertaken to introduce career development as the human resource umbrella. The

---

TABLE 1

THE SIX STAGES OF CAREER DEVELOPMENT

STAGE 1—Preparing
Analyzing
Planning

STAGE 2—Profiling
Identifying
Reality-Testing

STAGE 3—Targeting
Exploring
Specifying

STAGE 4—Strategizing
Understanding
Synthesizing

STAGE 5—Implementing
Acquiring
Demonstrating

STAGE 6—Sustaining
Maintaining
Evaluating

---

stages are introduced here and summarized in Table 1. They are described in detail in the ensuing chapters.

STAGE

1

PREPARING

Preparing, the first stage in the cycle, begins with an organizational response to a perceived need. Two distinct processes are involved: *analysis* and *planning*.

The combined processes involve several tasks: (1) analyzing needs and demands, (2) formulating objectives that respond to those needs, (3) developing programming to accomplish those objectives, (4) assigning responsibility for execution of the programs, (5) determining evaluation methodology, (6) outlining the ongoing human resource activities that can be linked to the program, (7) charting new activities that must be accomplished to make the program work, and (8) readying resources necessary for the succeeding five stages. The thoroughness with which this is done will largely determine return on investment that the organization can expect to receive from the program.

By the conclusion of the Preparing Stage organization members are introduced to the career development effort. The program design is determined, and resources are committed. These two outcomes—plans and commitment—largely determine the eventual effectiveness of the program.

STAGE

2

PROFILING

The Profiling Stage is the first to actively involve individual employees in the processes of *identification* and *reality-testing*.

The *identification* phase poses the question "Who am I?" The purpose of identification is to consider an individual's capacity (sum of personal skills, values, and interests, as well as work contexts or desired environments) in such a way that by verifying, changing, or adding information the individual's perception of self becomes more focused. Individuals are continually appraising themselves and being appraised by others. Identification seeks to make this process conscious and explicit, so that individuals become aware of the assumptions upon which they operate. Only then can positive change be effected.

The *reality-testing* process entails evaluation of personal skills as they are perceived by those who interact with the individual. For example, individuals might discuss the results of the identification phase with their leaders. This dialogue between employee and leader about overall capacity of the employee should be separate from the performance appraisal process. Although employees who enter the performance appraisal dialogue after working through the identification phase will be better prepared to discuss their own strengths and weaknesses and to evaluate the veracity of their leaders' reactions, keeping these processes separate will facilitate a candid exchange since the individual will not feel the extreme pressure of evaluation, or even judgment, often associated with performance appraisals. However, profiling by employees and their managers should strengthen the performance appraisal interchange.

Profiling culminates in a verified description of the participants' knowledge about their interests, abilities, attitudes, opinions, values, and desired work contexts. As a consequence, the participant develops more confidence and is often willing to consider varied development options.

STAGE

TARGETING

At the Targeting Stage individuals build on the information generated during profiling to investigate and select suitable career goals. The two processes involved are *exploration* and *specification.* Here, key decision makers must share information about the organization's long- and short-range plans so that individuals can develop realistic targets.

The *exploration* process involves employees and their leaders in an active investigation of the world of work. Leaders need to stay on top of the shifts in technological, social, political, and economic trends. They must make this information available to the employees in order for them to stay abreast of the trends that will affect their career plans. Individuals must broaden their frame of reference—not focus only on the effects on their current job, but also look at future shifts in the environment, the organization, and their profession.

The *specification* process involves assisting the individual in choosing a set of simultaneous options for movement within or out of the organization. Six possible career alternatives are available for the individual, including job enrichment and lateral movement as well as traditional vertical mobility. It should be kept in mind that the best option may be to leave the organization. The individual must therefore be able to apply this model to assess the industry, other organizations, and the environment. This assessment of the industry may even prove useful to avoid the "grass-is-greener" syndrome and to provide a more accurate comparison of the present situation with outside options.

The process also involves converting the goal from a vague concept into an action-oriented goal statement. This process involves testing each goal for its ease of attainability, relevance, and specificity. It involves using information discovered during the Profiling Stage and knowledge about present and future policies and career opportunities within the organization. The specification process is most effective if the individual has an idea about the range of available opportunities and has an understanding of the organization's future plans, so that personal goals may be synchronized with those of the organization.

At the conclusion of the Targeting Stage individuals have identified a set of career goals congruent with information about organizational needs and personal abilities, for use in the succeeding stages.

STAGE

STRATEGIZING

Strategizing involves developing plans to accomplish the goals set in targeting. Because of changes in the organization and in the individual, no one plan is adequate. Therefore, the Strategizing Stage is aimed at developing the contingency capabilities of employees. Strategizing consists of two phases: *understanding the system* and *synthesizing information.*

The first phase involves the individual in an attempt to gain an accurate *understanding* of the forces that influence life and potential growth in the organization. Individuals come to understand the informal system, with its subtle games of power and politics; gain insight into the culture, with its associated norms and boundaries; and continually attempt to gain insight into their own place within that system.

The second phase, *synthesizing,* involves formulating a specific course of action to reach a particular goal and planning for contingency capabilities. Effective action planning requires having certain organizational information, including knowledge of how people have moved before and of the interim steps necessary to reach certain positions in the organization. This information may be available in the career path progression charts already housed in the organization. By the conclusion of this stage individuals develop a written development plan (with deadlines) for acquiring the skills, training, experience, and resources needed to reach their goals. They also become aware of personal, interpersonal, and organizational forces that may tend to act for or against their plan and consider strategies for coping with them.

STAGE

5

IMPLEMENTING

The Implementing Stage involves putting strategies into action. Implementation involves the *acquisition* of specific resources for goal attainment and the *demonstration* of these new abilities in the organization. Action plans formulated during the Strategizing Stage suggest two types of plans that are pursued during the Implementing Stage: (1) plans to acquire the necessary skills, experience, visibility, and personal contacts required for goal achievement, and (2) plans to make new or better use of resources presently possessed by the individual, as actual steps toward goal achievement. The two phases that make up the Implementing Stage reflect these categories of action plans.

The Implementing Stage delineates the three principal sources of the necessary technical and managerial tools: (1) training and education—gaining skills through training programs sponsored within and outside of the organization, (2) learning based on experience—gaining skills through work on special projects or through on-the-job experience, and (3) support-guided development—gaining skills by learning from other people inside and outside of the organization. The individual must select appropriate resources, acquire or master the new skill or knowledge, and demonstrate that new learning within the organization. Although responsibility for the process rests with the individual, organizational support in the form of resources and development dollars can greatly affect the success of the employee during this process.

At the conclusion of the Implementing Stage employees will have selected their sources of learning. They will have investigated these learning sources, decided which seem most appropriate, completed the necessary learning, and demonstrated the learned skills. The resulting improvements in performance have been documented by the organization. In addition, employees will be aware of additional personal and programmatic resources available to them within the current organizational framework.

STAGE

6

SUSTAINING

Sustaining is defined as any follow-up procedures and accountability methods, designed early on in the process, that maintain the career development effort. The Sustaining Stage consists of two phases: *maintenance* and *evaluation*. Unless the players focus on sustaining mechanisms, the effort will die. An effective sustaining stage keeps the effort "evergreen."

The first phase of the Sustaining Stage is *maintenance*. In order to sustain the energy and momentum of the career development program, some steps must be taken to incorporate effective maintenance strategies into the process. The strategies vary from setting up follow-on meetings, continued learning, and planning teams, to ensuring managerial accountability for the effort.

The *evaluation* phase involves determining the appropriate evaluation methodology to best address the objectives set during the Preparing Stage. Although evaluation is a continual process and occurs throughout all six stages, it is at the Sustaining Stage that evaluation must be made visible. The evaluation results must be reported to all stakeholders, and depending on the results, processes may need to be revised.

Characteristics of the Model

Each of the stages previously described constitutes a vital element of a complete career development effort and exhibits important characteristics. Each stage, for example, is integrated with the other stages to the degree that it absorbs information from the preceding stage and contributes combined information to the succeeding stage. Effective career development occurs only when the program design facilitates progress through all six stages, and when involvement of all three players has been achieved.

Movement between the stages may proceed sequentially or oscillate among stages; yet all six must be traveled at least once for one complete cycle, ending at the Sustaining Stage. Repetition of any stage is assumed to produce "higher" knowledge or experience, that is, the individual has experienced it once and is, therefore, more sophisticated. For example, on the basis of an action plan formulated in the Strategizing Stage, an individual might return to school to acquire specific skills at the Implementing Stage. During that time a different application of those resources might become obvious, prompting a reconsideration of the goals set at the Targeting Stage. The individual's ability to select goals the next time around, however, will be enhanced by previous experience with the process.

Another characteristic is drawn from a law of physics that suggests that movement toward a higher level of order in one system will result in a greater degree of disorder in another system. The more isolated the career development effort, the greater the opportunity for causing disruption in the individual's work or nonwork setting.

While it is not possible to predict every type of disorder that will be generated during career development, understanding potential problems and working through them can help minimize some of the most common disruptions that result from career development efforts.

Because career development efforts exist within organizations whose environments are constantly changing, they are subject to a variety of forces that produce strain, tension, or conflict at each of the stages. Practitioners must be aware of the variety of forces that affect the career development effort and must be willing to modify each stage accordingly.

A career development effort is most effective when it is ongoing, integrated in the organization, internalized by the participant, and designed to include all six stages. It is synergistic when it combines all the conditions necessary for each stage in order to provide the maximum benefit to the individual, the leaders, and the organization.

An understanding of the career development framework and accompanying characteristics enables the practitioner to analyze, predict, and manage the processes underlying a career development effort. The framework also provides a mechanism for understanding other isolated human resource activities (described in the next chapter) as they relate to these six stages.

As long as the functional requirements of each stage are observed, a career development effort can be structured to meet unique needs. It can be simple or sophisticated, use very basic or highly advanced support technology, address administrators or vice presidents, and still be successfully described and understood in terms of the six-stage framework.

Payoffs: The Bottom Line

While an organization will not realize every possible payoff from a career development effort, an understanding of what the payoffs might be can help sell the program, by providing managers and career development practitioners with an additional tool for articulating the program's rationale and invoking the commitment of key individuals throughout the organization.

Table 2 describes potential payoffs for the organization and for others affiliated with the career development effort.

When fully implemented, career development can become the mission that gives meaning to the variety of human resource activities within the organization, thus strengthening the human resource links within the organization. Without such a linkage, communication between individual programs and the organization is often sporadic, blocked, or nonexistent.

A career development framework that has clear steps and that links other human resource activities to those steps can be a strong integrating force within an organization. A career development practitioner trained in building this framework can provide a focal point for individual, corporate, and human resource interests. The next chapter will describe the preparation necessary for the career development effort. It will showcase those human resource development activities that can be linked to the stages of the career development cycle and will suggest strategies necessary to prepare for a strong, integrated career development effort.

TABLE 2

POTENTIAL PAYOFFS

Payoffs for the Organization

- *Skill building.* Increasing the abilities of employees in their current jobs, as well as enhancing their abilities to adapt to task changes and technological advances.
- *Talent matching.* Providing information about employees' abilities and aspirations, in order to establish a match between organizational needs and individual capabilities.
- *Productivity and morale.* Reducing counterproductive forces—such as high turnover, absenteeism, and grievances—that may result from morale problems among employees who view themselves as having little opportunity for greater advancement.
- *Motivation.* Stimulating increased employee effectiveness among those who value a climate of growth, challenge, and shared organizational responsibility for personal development.
- *Revitalization.* Creating new challenges and opportunities for those who may have "retired on the job" to use their skills.
- *Advancement from within.* Developing a high-quality group of in-house candidates for promotion to higher positions.
- *Retaining potential.* Providing learning and growth opportunities, thus retaining key knowledge workers.
- *Recruitment.* Enhancing the attractiveness of the organizational climate as a place where talented individuals will want to work.
- *Human resource planning.* Providing additional information and resource identification for efforts that assist in determining future needs.
- *Problem identification.* Providing early information about staffing problems, including underutilization and competence deficiencies.
- *Image building.* Improving the corporate image as a forward-thinking, contemporary organization that strives to continually improve its operations.
- *Goal commitment.* Clarifying organizational goals for all employees and strengthening employees' understanding of their contributions to those goals.
- *Program integration.* Creating understanding of a system that links career development with other existing human resource processes, such as performance appraisal, pay plans, employee counseling, and career path planning.
- *Equal opportunity.* Helping identify women and minorities with potential for advancement and encouraging development of that potential.
- *Legal implications.* Helping meet legal requirements in areas such as equal pay, equal employment opportunity, and age discrimination.

TABLE 2 (CONTINUED)

POTENTIAL PAYOFFS

Payoffs for Leaders

- *Communication.* Increasing communication between leaders and employees about their current performance and future opportunities.
- *Information.* Providing leaders with better information about staffing needs, as well as about possibilities for addressing them by developing skills or changing the patterns of using talent.
- *Goal clarity.* Helping leaders clarify organizational and unit goals, and how they fit with individual tasks.
- *Developmental responsibilities.* Assisting leaders in acquiring skills to counsel and coach employees about developmental concerns.
- *Staffing justification.* Developing information to justify staff increases or cutbacks.
- *Identification.* Supporting efforts to identify employees who can be moved to other responsibilities.
- *Special projects.* Providing inventories of talents that may be called upon when special projects require assembling a task group to meet temporary needs.
- *Personnel decisions.* Helping employees to understand the leader's rationale for making difficult human resource decisions, including selections, promotions, transfers, and discharges.
- *Performance appraisal.* Setting the stage for easier performance review, by enhancing individuals' knowledge of their strengths and weaknesses before their managers formally appraise their work.
- *Motivation.* Establishing commitment and willingness on the part of employees to respond to requests for effective performance and new challenges.
- *Personal development.* Assisting leaders to become aware of their own career development needs and to plan strategies for fully developing and using their own talents.

Payoffs for Employees

- *Self-knowledge.* Understanding personal strengths and weaknesses, as well as desires and needs for life and career integration.
- *Organizational knowledge.* Gaining current information that provides greater understanding of personal possibilities and future opportunities within the organization.
- *Sense of purpose.* Focusing on clear multiple goals for the future and developing ways to meet those goals.
- *Self-determination.* Exercising control over aspects of life that may have been felt to be in someone else's hands, gaining a positive, active stance toward life and work.
- *Organizational identity.* Feeling a greater commitment to organizational purposes.

TABLE 2 (CONTINUED)

POTENTIAL PAYOFFS

Payoffs for Employees (Continued)

- *Skill building.* Learning new skills that can aid in accomplishing current tasks and also provide wider options for the future.
- *Experimentation.* Seizing opportunities to test new or potential talents and explore different areas of work and learning.
- *Supervisory relations.* Establishing more open communication with supervisors about developmental possibilities, personal performance, and organizational opportunities.
- *Peer relations.* Establishing opportunities for support and feedback from other employees.
- *Personal satisfaction.* Developing self-esteem from growth and learning.
- *Advancement potential.* Enhancing opportunities for advancement into higher positions.
- *Job enrichment.* Recognizing that career growth begins on the current job and that one can increase challenge and stimulation without necessarily moving "up."

Payoffs for the Career Development Practitioner

- *Integration of human resource activities.* Establishing a system that links together a wide range of human resource activities and enhances understanding and use of them in the organization.
- *Information dissemination.* Increasing information flow regarding important organizational issues and practices related to career development and, thus, clarifying to others the role of human resource development work.
- *Image building.* Enhancing professional image and worth by establishing a visible and systematic program that has bottom-line value to the organization.
- *Growth opportunity.* Developing personal talents by undertaking the challenge of planning and administering a far-reaching career development program for the organization.
- *Personal satisfaction.* Gaining a sense of satisfaction from contributing a meaningful service that assists others in personal and professional development.
- *Organizational involvement.* Obtaining involvement and shared responsibility from others—especially managers and supervisors—who may have previously seen human resource development as something "those other folks will take care of."
- *General program support.* Demonstrating success in a major program in a way that can help elicit support for ongoing or future human resource development programs.
- *Personal development.* Becoming more aware of one's personal development, and applying career development processes and strategies to one's own organizational life.

|2|

Readying Resources

THE PREPARING STAGE

*"We can't cross a bridge until we come to it;
but I always like to lay down
a pontoon ahead of time."*
—BERNARD BARUCH

C areer development efforts are complex and long term, they directly and continually affect the work lives of people at all levels and in all parts of the organization, and, very often, they can have tremendous impact upon the actual structure of the organization itself. The career development effort also touches upon a host of other ongoing human resource programs. To be successful, therefore, career development must be carefully planned, well supported, intricately linked with other efforts, delicately executed, and thoroughly monitored and evaluated.

The Preparing Stage is divided into two phases: *analysis* and *planning*. Leaders and practitioners are required to make a great effort; the more time they can give to these two thinking processes, the more chance there is of a successful effort.

Analysis

WHY CAREER DEVELOPMENT?

The first task of preparation is to determine the scope and nature of the career development effort through analyzing the needs, problems, and activities that led to the career development effort and that will, eventually, determine its objectives. There are many reasons why organizations undertake career development programs. Where does the need or demand for career development originate in this organization? What signals are organization members sending to suggest the need for career development? The answers to these questions require an examination of why career development is important, what problems it may help address, and who the beneficiaries of the program may be.

Chapter 1 outlined a variety of social, legal, and technological factors contributing to the current need to reassess the organization's responsibilities to its workforce. Underlying all these factors is the pervasive need to develop a workforce that is capable of and committed to maximizing organizational effectiveness—and thus to ensure the continued health of the organization. The best of advanced technology, efficient structure, and enlightened leadership is of little avail if individual employees are underutilized, underskilled, dissatisfied, or disaffected by organizational purposes.

Following the Trend

Addressing future trends will not only assist analysis of the need for career development but can also provide a valuable aid in selling the program to top management. All too often organizations find themselves fighting fires rather than aggressively planning to accommodate future trends and changes.

Table 3 presents the main trend categories and issues that have had an impact on organizations in the last two decades of the twentieth century, and will continue to do so well into the new millennium. Staying abreast of trends can provide valuable tools for brainstorming about the need for career development programs and organizational planning. They can be examined in light of two main issues:

- How these trends may affect the organization and its employees
- How a systemic career development effort could address these issues

Practitioners who can design and implement career development programs that address long-term organizational needs in terms of these trends will not only be making contributions to the human resource goals of organizations but could very well be providing leaders with tools with which to forecast and prepare for the future and, at the same time, selling top management on the need for such a program.

READYING RESOURCES ■ 23

TABLE 3

TREND CATEGORIES

Economic Trends	Foreign Investment
	International Trade
	Domestic Indicators (inflation, interest rates, and GDP)
Political Trends	International Business Law
	Federal Regulations
	Political Movements
Social/Cultural Trends	Diversity
	Spirituality
	Environmental Responsibility
Technological Trends	Information Superhighway
	Multimedia Technology
	Telecommuting

A Need in Deed

If career development programs and practitioners are to be effective adjuncts to the organizational effort, future trends and philosophies must be considered. However, the future is not the only area of concern. The feelings and attitudes of those in the organization who are actually concerned with career development must also be taken into account.

Message Analysis is one process that the practitioner may use to assist individuals and groups to uncover and discuss these factors. It may be used to identify how those working together feel about the need for a career development program or, on a larger scale, how division, group, or department heads see the need for (or may support) the effort. The purpose is the same—determining where the starting place is that has the most probability of program success.

Exercise 1 shows an example of a Message Analysis worksheet that was completed by members of an organization that decided to start a career development effort with a particular target group.

EXERCISE 1

A Technique for Finding a Starting Place

Questions that can be used by the practitioner to assess the group's attitudes toward the career development effort include:

1. If a spokesperson for each of the groups identified were to send you a clear, uncensored, unfiltered message regarding the career development (CD) effort, what would it be? Penetrate for the underlying meaning or underlying message.
2. Is the message real (true)? That is, do you like it? Do you agree with it? What in the organization maintains it as such? What can be done to turn the message more in support of the career development effort?
3. Is the message a myth (false)? If so, what in the system perpetuates it? What can be done to end or to debunk this myth?
4. Where does this analysis suggest we begin? Which group might be most supportive? Where would we be likely to succeed?

Resulting Diagram:

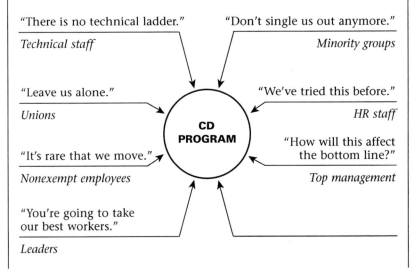

"There is no technical ladder."   "Don't single us out anymore."

Technical staff   *Minority groups*

"Leave us alone."   "We've tried this before."

Unions   **CD PROGRAM**   *HR staff*

"It's rare that we move."   "How will this affect the bottom line?"

Nonexempt employees   *Top management*

"You're going to take our best workers."

Leaders

The need for career development—and other human resource development programs that are linked to it—relates directly to the need for more effective employees. Profitability and performance are often seen as the bottom line, and career development is viewed as a means to that end. Career development can enhance the abilities, commitment, and appropriate skill utilization necessary to motivate and activate employees to increased effectiveness. In this way it offers a return on investment based on higher personal and organizational productivity.

Determining the sources of need for career development can help in setting relevant program goals, in designing appropriate activities, and not insignificantly, in justifying or selling the program to others in the organization. Organizational analysis and diagnosis is therefore a vital step in the Preparing Stage.

TO BEGIN, YOU BEGIN

Once it has been established that a career development program is actually needed and desired by the organization, the next step is to fully prepare for the long and arduous task of designing the most effective program possible.

Chance and Change

Of primary importance in this personal preparation is the recognition that career development is going to introduce change into the organization. It would be nice if change could be accomplished with no accompanying disruption, but because it is what it is, change disturbs, or totally alters, the status quo and often causes conflict. As a result, practitioners must be prepared to deal with a variety of actions, reactions, and counteractions once the program is introduced.

Why do organizations and the people within them resist change? A great deal has been written on this subject, most of which can be summed up as follows:

- Change is resisted because it creates an increased feeling of uncertainty about the future.
- Change is resisted because people may feel that they do not possess the skills that will be needed and valued in the new situation.
- Change is resisted because people may feel that it transfers control to those who are imposing the change.
- Change is resisted because key decision makers and leaders may feel threatened by shifts in power.
- Change is resisted because people may feel that the possible gain is not worth the time and energy invested in the effort.

In order to ensure the success of the career development effort, leaders and practitioners must be, or become, expert agents of change. They must recognize the ways in which organizations may resist change. Some of the resistance mechanisms identified by Donald Schon in his book *Beyond the Stable State* (1971) still appear today, in addition to new ways of resisting change:

- *Ignoring the change* by simply refusing to recognize that it has or is about to occur.
- *Compartmentalizing the change* by allowing it to take place in only a limited area or to a limited degree, for example, tokenism.
- *Limiting the change* to the least acceptable amount that will be allowed by the powers that be, for example, paying lip service to the change by showcasing only the most obvious part of it.
- *Co-opting the change* so that it serves the ends of the organization or individual rather than those intended, for example, distorting a change in order to allow the group or person to continue as before.
- *Outright sabotage* by deliberately derailing or damaging the change effort, for example, feeding inaccurate data to the reengineering firm.

How can this resistance be avoided?

Structure vs. People

Change can be effected by altering the structure in which people operate or by attempting to modify the behavior of the individuals themselves. Individual habits and behaviors are extremely resistant to change because they are ingrained and personalized. Normally, therefore, the most effective way in which change can be introduced is through the structure or organizational policies themselves. When the structure within which individuals operate is altered, they will by necessity change themselves in order to adapt.

Though the most effective way to introduce change is through structure, anyone who has ever attempted to modify a procedure or alter an existing reporting arrangement (or—heaven forbid—a performance appraisal program) knows that organizations will strongly resist any tampering whatsoever, regardless of its intentions or probability for increasing effectiveness. Therefore, most career development programs have followed the path of least resistance and aimed their efforts solely at individual behavioral change through workshops or counseling programs. This is not to say that such an approach is wrong or undesirable. The contention here, however, is that to ensure success and to effect lasting change, both the structure and the individual will have to be addressed.

In either case, practitioners must often be prepared to deal with hard-core resistance to change. They will be called upon to show why the change is needed and to get others involved in the problem-solving process. The change effort will need the active support not only of top management but also of the formal and informal opinion leaders of the organization. Practitioners would do well to find someone with influence to sponsor the change process.

It will be necessary to realistically consider all of the possible consequences of the proposed changes and provide options or trade-offs in order to make the changes and their ramifications more palatable. Practitioner agents of change may also find it necessary to help the organization's leadership realize the risks involved in the effort and develop reward systems for those willing to take those risks. They may find themselves at the forefront of dramatic structural or technological changes and be called upon to demonstrate how the changes will benefit those involved. Even those who are the most reluctant to accept the change effort may be convinced if the right tone is set.

One of the most effective ways to head off many of the problems associated with change is to set a tone of candor and realism at the very beginning about what a career development effort can and cannot do. This can also help defuse the "yes but . . ." responses from defenders of the organizational status quo and can steer program participants and others to a realistic level of expectations.

One way this tone of candor and realism can be designed into the effort is to involve as many senior managers as possible in crafting the philosophy of the initiative and to gain their buy-in. Briefings, planning meetings, and survey data can do this, but the practitioner does not always have the time and senior managers are not always easily snagged for meeting time.

As the word about career development spreads, it is also important to emphasize that career development does not deal with vertical mobility alone—"up is not the only way." This message should be reinforced throughout all program phases, as it will reduce those unrealistic expectations. Leaders and employees must remember that the traditional notion of upward mobility is only

CASE 1

A Working White Paper

A health care company found they had no time to do the consensus work they felt needed to be done at the Preparing Stage. Instead they devised a "walking-talking" white paper. In this paper, they presented a wide variety of ideas, philosophical approaches, intervention possibilities, and so on. Managers and employees were asked to jot down reactions and ideas and pass it around their departments. In the end, the practitioner was able to collate all the data, compare and contrast the data, and deliver a report to the executive committee with more "grounding" than they may have had otherwise. In addition, all department heads who received the data felt that they had contributed their input to the initiative.

one possibility in the career development realm. They must keep in mind that career development can also mean movement laterally, downward, toward enrichment within the current job, or out of the organization. The employee may take on new challenges or different tasks that are personally meaningful and rewarding but that do not necessarily require a move to the next higher rung on the corporate ladder.

It is also important to clarify (over and over) that career development is not a panacea for all problems. In all organizations there are a limited number of job openings, and movement into them can be slow. Furthermore, if career development equaled only upward mobility, the ultimate value to the organization would be slow to materialize and difficult to identify. Nothing about a career development effort is quick or easy. Clearly its greatest potential may take longer to realize than many leaders and employees would prefer.

"Small Is Beautiful"

All too often programs fail before actually getting off the ground because they are too massive in their approach and attempt too much too soon—before the organization is ready to accept the concept of career development. This can be avoided by beginning "small," only after a thorough understanding of organizational and individual needs and supports has been established. This may mean that some practitioners will have to deal with pressures to "make a showing" or "just do something." Handling the pressure to begin something big may be difficult, but those who persevere will be rewarded in the long run.

Rather than beginning with an organization-wide effort, practitioners may find it advantageous to begin with a focused effort in one particular portion of the organization, where support for career development has already been established. A close analysis of attitudes displayed in the Message Analysis conducted earlier may show one manager, one unit, one division, or one target group of the organization that is ready for career development. Beginning in a place where support is strong can accomplish a great deal toward ensuring success. In such case, beginning "small" may mean beginning with a guarantee.

Another aspect of the "start small" admonition is that it is not necessary to "reinvent the wheel" in order to begin a successful career development program. Certain departments or divisions may have built-in structural supports that are already providing a basis upon which to build. Massive change of the organization may not be necessary. The first step, then, is to investigate and analyze the sources of support and help that are already available.

Who Can Help?

Clearly, involvement and commitment from all the players identified in Chapter 1 are crucial at this stage, as they are throughout the remaining five stages. The organization should be closely involved in order to provide resource allocation, information, and reward systems. Managers, team leaders, and supervisors are key players, offering problem-solving advice, mentoring, and contextual limitations, and providing long-range goals. It is crucial to obtain full "sponsorship"—not just lip service—of key leaders for two reasons: (1) If uncommitted, they can easily sabotage the program by discouraging (or failing to encourage) employee involvement and revoking resources, and (2) if committed, they can substantially promote program visibility, which signals others to assist in making it succeed. If top management is involved at early stages and if they can see clear benefits for themselves and for the organization, the success potential for the career development effort at later stages is greatly enhanced.

■ **ACTION PROVOKING QUESTIONS**

FOCUS GROUP QUESTIONS

- When we say the word *career development,* what does it mean to you? To your peers?
- What kind of career development questions do employees come to you with, or have you asked of your leaders?
- What (skills, knowledge, behaviors, abilities, information) do you feel leaders here need to be effective at developing their people?
- Who do you feel is responsible for career development? Who should be? Who should initiate the discussion?
- What kind of advice do you wish you could get or would have gotten from your own leader?
- What do you think employees need to know about career development? Are career development needs unique for the technical population? How are they different from those of other parts of the organization?
- What's in it for leaders to support career development? What would have to be in it to gain *commitment/involvement* and *participation*?
- If we were designing a career development program for you—personally—what would it have to have in it? What would you want us to help you do?
- In what ways do you presently see HR supporting career development? What would you like to see more of?
- What obstacles/roadblocks will a career development program face here?
- How directed are your employees/you toward *one* career goal? Do you feel other options are available?
- What specific resources does the HR department offer that you feel make a good contribution to career development?
- What have you learned about how to manage or not to manage your career—what do's and don'ts do you think are alive and well and enforced in our particular culture?
- Do you think career discussions should be enforced? How would you enforce them? How would you track them?

The involvement of select human resource development professionals (in addition to the practitioner) is also vital. If the human resource (HR) staff is not committed as a staff, the program will lose support necessary for its success. Often members of the HR staff do not see the relevance of their own units to the career development effort. Attempts by the practitioner to assist colleagues in recognizing their special contributions to career development will result in substantial payoff.

EXERCISE 2

Career Development Task Force Planner

CAREER DEVELOPMENT TASK FORCE: PROSPECTIVE PARTICIPANTS

Use this chart to jot down names of potential task force members as they occur to you.

Leadership	HR Professionals	Employee Representatives
Who will best articulate the feelings and insights of the top? Who can most easily carry back information?	Who has information and expertise to contribute?	Whose area will be affected? Which team leaders and members can make important contributions?
_____	_____	_____
_____	_____	_____
_____	_____	_____
_____	_____	_____
_____	_____	_____
_____	_____	_____

One way to ensure involvement and build commitment is to conduct focus groups with leaders, HR professionals, and employees from various areas of the organization. Participants not only *feel* that they are making a contribution to the effort, they really *are*, since if well managed, focus groups actually can provide a tremendous depth and breadth of information. The Action Provoking Questions on page 30 are useful in conducting effective focus group sessions.

In addition to involving top management and HR professionals, the wise career development practitioner will also involve line managers and team leaders as representatives of the user department(s) to be addressed in the program, or if one has not been defined, representatives of various levels and functions in the workforce. Such representation would complete the necessary cast of players discussed in the preceding chapter. Exercise 2 is a guideline for developing a list of prospective participants.

At the earliest time possible, all of these representatives should be organized into an advisory group to act as a guiding and reference task force throughout the program. The payoff for forming this group will be great. Such a task force will provide the practi-

CASE 2

A Blueprint Conference

A manufacturing organization kicked off its development effort by calling together a group of 25 line managers from every business unit in the organization. These managers were selected for their ability to be opinion leaders and represent the ideas of their constituencies. A "Blueprint Conference" was convened so that this group could come together, with the help of a consultant, to define their philosophy, decide on training rollout, and determine the new information avenues that were necessary to make the program more effective. Within one day (with a lot of preplanning), the practitioner was able to gain input and buy-in from a great variety of employees. This helped to sell the effort, since in this case an ongoing task force was impossible to arrange, so the one-day conference was used as the major buy-in vehicle.

tioner charged with the overall "get it off the ground" responsibility assistance in the form of sounding boards, channels to the "outside," stimulation, and challenge. The task force participants are sure to gain new skills in program design, interpersonal awareness, and sensitivity to organizational needs. For many, participation in a task force of this type will be in itself a kind of job enrichment. The organization also benefits when this effort becomes not just one more program designed in some dark corner by a practitioner, but a collective effort that requires active involvement from disparate parts of the organization.

An advisory group is more likely to be effective if it possesses what can be referred to as the "Seven C's": clout, compensation, contemplation, conviction, conversion, competencies, and closure (1992). The groups must have *clout*—the power to make a difference. There must be an element of *compensation*—their work must be rewarding and rewarded. The groups must *contemplate*—they must possess both content and process knowledge. They must have a strong sense of *conviction*—they must believe in the effort. The groups must go through a *conversion*—they must buy into the process. Their work must enhance their *competencies*—they build broader and more transferable skills. Finally, when a project or a

EXERCISE 3

A Checklist for Advisory Groups

An example of a checklist for advisory groups. For each of the following, rate on a seven-point scale how the group is doing:

	Stuck off course			Riding the Rough C's			On course for clear sailing	
Commitment Investment in the process is evident	1	2	3	4	5	6	7
Contemplation Everything is up for debate	1	2	3	4	5	6	7
Conflict Forming/storming/ norming/performing	1	2	3	4	5	6	7
Creativity Open to new ways before closing down	1	2	3	4	5	6	7
Challenge All members are pushing their own limits	1	2	3	4	5	6	7
Courage Not playing it safe and easy	1	2	3	4	5	6	7
Compensation Investment is valued and rewarded	1	2	3	4	5	6	7
Celebration Successes along the way are recognized	1	2	3	4	5	6	7

Adapted from Kaye, 1992

phase is completed, the *closure* and contribution of the effort should be celebrated. Exercise 3 offers a useful checklist for advisory groups.

The analysis phase of the Preparing Stage is aimed at giving leaders and career development practitioners a clear picture of how the organization's current needs, opportunities, and activities relate, or may eventually become related to career development. This can substantially aid the organization in clarifying rationale

---

CASE 3

A Customer-Oriented Design Team

A large oil company spent ten months in the Preparing Stage in order to assure that all eight operating companies could deliver a development effort that was somewhat consistent across the organization. The effort involved a senior-level advisory group (who devised the original vision), a middle-manager project team (who scoped the project and sold it to top management), and five development teams (who took on challenges such as accountability, information sourcing, communications, and education). All groups met together in a total community several times during this phase so that communication between teams could take place.

---

and goals of career development, in determining the necessary components of preparation, and in developing criteria by which the eventual success of the program can be measured. The end products of serious analysis are clear program intentions and objectives. The activities undertaken during this phase are not necessarily chronological steps and, therefore, many of them may be undertaken simultaneously.

Now is the time to dust off corporate goal statements, internal reports and reviews, growth and human resource plans, and issue papers. These can provide a wealth of information for analyzing why and how the organization might benefit from a career development program; they can aid in making the goals of the program consistent with overall plans and needs.

LINKING HR ACTIVITIES: THE STRUCTURAL SUPPORTS

During this stage the practitioner will also want to fully review existing human resource activities to determine which ones represent necessary links to the career development effort. Typically, these have already been established through a variety of efforts that fall under the aegis of human resource development, but they may not have been integrated into a system that is recognized as a coordinated career development approach. Also, it is likely that some programs of activities that are needed to support career development are either incomplete or missing, and it may be necessary to get them in place before the effort is formally announced to employees.

It is during this analysis that prior inclusion of other HR staff on the career development task force will prove to be valuable. With these professionals taking part in the review and analysis of programs, there will be less possibility that they will see the career development effort as competing with their own programs. Rather, they will probably appreciate how ongoing human resource events can actually complement and mutually support the career development effort.

The HR links described here are those activities that can both reinforce and be reinforced by an integrated organizational career development effort. They affect the various stages and in turn are affected by them. They provide information vital to the career development program and assure its interaction with organizational principles and policies. Establishment of the six-stage career development framework suggested here benefits these other programs by providing an integrative and coordinating element and encouraging employees to be more responsible in using the programs. There are several generic human resource links suggested here that provide input to various stages of the career development process. Although these links may differ from one organization to another, they are discussed more to suggest ways in which leaders and practitioners might look at their own unique systems to select appropriate activities than to be seen as *the* HR activities vital to a successful program. Figure 1 demonstrates the relationship between the career development process and HR activities.

At the Preparing Stage, for example, the practitioner must know the basic direction of the organization—its *forecasting* of changes within the organization and in its environment, its *development of a diverse workforce,* and *leadership training.* The necessary training must occur prior to the program's inception.

A face-to-face interchange between the leader and the employee must be established. During a *performance appraisal,* leader and employee can discuss what competencies the individual possesses and which skills need to be developed to satisfy individual and organizational needs. Skills identified during the Profiling Stage are useless unless they are tested against reality. The skills identified and tested against reality must be documented and catalogued if the organization is to benefit substantially—a *skills inventory* can store such information.

FIGURE 1

The Career Development Process
and Human Resource Links

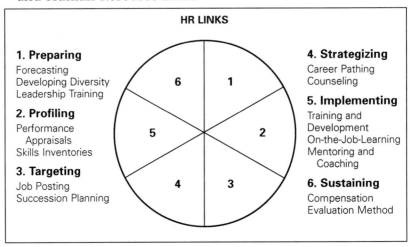

HR LINKS

1. Preparing
Forecasting
Developing Diversity
Leadership Training

2. Profiling
Performance
  Appraisals
Skills Inventories

3. Targeting
Job Posting
Succession Planning

4. Strategizing
Career Pathing
Counseling

5. Implementing
Training and
  Development
On-the-Job-Learning
Mentoring and
  Coaching

6. Sustaining
Compensation
Evaluation Method

At the Targeting Stage, not only do individuals and their leaders need to once more make use of organizational *trends and forecasting information;* they also need to know the *succession plans* that have been outlined so that employee goals can be set in light of these organizational plans. It will further help in determining realistic goals if the employees can make use of a *job posting system* to see if they have the skills required for particular positions and to determine the scope of job opportunities available.

Similarly, at the Strategizing Stage, employees will have an easier time developing an action plan if they can be apprised of the *career paths* followed by others in similar jobs, to determine if the action plan they are pursuing makes sense. When strategies indicate unexpected directions, employees may wish to avail themselves of specific *counseling* services, such as preretirement or outplacement services.

During the Implementing Stage, the employee is expected to follow through on an action plan. This may mean taking advantage of certain *training and development* opportunities, gaining skills through *on-the-job learning,* specific learning assignments and tasks, or learning from *mentors and coaches* (inside and outside of the organization).

Although rewards come throughout the six-stage process, it is at the Sustaining Stage that the organization witnesses movement and responds with fair *compensation* and rewards that meet the needs of a diverse employee population. *Evaluation* mechanisms are implemented, assessing the program in terms of what gains the employees are receiving from the process and how organizational needs are being met. If found to be effective, methods are constructed to maintain rewarding efforts.

Minimally, the concerned leaders and practitioners could respond to the career development call by organizing a few specialized activities, such as a workshop that covers or alludes to most of the stages in the model. Clearly, a workshop could present appropriate and meaningful profiling, targeting, and strategizing techniques. It could even introduce the Implementing Stage by describing the availability of in-house resources or by distributing a catalogue of courses and tuition reimbursement policies.

However, *a workshop is seldom sufficient.* If there is sincere desire to see maximum career growth and change for the organization, structural supports must be introduced. Structural supports are those human resource activities that can be institutionalized and adopted systemwide. They exist as a clear statement of the organization's commitment to individual growth and development. The human resource development links just described are examples of structural elements. They must be *identified, studied,* and if necessary, *upgraded* so that they truly support each career development stage.

The beauty of such a system is that the benefits are twofold. Each of the human resource development activities reinforces a particular career development program stage and is, in turn, reinforced by that stage. The information available through job posting, for example, adds valuable supplemental data to the process of targeting career goals. In turn, employees' awareness of and ability to intelligently use the job posting system is reinforced by knowledge gained during the activities of the Targeting Stage—more employees are apt to make appropriate use of job posting, if only to gain more information for use in formulating their career goals. In this manner, one clear benefit of career development will be more active use of current human resource development systems by employees. (Granted this may be frightening to some practitioners and some organizations!)

■ **ACTION PROVOKING QUESTIONS**

DETERMINING FUTURE HR NEEDS

- Do we have a formal system for forecasting future human resource requirements throughout the organization?
- Is the data in this system regularly updated or challenged as to accuracy?
- Are we clear on our human resource needs for the next five years? Ten years?
- Is this system visible to and used by leadership for decision-making purposes?
- Do employees know of and understand this system?
- Do employees have access to relevant outputs of this system?
- What steps must we take to create a forecasting system that will adequately support the career development program?
- How can data generated by the program help us inventory our current workforce supply?

Each of the succeeding chapters will discuss these development links as they apply to the stage that seems most relevant. Readers are advised to determine those links that are familiar in their own organizations and to affiliate them with stages that they consider significant. All human resource activities must be investigated and considered to determine how they will support or influence the career development stages. The suggested questions may serve to help leaders and practitioners further analyze those activities currently in place.

At Preparation

Forecasting. Forecasting is an integral component of human resource planning. It requires collecting and analyzing information about future human resource needs, including a continual examination of relevant factors within the organization (such as talent resources and expected structural and human resource changes) and in the outside environment (such as potential technical, social, political, and economic changes). This information is vital to the career development cycle. Without it goals are set in a vacuum. The Action Provoking Questions above will aid in determining the organization's future needs.

Forecasting is one of the human resource functions that will normally have applicability during a number of stages, for exam-

---

■ ACTION PROVOKING QUESTIONS

EVALUATING DIVERSITY DEVELOPMENT

- Are we satisfied with the state of the art of this organization's development opportunities for special needs groups?
- How will each career development stage make our organization more responsive to diversity needs?
- Are we using the skill identification information developed at the Profiling Stage, to give us a better picture of needs of any underrepresented groups?
- Are the goals for developing diversity, set at the Targeting Stage, realistic?
- Is the organization doing all it can to support these goals?

---

ple, during the Preparing Stage, the Targeting Stage, and the Strategizing Stage.

Developing Diversity. A diverse workforce poses both challenges and opportunities. On the positive side, it offers a broader knowledge base and more flexibility. The challenge is, however, to offer the development opportunities that will access this knowledge and flexibility to its fullest potential. Too often, career development efforts aimed at minority employees are resented as "special treatment." In a personal conversation, Sharon Jordan-Evans, leadership consultant, used an analogy to suggest that the situation often puts minority employees "in a three-foot hole" in terms of the experiences required to develop many skills—especially leadership skills. Development, she suggests, requires leveling the field—getting them out of the hole by providing developmental opportunities. Effective programs bring minority employees up to a level playing field. Roosevelt Thomas (1991) suggests that truly managing diversity requires developing an environment that simply works for all employees. Such an environment would require the maximum utilization of all employees' skills that are in sync with the direction of the organization. A well-planned career development effort will teach employees how to inform the organization of these skills and abilities and will, simultaneously, teach managers and the organization how to recognize and deploy that talent. Leaders and practitioners interested in the greatest payoff from their career development effort should consider the Action Provoking Questions above.

Leadership Training. If frontline leaders are the primary contact for each employee's career development, they must be prepared to act as a catalyst and an advisor. Through an assessment process (written questionnaire, 360-degree feedback, or oral interviews), the organization can determine what leadership skills are already available and which are needed to function in this capacity. Coaching and training can be provided to supplement existing skills. The first set of Action Provoking Questions focus on evaluating existing skills.

At Profiling

Performance Appraisal. Typically, performance appraisal is one of the few existing opportunities for dialogue concerning present skills, career futures, and developmental needs. Often, however, it is implemented simply as an annual checklist of employee characteristics, with few persons taking advantage of its potential for communication and testing against reality. Ideally, performance appraisal should include face-to-face interchange between leader and employee and should involve setting mutual objectives, establishing methods to monitor performance, discussing past performance success and deficiencies, examining career aspirations and opportunities, and discussing career development needs. Organizations should separate performance feedback from career development discussions to ensure that *both* happen and that *both* are seen as important to the organization. The second set of Action Provoking Questions on page 41 might be asked about the organization.

Skill Inventories. Skill inventories, also called Human Resource Information Systems (HRIS), are information storage, update, and retrieval systems that monitor employee backgrounds, training, experience, and skills. If it is to be used as a resource database for replacement and advancement, the inventory must be continually updated, easy to assess (tabular and graphic formats), and readily available for use. Skill inventories store and catalogue the precious skill identification data that is generated during the Profiling Stage. The last set of Action Provoking Questions on page 41 are helpful in assessing the skill inventories.

At Targeting

Job Posting. Announcing job openings visibly throughout the organization enables potential candidates to learn about the kinds

■ ACTION PROVOKING QUESTIONS

EVALUATING EXISTING LEADERSHIP SKILLS

- Do leaders have basic skills in counseling and coaching employees, providing performance feedback, setting mutual goals, and assessing training needs?
- Do leaders have full awareness and understanding of the organization's existing human resource development programs and of the need for career development?
- What training is needed to prepare leaders for the career development program?
- What information needs to be developed before we can conduct this training?

■ ACTION PROVOKING QUESTIONS

EVALUATING PERFORMANCE APPRAISALS

- Do our performance appraisals aid leader-employee communication about current performance and future plans?
- Are leaders skilled, and willing, to give frank, honest performance feedback regarding employees' personal, technical, and conceptual skills?
- Do employees view performance appraisal as an opportunity to test their self-perceptions against reality? Are they assisted in preparing for this dialogue?
- Is the career development discussion seen as distinct from performance feedback and seen as an equally important dialogue between leaders and employees?
- What steps should we take to improve our performance appraisal vehicle so that it supports the career development effort?

■ ACTION PROVOKING QUESTIONS

EVALUATING SKILL INVENTORIES

- Is information fed into the skill inventory in a timely, consistent manner?
- Are employees consistent about updating their own inventories?
- Do leaders adequately use the inventory—or do they bypass it when they have staffing needs?
- What steps must we take to create an inventory that will document information generated by a career development effort?

■ ACTION PROVOKING QUESTIONS

EVALUATING JOB-POSTING SYSTEMS

- Do employees sometimes feel that jobs are filled before they even hear about the vacancies?
- Do employees frequently complain that they can't find out about the kinds of jobs they could qualify for in other parts of the organization?
- Do leaders resist openly advertising vacancies because they feel it will hinder their ability to select who they really want?
- When jobs are posted, are interested applicants given enough information to understand how those jobs fit with their past experience and training and their future career goals?

---

of positions that become open and to apply for those that fit their qualifications and career aspirations. The existence of a comprehensive and visible job posting process can help set a favorable organizational climate, provide the organization with the benefit of a broad applicant pool, and assist employees in identifying career goals. Most larger organizations post job openings electronically. Ideally, posted jobs should include information about possible career progression stemming from them, as well as the necessary job description and qualifications. They are especially helpful during the Targeting Stage, because they provide an idea about the range of opportunities that might be goal alternatives. The Action Provoking Questions above are useful in assessing job posting policies.

Succession Planning. Succession planning requires formally charting replacement needs and time frames and looking internally for those who may be ready to move into upcoming vacancies. These individuals may be groomed for succession when titles such as assistant, deputy, or associate carry with them appropriate responsibility and exposure. Recruitment and selection should also take into account succession possibilities. Succession plans can be integrated with goals developed by employees during the Targeting Stage. The Action Provoking Questions on page 43 are useful in evaluating the succession plans.

At Strategizing

Career Pathing. This method of planned job progression generally involves delineating on-the-job learning and experiences

■ ACTION PROVOKING QUESTIONS

EVALUATING SUCCESSION PLANNING

- Do we have adequate plans for succession into key positions?
- Do we too often have to search outside our own organization for candidates for key positions?
- Do we have programs for identifying and developing high-potential individuals?
- Do our recruitment, selection, placement, and training practices reflect future succession needs?
- Are leaders involved in and aware of the organization's succession plans?
- What steps must we take to improve our succession planning, so that it reinforces actions taken in the career development effort?

---

that can lead to appropriate movement in the organizational hierarchy, or structure, since establishing career paths also entails plans for lateral movement. Since the timing and availability of vacancies is subject to constant change, establishing career paths can also be a series of short-term (one- to two-year) plans that are continually revised, supplemented by a more general, longer-range plan. Information about career paths can provide valuable assistance to employees in developing realistic action plans during the Strategizing Stage.

Many organizations are foregoing their career-pathing presentations because they find they bring more problems than results. One problem inherent in career pathing is that employees may perceive an implicit promise such as "if I follow these steps, and hold these positions, I'm owed this promotion." In this sense, career pathing may create a misguided sense of entitlement. A second problem concerns the increasingly dynamic nature of organizations today. Organizational structures are changing so rapidly that it is impossible for the career pathing program to keep up. With these words of caution in mind, the Action Provoking Questions on page 44 can be used to evaluate the existing career paths.

Counseling. As the business environment goes through major changes, many organizations make specialized counseling services available to employees. Three such specialized services are executive coaching/directional counseling, focused on derailed or stalled

---

■ ACTION PROVOKING QUESTIONS

EVALUATING CAREER PATHS

- What are our formal mechanisms for creating career paths?
- When was our career path information last updated?
- Do leaders have access to career path data?
- Are leaders able to explain career path data to their employees?
- Do employees have access to career path data?
- Do employees have any informal mechanisms that can help them develop insight into their own individual paths?
- In the environment in which we operate, is it realistic to develop specific career paths (with specific job slots in mind), or do we need to develop more generalized lines of career progression?
- What steps do we need to take to create a career path system that will provide valuable input to the career development effort?

---

employees who nevertheless are valuable to the organization; pre-retirement counseling, which prepares mature employees for plans and decisions they need to make regarding their non-full-time work years; and outplacement counseling for employees who are, for whatever reason, being asked to leave the organization after rendering years of service. These counseling services are performed by individual specialists or external consultants, who serve employees on a full- or part-time basis. Needs for these services may be evidenced during the Strategizing Stage. The Action Provoking Questions on page 45 address the viability of these counseling services.

At Implementing

Training and Development. Training and development involves sending employees to special workshops and seminars, generally outside their immediate work setting. To be most effective, such training must relate to immediate or realistic future work needs, and it must be linked to employees' own expectations and desires about their career development. If training and development is linked to both organizational needs and employee career development goals, it will be more cost-effective. Training and development experiences can include, among other things, tuition

■ **ACTION PROVOKING QUESTIONS**

EVALUATING COUNSELING SERVICES

■ Have we established services to meet special employee needs?
■ Have we framed adequate policies to allow employees to seek the help they need outside the organization?
■ Are we cognizant of the areas that need development as suggested by the number of employees seeking special services?
■ Are we aware of the quality of counseling services available through our own organization?
■ Do we have a statistical summary of the increasing or decreasing number of employees seeking services and the implications of those numbers?
■ Have we kept up-to-date with trends in the counseling field and services that other organizations are performing?
■ Are our counseling practices supportive of the career development program?

reimbursement programs, one-time workshops, or seminars for entire groups of employees. They may involve going out to specialized programs, or they may include programs conducted by internal resource persons who have adequate experience in the subject matter being taught and have skills in designing and conducting training. During the Implementing Stage, employees will select those training and development programs that will aid them in achieving their goals. The Action Provoking Questions on page 46 might be asked regarding the existing training and development programs.

On-the-Job Learning. Actual work experience and developmental assignments are some of the most effective means by which employees can gain or update skills. Often, however, the system is so ad hoc that employees are just plain lucky if they get to work with someone able to give them necessary training and willing to expose them to new experiences. Learning from experience may include formal orientation and training sessions conducted by experienced employees; deliberate efforts to pair employees with resource individuals responsible for their learning (mentoring programs); formal feedback mechanisms; task force assignments; or job rotation, for exposure to a variety of experiences. On-the-job learning may be another developmental resource for employees during the

---

■ ACTION PROVOKING QUESTIONS

EVALUATING TRAINING AND DEVELOPMENT PROGRAMS

- What training and development experiences are now available?
- Is training and development available to all employees who can show a need and desire, or is it more often used selectively as a reward (or punishment) process for certain levels of employees?
- Are employees selecting training and development opportunities that are in line with their career goals? (If so, are we measuring the results of those efforts in helping them meet their goals?)
- Have we conducted any formal assessment of the organization's training and development offerings? Selection procedures?
- Are leaders able to identify training and development needs and suggest ways in which they might be met?
- Are leaders able to counsel their employees regarding the training that should be selected?
- Is there top-level commitment to training and development as an appropriate way to help assure organizational health and maximum return on investment in human resources?
- What steps must we take to create training and development that is tied to the variety of career goals selected by employees?

Implementing Stage. The first set of Action Provoking Questions on page 47 consider the effectiveness of on-the-job learning programs.

At Sustaining

Compensation Practices. Compensation is a complex network of processes directed toward rewarding people for services performed and motivating them to attain desired goals of performance. Among the intermediate components of this process are wage and salary payment; the awarding of insurance and vacations; and the provision of essentially noncost rewards such as recognition, privileges, and symbols of status. A wide variety of systems and policies are used to facilitate the administration of the process. Organizations also supply a wide variety of fringe benefits. Careful attention must be given to the planning and installation of fringe benefits if they are to be useful incentives for the development of organizational careers. Compensation policies have a profound effect on the recruitment, retention, satisfaction, and motivation of employees. The second set of Action Provoking Questions on page 47 can be asked regarding the compensation policies in existence.

■ ACTION PROVOKING QUESTIONS

EVALUATING ON-THE-JOB LEARNING PROGRAMS

- What efforts are now going on that could be characterized as deliberate (not ad hoc) development strategies?
- Does on-the-job learning occur throughout the organization or only in isolated departments?
- Do leaders feel they have a responsibility for assuring that on-the-job learning occurs?
- Are employees encouraged to actively pursue developmental opportunities?
- Have we conducted any formal assessments of our on-the-job learning needs or of the abilities among leaders to create developmental experiences?
- What steps must we take to create on-the-job learning opportunities that prepare employees to move toward the goals identified in the career development program?

■ ACTION PROVOKING QUESTIONS

EVALUATING COMPENSATION POLICIES

- Do our compensation policies support movement other than vertical?
- Do our employees have a sound understanding of our compensation system?
- Are we aware of all the possible benefit plans that can be used to support various kinds of career mobility?
- Is there a way for us to reward leaders who do an excellent job in the career development of their subordinates?
- Are we aware of the ways in which our present practices may hinder the motivation of individuals in the career development effort?

Evaluation Methods. It is important to establish effective evaluation mechanisms, and although addressed at the final, Sustaining Stage, they need to be in place from the start and operated throughout the process. Evaluation can take place through examination of records, answering questions such as, What events took place and who took part in them? Another method is the observation of behaviors, noting any changes. And finally, evaluation can take place through the collection of self-report data: Participants can, for example, be interviewed or surveyed on experiences or perceived results. The data collected by any of these

---

■ ACTION PROVOKING QUESTIONS

EVALUATING THE EVALUATION METHODS

- Do the evaluation methods address all stakeholders (employees, managers, and leaders)?
- Do the evaluation methods provide effective qualitative and/or quantitative data?
- Do the data suggest good implementation steps for the leaders and practitioners?
- Do leaders and practitioners have a good plan for how the evaluation results will be used and disseminated?
- Do the evaluation methods present a balanced view of positive and negative results?
- Have leaders and practitioners considered the appropriateness of the evaluation methods for the culture?

---

methods needs to be analyzed and interpreted in order to establish such bottom-line figures as total cost savings for the organization. It must be kept in mind that the quality and usefulness of the data will depend on who is the source, what is considered evidence, when evaluation is carried out, where it takes place, and how information is gathered. The Action Provoking Questions above consider the effectiveness of evaluation methods.

Warning

In analyzing these links, it is not essential to find that they are all in perfect harmony with the career development effort before starting the program. In some cases, action may be taken immediately to provide more effective program integration; in other cases, action may be initiated but not completed until later. An organization that waits until it finds that all supporting human resource links are letter-perfect is probably stalling for other reasons on the installation of the career development effort. At this point, the emphasis should be on becoming aware of the potential weaknesses in the current structural systems and considering some action to strengthen them.

CAREER DEVELOPMENT PROGRAM APPROACHES: THE PEOPLE SUPPORTS

In addition to structural supports, leaders and practitioners must also be ready to develop mechanisms that directly affect people and influence their behavior. In other words, if change is to be effective, it will also affect those who make up the target audience of the career development effort. It may be easier to gain commitment and assistance from the organization in this area since the organization itself can become involved to some extent.

This involvement can be translated into four major categories of activity that can be used to deliver some of the important steps of the career development process. Each has its array of benefits and drawbacks, strengths and deficiencies. Practitioners who are familiar with each of these types of activities can more effectively pick and choose in deciding which approaches will be most effective, given the organization's degree of involvement and its basic style, culture, norms, and ideology. The choices include:

- Self-directed activities
- Counselor-guided activities
- Group-supported activities
- Combinations of the above

Self-Directed Activities

Self-directed activities rely heavily on the employees' desires and abilities to map out career development strategies for themselves. Organizations using this approach generally support individual efforts by providing programmed workbooks that can help employees conduct personal assessments. The workbooks may be the off-the-shelf variety, published nationally and widely applicable to various organizational settings, or they may be especially designed by and for the organization at hand. Obviously, the latter allow greater opportunity for specifying issues that relate directly to the individual's career potential within the given organizational setting.

Workbooks usually are highly diagnostic in approach, offering exercises and questionnaires that require the individual to assess personal values, career preferences, life satisfactions, and career-related strengths and weaknesses. They may include self-scored tests to pinpoint individual styles and priorities, and they may contain instructions for sharing and validating the information with others. Generally they conclude with goal-setting and planning exercises and an admonishment to set firm timetables, periodically review progress, and revise as necessary. Sometimes these workbooks have companion versions for counselors or leaders, so they can assist employees in the development process.

Workbooks are most useful when supported by a good deal of written communication to employees about HR activities, such as job openings, possible career paths within the organization, and other developmental opportunities. In this way the employee can incorporate both personal knowledge and organizational knowledge to realistically pursue plans for career development.

Self-directed career activities are increasingly relying on computers. Using computer workstations, employees can access the hundreds of Web sites sponsored by corporations, nonprofit groups, and government agencies to explore career options, look at salary surveys for specific job titles, correspond with professional career counselors, even take classes over the Internet. Many companies offer internal job posting systems that allow employees to examine requirements for open positions, apply for jobs electronically, and on some systems, post their resumes on electronic bulletin boards.

Another branch of self-directed activities is the growing library of computerized assessment tools. Like workbooks, these instruments allow employees to learn about their aptitudes, personalities, "best fit" job profiles, and general career strengths and weaknesses. Computerized 360-degree feedback systems allow superiors, subordinates, customers, suppliers, colleagues, and even family members to offer individuals feedback while preserving confidentiality. In addition to being more interactive and user-friendly than workbooks, computers also automate the scoring and reporting processes.

Another self-directed approach in a number of organizations has been the establishment of career resource centers. Such centers are usually staffed by full- or part-time specialists who can guide employees to the particular information necessary. Centers are sometimes seen as libraries, and sometimes as storehouses where employees can come to read, review, and search for particular information related to career concerns or questions. Career resource centers contain books, cassettes, and information on specific careers within and outside of the organization. Some also possess computer terminals that provide access to a local computerized career information system.

The drawbacks encountered in the self-directed career development approach often stem from the level of individual self-motivation required to make this approach operative. It is extremely difficult for most people to maintain the impetus for

READYING RESOURCES ■ 51

CASE 4

Using Technology for Powerful Self-Directed Development

A telecommunications firm started a process to address diversity issues, but along the way the issue broadened to involve developmental issues in general. The firm's management wanted a process that would give them a baseline assessment of their competencies, along with the creation and implementation of individualized development plans. They used a computerized 360-degree feedback tool that would allow the learners to develop greater depth of information about themselves than they would get from a paper-and-pencil instrument. They then used another computerized program to create customized development plans for each employee and manager. The firm's management believes that technology is providing greater depth and research-supported development solutions, making development less of a guessing game.

career development when it appears that nobody but themselves is either knowledgeable about or interested in their plans, and when they have little opportunity for dialogue with others. In addition, self-directed activity is an operation in a vacuum. Employees are almost totally reliant on the resources and information provided them, with nowhere to turn if additional assistance or information is needed.

However, self-directed activities do allow those who are highly dedicated to career development to voluntarily pursue a course of self-assessment, to design career plans to individual specifications, and to exercise total personal involvement and responsibility. And this generally can be done at a relatively low cost to the organization.

Counselor-Guided Activities

Counselor-guided approaches entail one-on-one discussions with someone specially trained to help guide an individual's perceptions of his or her career future. This approach may involve professional counselors (often psychologists) from outside the organization, specialized staff within the organization (generally employee counselors in the human resource department), or lead-

CASE 5

*Using Specially Trained Managers
as Employee Counselors*

ndividual counseling is available from specially trained managers at a large R&D lab for any employee who requests this service. Employees seek counseling for a variety of reasons. These reasons range from request for simple factual information on available educational courses or for assistance in developing educational and occupational goals, to request for feedback on the reality of career goals. Employees are given whatever assistance and information is available. When appropriate, they are referred to specific sources of factual information in a selected career. The major focus in the career counseling sessions is on assisting employees in the process of decision making around careers by providing them with the tools and techniques they can use to gather appropriate information and data and to make informed decisions for themselves.

ers who initiate career conversations with subordinates. Counseling may range from the formal administration and analysis of aptitude and personality tests to the informal rap session.

Through this approach the employee receives highly individualized advice and support, as well as substantial motivation stemming from the notion of shared responsibility for career planning. Counseling staff from outside the organization can contribute a sense of anonymity, objectivity, and some specialized professional capabilities. However, they also contribute a hefty price tag and, occasionally, a sense of reluctance among employees who feel they would be visiting "the company shrink." This approach is especially helpful, though, when employees need guidance or support in moving out of the organization. When the individual's goals and needs no longer match those of the organization, or when the organization is downsizing, formal outplacement services are needed.

Ideally, counseling by the team leader should be available to the subordinate in some form, even before the decision to prepare for a career development program is made. In reality, however, this is rarely the case. Instead, the annual performance appraisal is often the only occasion where such discussion takes place. And often, it

---

CASE 6

Using Workshops for Leadership Development

A high-tech manufacturing company, as a part of its ongoing Leadership Workshop, has spent a great deal of time and effort developing leaders' counseling skills. These include coaching, communicating, and helping skills. The high point of this experience is a twelve-hour exercise in which participants take the roles of workers, supervisors, and managers. The workers solve a problem as a "problem owner" and "helper." Each of these role players then is evaluated on his or her performance by individual supervisors who are, in turn, given an appraisal by a management board. By the end of the workshop, performance evaluation, a theretofore dreaded task, is seen as an exciting and valuable experience.

---

is an occasion of mutual discomfort where both parties are happy to just put check marks in boxes or move through the routine. There is little offering or seeking of any real counseling. This is particularly unfortunate in the area of career development, since leaders are often in the best position to provide realistic information about the organization and possible career paths, as well as to understand the capabilities and needs of their subordinates.

To take advantage of the potential benefits of leader-employee counseling, an organization will need to commit resources and time to training leaders in basic counseling techniques. It will also need to establish systems of reward and accountability for the counseling function as an ongoing, required leadership responsibility. At a minimum, the leader will need skill in listening, questioning, and providing feedback, and a capacity for knowing and explaining career-related resources and options within the organization.

Group-Supported Activities

Group-supported activities generally take the form of workshops aimed at generating collective discussion and mutual support for career development. A typical career planning workshop is one to five days in length and is often used to kick off a larger, more integrated effort. A well-designed and conducted workshop will give participants an opportunity to at least partially work their

CASE 7

Using Workshops for All Employees

A medium-sized manufacturing company designed a Career Development Workshop Series, which has since been regularly offered to employees at all company locations. The Career Development Workshop Series consists of a group orientation session and four formal career workshops. During the group orientation, employees share their expectations with the staff and learn about what the Series can do for them. Interested employees can then enroll in the formal career workshops. The first of these is the Career Awareness Workshop, which involves participants in basic career and life planning exercises. This is followed by workshops in Resume Writing and Interview Skills, which give participants practice in organizing their skills and experience and presenting them to a hiring supervisor. The final Career Search Workshop then teaches employees how to gather information about company job opportunities and how to best use the job posting system.

way through the career development cycle in a highly supportive low-risk environment. Using a variety of instruments and appraisals, participants help each other to *profile* their personal traits and career preferences. Career goals and objectives are *targeted* as participants discuss with one another the opportunities and paths available within their organizations. Action plans are *strategized* and tested on one another for realism and practicality. Mutual support is often pledged and provided after the workshop, as participants return to the workplace to *execute* their individual plans.

The "we're in it together" aspect of the workshop setting can make this approach a powerful strategy for initiating career plans that have maximum potential for follow-through. The workshop strategy can be used to initiate career decision making and to inform participants of available options and relevant organizational directions. In this manner, each individual is provided with a support system of others who are having similar experiences and who can contribute assistance after the formal workshop is completed. Though workshops can provide a great deal of organizational information, they have their greatest impact and return on

CASE 8

Using an Integrative Approach

A public sector organization has developed a unique and comprehensive program of services that combines both counseling and career development. It provides confidential individual and group assistance to all employees on personal, performance, or career-related matters. Specifically, the guidance and counseling services offered are (1) orientations and developmental workshops, (2) a Career Resource Center, (3) individual counseling appointments with psychologists, and (4) consultation to leaders in the areas of problem identification, the referral process, performance counseling, and career development.

investment when follow-up activities, specifically designed to keep the process active, are provided.

Integrative Combinations

Many very comprehensive career development programs incorporate self-directed, counselor-guided, and group-supported activities at various stages of program implementation. For example, self-directed activities may initiate personal diagnosis, counseling may help individuals understand and apply that diagnostic information, and workshops may generate goals for future action. Then the program can be sustained with further available counseling, group activities, and tools to facilitate individual reflection.

A typical integrative approach might ask employees to complete a workbook or some career preference tests before attending a career workshop, or it might provide a workbook at the close of a workshop, so that individuals may delve further into special career considerations after the workshop has concluded. During and after the workshop, one-on-one counseling is available to provide further assistance on an individual basis.

While these approaches and their differences are important for the practitioner to know, it is extremely important to recognize that none of these activities alone is enough to produce an effective career development effort. A workbook, workshop, or counseling session may stimulate planning, but it will usually not in and of itself provide all that is necessary to ensure organizational mobility. Each must be carefully linked with the other human resource development activities discussed earlier, in order to provide the true supportive structure for carrying out a successful career development effort.

Come One, Come All?

No matter what approach is introduced, deciding on the level of participation in the career development program will be crucial. There are four general arrangements for dealing with the issue:

- Everyone in the organization participates—all levels and all divisions.
- Volunteers are solicited from throughout the organization on a first-come, first-served basis, with a ceiling on the total number that can be accommodated by the program.
- Special groups of employees (such as women, minorities, high-potential candidates, middle managers, or preretirees) are offered the program.
- Employees in certain divisions or units of the organization are offered the program.

Clearly, anything less than full organization-wide coverage requires grouping employees for selection. This may be done by using place of work (unit or division), personal or professional characteristics (level attained, future potential, or minority status), or leaders selecting certain subordinates based on certain criteria.

Groupings by division or unit can provide an opportunity to selectively install a pilot program, in order to work out kinks and test various strategies. In addition, careful selection of units where commitment and enthusiasm is greatest can give the program the impetus of early success and favorable word of mouth. In fact, organizations that set out to fully implement career development throughout all units often find a substantial differential among how various offices put the program into practice—ranging from some that embrace all phases on a comprehensive basis to others that simply undertake certain discrete events without installing a truly systematic approach.

The possible drawbacks in selecting only certain organizational units arise from the difficulty of making appropriate choices. The unit(s) selected should provide a good pilot example of how the program will be received and what problems might occur; but it should also be assured (as much as possible) of initial success and the opportunity for transference to other units.

Organizations that select special groups of employees most often choose to conduct career development for management trainees or high-potential candidates. This executive development approach allows for succession planning at the highest levels, but it may limit career development opportunities to those who would be likely to take the effort into their own hands even if no organizational assistance were available.

Organizations may also single out women and minority employees, midcareer employees, preretirees, or others. Whatever the group, the stages of the career development process remain essentially the same, so that this approach may also be considered a limited experiment to be expanded to other employees at later dates.

The question of grouping participants will always be one that stimulates a great deal of discussion. Should participants be from one homogeneous work group, or should they be representative of the organization at large in a cross-sectional heterogeneous group? There are pros and cons of both approaches.

Homogeneous work groups tend to know each other, have common problems, and can deal with each other openly and frankly. However, they tend to be parochial in their view and to have common well-defined biases, prejudices, and opinions. They are often cliquish and tend to be somewhat closed to new ideas and approaches.

Heterogeneous groups have a broader organizational view, represent a wide variety of backgrounds, and can stimulate each other with new ideas, new material, and different options. However, heterogeneous groups tend to be somewhat closed at the beginning and are sometimes difficult to "open up" in order to begin the sharing of data. Representing, as they do, a wide diversity of backgrounds and attainment levels, they bring to the group a diverse set of prejudices, biases, and opinions, and these must be dealt with before the larger task can be addressed.

Time, resources, and practitioner skill must all be considered before deciding whether to work with homogeneous or heterogeneous groupings. If time is not a factor, if resources are relatively unlimited, and if the practitioner is experienced and highly skilled, the approach that is more difficult in the practitioner's view may be undertaken. If the opposite factors are present, the practitioner may wish to work with an easier arrangement.

It is important to recognize that not all employees will be interested in career development. And it is unlikely that mandatory participation will provide them with an incentive to wholeheartedly implement career plans. While employees may need strong encouragement to participate in the program, those who feel that the final decision has been voluntary are most likely to realize the full benefits of the career effort. It is interesting to note that while many organizations make their manager training mandatory and employee training voluntary, some are changing this direction. In light of the new employment contract that promises no security and the message of career self-reliance, some organizations are in fact mandating their employee education efforts. Their belief is that no employee can afford to sit back and be comfortable with his or her current position. Development is a *must* for all! The organization and its leaders can offer information, opportunities, and assistance, but the primary responsibility for career development still remains with each employee.

The Planning Process

The second essential component of the Preparing Stage is planning—mapping the specific strategy and methods of the career development effort. It involves setting objectives, designing an evaluation scheme, assigning responsibilities for the entire effort, and determining methodologies, resources, and support.

THE SETTING OF OBJECTIVES

Most objectives are defined in terms of what activities will be undertaken and who will be responsible for them. These are the inputs of the career development effort, and though they are important, they do not provide a means by which a program's effect can be measured. For this reason the concept of writing objectives in terms of *outputs, impacts,* or *results* is emphasized here. These are the projected accomplishments of the proposed effort and the effect of those accomplishments on the organization and program participants.

Results can be measured; they can be seen, touched, heard, smelled, and tasted; they are real. An *input* objective might call for establishing a series of workshops and training programs for administrative staff. Once these efforts have begun, the objective has been accomplished, but to what organizational benefit? A much more effective *output* objective, addressing the same end, might call for creating a qualified in-house administrative applicant pool and reducing the turnover within administrative ranks. When this objective has been reached, something measurable has been accomplished, and the organization can see what has happened. Instead of merely monitoring the progress of the establishment of a program, the organization has a benefit that is real.

As indicated earlier, objectives of career development efforts in most organizations relate to increased organizational productivity and individual efficiency. They include such factors as improved performance, reduced turnover, and increased flexibility. While internal pressures to quickly and measurably demonstrate the program's material benefits will tempt the organization to state objectives only related to more productive performance, it may be valuable to reach beyond these to include more pragmatic and measurable factors, such as improved performance, skills, abilities, and productivity; increased adaptability; improved morale; and a greater feeling of personal identity and job involvement.

It is unlikely that a single objective statement will adequately account for such a great variety of desired outcomes. Objectives should take into consideration intrinsic payoffs to employees, as well as dollars-and-cents benefits to the organization.

The chart in Exercise 4 is designed to serve as a checklist for human resource problems, which could generate specific outcome objectives. Before moving ahead, practitioners may want to consider whether their organization is facing any of these problems and whether solutions to the problems should be included among the objectives for the career-developing effort.

APPROACHING EVALUATION

Developing an evaluation approach at this early stage provides a guide for further specifying objectives in terms of outputs, for setting in motion systems to monitor progress of the effort, and for measuring its success.

The time has now come to make certain that program objectives are stated in terms that are clearly measurable. What is each objective specifically intended to accomplish? How can this be stated in terms of measurable results? Many repetitions of this step, with review, critique, and inputs by others in the organization, may be necessary. For example, one of the objectives may now read, "to increase frontline leaders' understanding of their human

EXERCISE 4

Human Resource Problems

In what ways can a well-thought-out career development program help solve any of the problems faced by your organization?

- The rate of turnover requires us to continually train and retrain employees.
- Absenteeism, grievances, and other counterproductive employee activities are creating problems.
- Some jobs leave employees with little opportunity to advance, other than by leaving the organization.
- We hear some grumbling about low morale, but we're not really sure what causes it.
- Through our equal opportunity efforts we have been able to recruit women and minorities, but they tend to stay clustered in certain jobs, job categories, or classes.
- We have problems effecting lateral transfers when employees reach a plateau in their current positions.
- We don't have a complete picture of inhouse talent and skills that might be resources for future needs.
- Our leaders are not generally able to counsel employees about their career development.
- Performance appraisals are more a necessary formality than an opportunity for real information exchange between supervisor and subordinate.
- Many managers have unrealistic aspirations toward advancement.
- People tend to know very little about the organization and its direction beyond their immediate workplace.
- Many people seem to be unaware of how the accomplishment of their jobs fits into larger organizational goals.
- We do a lot of things that could be called career development, but they are isolated and vary among departments and levels of employees.
- Many employees don't really know their mobility options within the organization.
- People don't seem to know how to go about preparing for development.

resource development function." Restated in more measurable terms, this may become, "to increase the number of leaders who use counseling, coaching, and on-the-job learning as means to develop employees' potential." Before this objective is completely acceptable, several further iterations of this statement may be necessary. Developing performance criteria, which can function as measures of program outcomes as they relate to objectives, will bring even more clarity. In the above example, performance criteria may include a specific increase in the number of reported counseling instances, a precise increase in hours spent in on-the-job training, or a targeted decrease in the number of employee complaints related to insufficient understanding of tasks.

Establishing performance criteria at this point will often uncover a need to collect baseline data about current activities, to be used later as comparisons. If increases or decreases are to be used as indicators, they will be useful for comparison only if there is a clear understanding of what existed before implementation. In this way, change can be measured and analyzed for its significance and program relevance. Clear performance criteria also enable timely determination of the data collection and analysis methods to be used in the career development program. Data collection may entail looking at numbers on staffing reports, constructing tests of performance, and designing attitude surveys. Often, to increase the validity of eventual evaluation results, data will need to be collected and analyzed before the program begins and at various points during its implementation. As practitioners will discover, if they have not already done so, establishing an effective program will require a great deal of dexterity in moving from one stage to another and in carrying on several functions simultaneously.

Depending on the rigor with which evaluation is undertaken, practitioners may find the assistance of statisticians and other numbers wizards useful. However, much valuable information can also derive from less formal and rigorous methodologies, as long as care is taken early on to define objectives and indicators in measurable, outcome-oriented terms.

Success Indicators

One helpful step in preparing for evaluation is articulating what specifically will constitute success. A description of the essential program components that contribute to a successful career development effort will help to further determine evaluation criteria. These components relate to both the process—how the program will be carried out—and the product—what will happen—and vary greatly from one organization to the next, depending on needs, objectives, and activities already in place. One way of actively involving the planning task force (described earlier in this chapter) is to engage them in selecting the success indicators that would be relevant to the career development effort of the organization. Success indicators describe an effective program and its impact on all individuals involved. Success indicators and ideas for their measurement can be collected from top management, leaders of prospective participants, various levels of employees throughout the organization, and even human resource employees. The planning group could determine those indicators that are most vital as a demonstration of program success and those that, in addition, are most easily measured. The data collection process will stimulate interest in the program and build commitment from others not yet involved.

What constitutes success varies with one's point of view. Participants might measure program success in terms of personal learning, discoveries, and accomplishments. The leaders of participants might determine success of the program by looking at employee performance, productivity, and reduced conflict. Top management might measure success by examining participants' contributions to organizational effectiveness and reduced turnover. The lists of success indicators and means of measuring them presented in Table 4 are designed to serve as suggestions or stimulants for practitioners wishing to establish success indicators for their own organizations.

Success indicators can be used to form program objectives and to design evaluation procedures that each group sees as valid and acceptable proof that the career development program does actually bring a return on their investment. The Action Provoking Questions on page 65 concern the areas of activities, processes, and results. They can also be helpful in drawing up meaningful success indicators.

Additional areas concerning success indicators need to be considered. McMahon and Yeager (1976) suggested the following essential program features, which still ring true today:

- *Dialogue* between individuals and their leaders, which is essential for successful career development and should serve to generate openness and trust among the parties involved.
- *Context,* the means by which individuals are provided with an understanding of the career milieu in which they operate —including information about organizational goals, opportunities, and options.
- *Involvement* of individuals in their own career development processes, which is required to enable employees to set goals and timetables that are personally meaningful and to under take activities that reflect personal needs and aspirations.

TABLE 4

SUCCESS INDICATORS FOR PARTICIPANTS, LEADERS, AND TOP MANAGEMENT

	Success Indicators	Potential Measures
Success Indicators for Program Participants (I am able to . . .)	Learn what I want to do	Identified three potential career options
	Get feedback on where I need to improve	Requested feedback from leader and completed exercises in workshop, which proved to be valid
	Identify my strongest skill(s)	Was able to list and discuss these skills and receive reinforcing feedback
	Identify jobs for which my skills are transferable	Listed four other jobs that fit my present skills
Success Indicators for Leaders of Participants (My employees are/have . . .)	Fewer complaints; more satisfied with their status and appraisals	Check for decrease in number of harassment or diversity-related complaints
	More productive	Ascertain quality/quantity measurements; less turnover over fiscal year
	Less dependence on me for guidance; taken more initiative on career matters	Record number of individuals who ask for time to discuss career plan with me and come in with a plan in hand
	More realism regarding their strengths and weaknesses	Better preparation by employees for performance appraisal, and more realistic self-assessment during appraisal
	Retained longer; effective job enrichment	Less turnover due to lack of job challenge, as ascertained from exit interview data

TABLE 4 (CONTINUED)

SUCCESS INDICATORS FOR PARTICIPANTS, LEADERS,
AND TOP MANAGEMENT

	Success Indicators	Potential Measures
Success Indicators for Leaders of Participants (My employees are/have . . .)	More opportunities for transfers	Increased number of lateral transfers into my department and from my department to others; greater cooperation from my peers
Success Indicators for Top Management (I witness the following . . .)	Reduced turnover	Statistics at end of fiscal year
	Improved productivity	MBO goals met; improved performance appraisal reviews
	Succession planning	Identification of back up employees for key positions
	Improved morale	Pre/postattitude surveys show substantial changes
	Change in use of human resource activities	Active use of present systems; more knowledge about company's present HR activities
	Loyalty to company	Less dollars spent on recruitment; length of stay with company improved

- *Feedback* to individuals, often in the form of leader-employee discussions, which enables employees to assess their learning and to plan appropriate changes as they go through the career development process.
- *Process mechanisms,* the techniques and methods (such as workshops, counseling, on-the-job learning, and performance appraisals) by which career development is brought about and which must interface with one another as a systematic developmental approach.

These important process elements can further help in identifying the components of a successful program.

■ **ACTION PROVOKING QUESTIONS**

DEVELOPING SUCCESS INDICATORS

Activities

- Have we undertaken necessary structural adjustments to link career development to other human resource development programs?
- Have orientation activities been conducted for leaders?
- Have career development assessment and planning activities been conducted by and with employees?
- Has a forum for discussion/counseling been made available?
- Are educational and training and developmental experiences (on and off the job) available?
- Is there evidence that employees are pursuing their plans toward career goals?
- Have we established a system for monitoring and updating the career development program?

Processes

- Is open dialogue among and between levels of employees being used as a mechanism to facilitate the program?
- Are information sharing and personal guidance being undertaken to help individuals understand career opportunities and options?
- Is participation being sought and used as a means of helping employees be involved in undertaking career development that is specifically relevant to individual needs and goals?
- Do we use feedback among and between levels of employees as a means of helping employees to set realistic goals and monitor progress on career plans?

Results

- Do employees, leaders, and others report changes in attitude or morale?
- Do employees, leaders, and others report improvements in utilization of skills?
- Do employees, leaders, and others report changes in career directions or expectations?
- Has workforce planning and forecasting been made more effective?
- Have we reduced turnover, absenteeism, and grievances?
- Have we improved our ability to meet the needs of a diverse workforce?
- Do we have more effective means of leader employee communication, including performance appraisal?
- Do various units report more effective means of having the right people in the right places at the right times?
- Do our tracking systems show we are making progress toward meeting the impact–oriented objectives we stated for ourselves at the outset?

TABLE 5

LEADERS' ROLES DURING THE PLANNING PHASE

Role model	Leaders demonstrate interest and activity in their own career development
Information source	Leaders provide information to employees about career development and career opportunities
Motivator	Leaders encourage employees to undertake career development and reward these activities
Counselor/Coach	Leaders conduct counseling interviews with employees to help guide and monitor their career plans
Diagnostician	Leaders assess strengths and weaknesses of employees on the job and give feedback about how these apply to career opportunities
Training specialist	Leaders create on-the-job learning opportunities and guide employees to other, off-site opportunities

---

WHAT'S A MANAGER TO DO?

Another essential task in the planning phase involves clarification of leadership roles in the career development process. The key question that will pop into most leaders' minds when they hear that a career development program is in the works is: "What will I have to do?" In many cases, they are really asking, "Will it mean more work and responsibility replacing employees?" or "Will I have to conduct a bunch of soul-searching discussions with my employees?"

The options for leadership responsibility are numerous, and the degree to which leaders take an active role in carrying out those options depends on the preference of the organizations, their assessment of the current leadership capacity, and their willingness to provide leaders with the time and resources (possibly including training) that may be required. Some roles in which leaders may be involved are listed in Table 5.

The role model, information source, and motivator roles may require only that the organization clearly state to leaders that these responsibilities are expected of them and provide some basic orientation information to aid them in carrying out these responsibilities.

CASE 9

The Managerial Role in an Informal Work Environment

The informality of the work environment in a high-tech company fosters frequent discussions between managers and their employees. While many of these discussions may center on a specific job task or rescheduling of work hours, it is common for employees to initiate general talks with their managers about their future career directions. As a rule, managers are highly supportive of career development and career change options for their employees. Most managers have made several job changes in the course of their own careers and tend to view this employee desire for change in work content and setting as a natural phenomenon. Some managers will actively facilitate such changes by making contacts with other managers in areas of the company that interest their employees. This kind of cooperation usually exists whenever there is rapport between a given employee and his or her manager.

CASE 10

Training Managers for a More Formal Role in Career Development

Recognizing that supervisors at a large high-tech firm needed to acquire skills to carry out their career development responsibilities, a workshop series was designed. The objective of the workshop was to help utilize employees productively. The workshop was based on a collaborative career-planning approach, emphasizing the critical link that line managers must play to ensure the success of the organization's career development program. Specific objectives included:

- Identifying work requirements
- Identifying employee skills, abilities, and motivations
- Matching employees to work
- Communicating with employees

To demonstrate management support and commitment to this process, the general manager met with participants of the workshop. The purpose of the meeting was to review supervisor action plans constructed during the workshop and to identify organizational obstacles that might impede implementation of the plans.

TABLE 6

ROLES OF PRACTITIONERS AND LEADERS

Career Development Stages	Practitioners	Leaders
Preparing	Review existing programs and plan for their linkage to career development Gain commitment/ understanding of others Set program objectives Determine delivery vehicles Design evaluation Assign staff roles	Allocate resources the system Demonstrate commitment Collaborate on program objectives Provide information
Profiling	Provide surveys/ questionnaires for self-assessment Administer workshops Make computer assessments available Assure linking programs (skill inventories, performance appraisals)	Provide encouragement Listen to employees' self-assessments Allow time for employees profiling efforts
Targeting	Encourage top management to share organizational information Disseminate information for employees Instruct in career alternatives Instruct in goal setting	Share organizational information Give feedback on goals Refine support programs as necessary Provide advice and coaching
Strategizing	Instruct in analyzing the system Assess and refine linking other HR programs as necessary Encourage management support	Encourage employees Provide information Provide guidance on developmental plans

TABLE 6 (CONTINUED)

ROLES OF PRACTITIONERS AND LEADERS

Career Development Stages	Practitioners	Leaders
Implementing	Examine and refine existing educational programs Develop additional programs for education and training, on-the-job experiences, professional support Provide information about developmental resources	Allow time necessary for employee development activities Establish means for utilizing new employee abilities Provide ideas for training and development Suggest development assignments
Sustaining	Monitoring progress Document activities Develop reward and recognition systems Design tracking system Evaluate program progress Analyze need for program revision Demonstrate to top management return on investment of program	Provide feedback and rewards Provide information that contrtibutes to program valuation Continue utilization of new employee abilities

The counselor, diagnostician, and training specialist roles, on the other hand, may necessitate specialized training that begins well in advance of the program. Although career development is ultimately an individual responsibility, the process is usually strengthened when leaders lend their support to the effort. Leaders are often the most available resources to employees for feedback on strengths and weaknesses and for information about opportunities within the organization. With adequate training and coaching skills they can often offer the assistance that employees need in order to formulate adequate self-assessments, goal statements, and action plans. If leaders are also encouraged in this effort by their own superiors, the impetus to offer this service will be even greater.

Often practitioners find that their roles and tasks intermingle with those of leaders. In systems where the leader is to be clearly involved, yet not carry the major responsibility for the program design and implementation, the roles and tasks may look something like those suggested in Table 6. This delineation may help in further outlining responsibilities or in just clearly articulating the sometimes subtle differences between practitioner and leader.

WHAT HAVE WE GOT TO LOSE?

The final step of the planning phase is to realistically account for the possibility of snags, snafus, and other undesired circumstances or consequences. While there is no need to be pessimistic to the point of creating a self-fulfilling prophecy, it is only good sense to prepare for constraints and problems that might occur.

All of the players involved in the career development process are taking some risks by launching and participating in the program. Table 7 outlines some of the risks involved.

All of this is not to say that every career development effort is going to meet with an endless mass of problems. Some, in fact, meet with very few problems; they are conceived as necessary by top management and welcomed by people at every level of the organization. Others, for a variety of reasons, are resisted or misinterpreted from the beginning.

Practitioners who are aware of the possible problems and make allowances for them are those who conduct successful programs. They plan in advance and are rarely surprised.

REWARDS FOR THE WEARY

Oddly enough, one of the major problems, and one that should be addressed during the Preparing Stage, deals with the rewards and incentives that can do much to make the program successful after it has been launched. Although this will be dealt with again in the Sustaining Stage chapter, it is essential that it also be mentioned here.

Traditionally, career programs reward only upward movement within the organization. The theme of this book, "up is not the only way," means, as will be shown, that all sorts of mobility should be encouraged (by necessity)—upward, lateral, and even downward or out of the organization. Unless the organization is prepared to recognize and reward these other directions of move-

TABLE 7

RISKS INVOLVED WITH A CAREER DEVELOPMENT PROGRAM

Organizational and Leadership Risks

Risks for leaders and the organization are varied and vital for the practitioner to consider before launching a program. They include:

- Inability to meet increased demand for career mobility
- Loss of some valuable employees who find a better career fit elsewhere
- Excessive internal mobility
- Need to commit greater resources than anticipated to training, job restructuring, incentives, and new HR practices
- Newly surfaced employee dissatisfactions with organizational practices
- Inability to demonstrate a quick payoff of developmental efforts
- Employee desires for more human resource development activities than the organization is prepared to deliver

Individual Risks

Risks for the individual differ in many respects but are just as important to consider. These factors include:

- Unmet expectations about career alternatives within the organization
- Dissatisfaction on discovering that career desires may not mesh with personal strengths and weaknesses
- Frustration of personal inability to follow through on career plans
- Uncertainty or anxiety among those who are satisfied with current job and responsibilities and do not desire career development or change
- Competition among employees for scarce career opportunities
- Surfacing fears of change, personal inadequacy, loss of job security

ment, practitioners will find their programs falling flat—individuals will discover that upward mobility is the only kind that is rewarded, and other career goals set at the Targeting Stage will become meaningless. Therefore, during the Preparing Stage, before the effort is ever launched, these reward systems must be addressed and provided.

Second, leaders do not like to lose good people—many do not like to lose even their marginal performers. A successful career development program should make good performers out of the marginal people and outstanding performers out of the good ones. Employees want to move in all directions. Unless leaders are rewarded for encouraging employee mobility in a variety of directions, they will witness only problems—that is, the loss of good people. The organization must also provide a reward system to compensate (monetarily or otherwise) leaders for their developmental efforts and encouragement of subordinates. Simultaneously, they must reward employees who opt for other than vertical mobility. Practitioners, in consort with their colleagues in compensation, must address these problems early on if the effort is to succeed. Creativity and imagination are the tickets to success.

ON YOUR MARK, GET SET

Clearly one could go on preparing forever! But that would not launch a career development program, nor motivate employees in career paths, nor provide much return on investment for the organization. The Preparing Stage comes to a close when the practitioners, to the very best of their ability, feel that the necessary groundwork has been laid and that both the people and the structural interventions have been determined and comfortably established.

Table 8 outlines some typical errors that, according to organization development professional Dave Nicoll, seem to snag human resource practitioners when they get ready to launch a new program. Any of these can snag you. So beware!

In delivering effective career-developing efforts, the practitioner has to be aware of two very specific killers—underdoing, beginning before the program is well thought out and before organizational support functions are ready; and overdoing, readying resources to such a degree of perfection that leaders and employees alike lose impetus and commitment and feel that all the career development talk was just that—talk!

Either extreme can adversely affect the remaining five stages, which will be described in the ensuing chapters.

TABLE 8

ERRORS OF A GRIEVOUS KIND

Acting Without Direction

- Moving away from something, rather than toward something
- Not knowing what you want, but acting anyway

Spurning Half a Loaf

- Rejecting partial success
- Refusing to attempt minor achievements

Deciding the Task Is Too Big

- Not starting on a small part of the job, because the whole job looks too enormous

Leaving the Backyard Unattended

- Ignoring the people whose support you will need

Building Foundations on Sand Dunes

- Acting on what you want, even though you know others don't agree

Not Knowing What You've Got When You've Got It

- Failing to determine what constitutes success, and not stopping to look for it

|3|

Tapping Talent

THE PROFILING STAGE

"Our options are to learn this new game,
the rules, the roles of the participants
and how the rewards are distributed,
or to continue practicing our present skills
and become the best player in a game
that is no longer being played."
–LARRY WILSON

The essence of the Profiling Stage is to assist the employee in answering the question, "Who Am I?" Because that question is often difficult to answer fully and honestly, employees need strong encouragement throughout their efforts to identify existing skills and to recognize their potential for transferring present skills to future career settings. During the Profiling Stage, the employee is responsible for identifying skills and interests, the leader must support the effort by providing opportunities for discussion, while the practitioner makes a variety of assessment tools available.

The Components

The Profiling Stage occurs in two distinct phases: identification and reality-testing. During the identification phase, employees are assisted in using a variety of methods to uncover their range of skills, knowledge areas, values, and work context preferences. This enables them to develop a personal profile that provides direction for selecting appropriate goals at the Targeting Stage, which follows.

During the reality-testing phase, employees test these self-perceptions by soliciting feedback from other individuals and by cross-checking with existing organizational resources, such as past performance appraisals and job descriptions. Skill identification without reality-testing encourages the individual to select goals based on skills that are only self-perceptions. Reality-testing forces a system of checks and balances on the individual. While skill identification usually begins the Profiling Stage, one need not wait until all skills are identified to begin testing them against reality. There is much oscillation between the phases throughout the Profiling Stage. It is also possible to invert the two phases, that is for the employee to receive data about an area of expertise from a colleague or boss and then proceed to identify more specific skills involved or to identify other situations in which that skill was used. What is important to remember is that each skill identified must be verified—before the Profiling Stage concludes and the individual begins to determine career goals at the Targeting Stage.

A BEVY OF BENEFITS

Although profiling is largely an individual activity that results in information for the employee, its output extends to the organization as a whole. Typically, organizations have only scant knowledge of the depth of human resources in their workforce. Many companies that have developed formal skill banks have often catalogued only the abilities now being used on the job and have not assessed additional skills or current ones that may be available to fill future needs. Employee-profiling activities can provide useful information to the organization, suggesting strategies for further employee training and human resource planning.

The value of profiling for employees lies in their increased ability to articulate their skills and abilities, thereby enabling them to more intelligently choose career alternatives. Even if employees stopped the cycle after having done only this self-assessment process, they would have gained a great deal. Most would have learned that their skills are much more extensive and transferable to a wider variety of job settings than previously imagined. Such discovery builds self-confidence, with benefits extending beyond the job setting. The profiling process also encourages employees to discuss self-perceptions with leaders and to formulate a wider base for defining career goals and performance standards. Such an understanding of personal abilities and preferences increases productivity on current jobs and helps in projecting career futures. The Profiling Stage is a crucial step with immediate payoff, but only a first step in the total career development cycle.

NOW, FOR THE HARD PART

Unfortunately, skill identification is no simple task. Individuals are often prevented from verbalizing their skills by a cultural norm that gives high priority to personal modesty. It is, therefore, often difficult for employees to sell someone on their skills, even when it is appropriate to do so. Complicating matters is the fact that jobs are often identified by vague labels rather than by specific activities or skills. The question asked is "What do you do?" not "What are your skills?" And the reply is "I'm a human resources analyst," not "I organize, write, interview, and analyze." The ability to articulate specific skills used on the job is often the most difficult to master. And many individuals take their abilities for granted, failing to recognize the multitude of skills they use in accomplishing even routine tasks. For many it is easier to define skill deficiencies, since negative feedback from leaders may be more common than positive. Even when skills are well defined, most people contribute to this negativism by putting themselves down in order to appear "humble" and "worthy." Furthermore, employees often fail to consider skills used less frequently, on prior jobs, or in personal endeavors. The challenge for practitioners and leaders at the Profiling Stage, therefore, is to assist employees in exploring their wide array of personal capacities. This requires a deeper understanding of how present work activities encompass specific skills that can become future building blocks.

The Identification Component

The identification phase of profiling entails examination of three of the key attributes that can influence the selection of future career goals: skills, values, and work contexts. Employees will need to embark on thoughtful self-exploration in each of these three areas before gaining the clear composite picture needed for the Targeting Stage.

THE SKILL OF IT ALL

Before undertaking skill identification activities, the practitioner needs to understand the nature of skills and their use at different levels of the organization. A skill may be defined as specific behavior that results in effective performance. During the Profiling Stage, it is important to remember that a skill must be demonstrated in performance, not merely in potential.

Skills can be learned in three specific ways: theoretically, through simulation, and by on-the-job experience. In the first approach an individual is exposed to knowledge by reading or listening to a lecture. In simulated learning the individuals actually practice a skill in an artificial situation and receive feedback on their performance. Skills are learned through on-the-job experience when individuals perform a skill as a natural component of their work. Skills are most effectively learned when individuals can actually perform the skill in a realistic situation and then explicitly analyze their performance.

Many organizations have adopted the term *competency* and are careful to distinguish between the words *skill* and *competency*. Those who do this maintain that competencies are clusters of related skills, and that skills are the specific behaviors that make up competencies. The use of the word *competencies* allows the organization to describe requirements in much broader terms than the word *skills* would. The term *competencies* thus allows for flexibility and makes for an HR system that is much more resilient and adaptable.

However, the "classic" approach, and still one of the most common means of classifying work-related skills, is to categorize them as those that are technical in nature, those that deal with human relations, and those that pertain to the conceptualization of problems and situations. Because of its many applications, this classification system has been selected for use in this book. (At this and subsequent stages reference will be made to these three skill areas.)

Nearly every job can be broken down into requirements for skills in technical, human, and conceptual areas. All employees possess skills in these categories, and success in almost any career field will require proficiency in them. Analyzing the relative importance of these skills will show what areas are potential sources of strength.

Technical Skills
Technical skills are the most concrete and most easily identifiable of the three types. They are represented by proficiency in a particular activity or process related directly to the job. These skills

are acquired through training and experience in using whatever tools, processes, or techniques apply to a specific function. Work specialization has put a high priority on technical skills—ranging from surgery to accounting to pipe fitting to computer systems design—and they are typically emphasized in most professional, vocational, and on-the-job learning programs.

While they may be easily identifiable, technical skills are probably the least transferable of the three—they are the type of skill that an individual would be most likely to change or leave behind as one moves through the organization.

Human Skills

Human skills are primarily related to working with people. While they can be developed through conscientious effort, these skills require a strong natural inclination and must be consistently demonstrated if they are to be successful. An asset at all job levels, these skills are reflected in the way an individual understands, communicates with, and motivates others. They facilitate cooperative efforts, from effective delegation to teamwork to negotiation; they are marked by productive relationships with colleagues, subordinates, and leaders. An individual skilled in this area is sensitive to the personal needs and capacities of others, as well as to the functional needs of accomplishing a task. These skills permit one to develop and maintain a network of contacts, in order to do favors for one another and pass along information; to motivate, train, counsel, and guide a staff; and to mediate conflicts between individuals.

Conceptual Skills

Conceptual skills are the most complex to identify because they involve a mental coordinating and integrating ability that embodies both technical and human skills. They include the ability to visualize various components of an enterprise, problem, or decision as a whole, to recognize the overall functional relationships of those components; and to sense what action is appropriate in terms of the total situation. This skill enables individuals to base decisions on creative thinking about the past, present, and future, by being able to visualize a mental model of the organization as a whole unit.

For any particular organization and its structures, the functions and specific skills required in each job or area will vary. Employees

---

CASE 11

Active Identification of Skills

The home office of a major insurance company has developed a career-planning program for its more promising clerical employees. The program is based on a job family concept that makes the tasks people actually do and the key skills inherent in doing them more comprehensible to employees.

During the sessions, participants analyze key job duties and skills required for successful performance and listen to a series of taped interviews with present jobholders from the various job families. On their own, employees fill out a self-assessment of job interest and abilities. Then they undertake an eighty-six-item personal job analysis survey and fill out a set of scoring keys for each of the four job families, which enables them to relate their interest patterns as shown by the job analysis survey to each of the job families.

---

need to identify their specific technical, human, and conceptual skills and match what they see as their current abilities against those required for their future work. It is important to gain leaders' support in defining and specifying skills in order to accurately determine them. The Action Provoking Questions on page 81 are helpful in identifying skills, interests, and values for both employees and managers.

TRANSFERABILITY OF SKILLS

One outcome of the identification phase is the ability to determine which skills are potentially transferable to other locations within or outside the organization. Without transferable skills, individuals would not move at all from one position to another within an organization. The more the individuals can become aware, not only of the specific skills relevant to their particular job, but of those skills that are transferable to other jobs, the broader the range of goal options that can be opened to them.

A transferable skill means that an individual has gained particular knowledge that is necessary to move from one area of an organization, or one kind of work, to another. If an individual can see that a particular skill is transferable, abilities acquired elsewhere and at other times in that individual's life can be considered acceptable background for a particular position.

■ ACTION PROVOKING QUESTIONS

QUESTIONS BETWEEN MANAGERS AND EMPLOYEES

While there are a myriad of instruments and inventories that the practitioner can recommend to employees as well as to managers that help to identify skills, interests, and values, the following set of questions can also be utilized to help spark a discussion that surfaces this information:

Skills
- What are three skills that it takes to do your current job well?
- What skills have you used consistently across the past several positions you've held?
- Which skills would you like to develop further?
- If you were to mentor someone around one skill that you possess, what would it be?
- When you have a really good day at work, what kind of skills are you drawing on?
- Which skills seem most portable to you?
- What's one skill you haven't used for a long time?

Interests
- Which interest areas would you most like to develop further?
- What activities have you lost interest in? Would you want to rekindle any?
- What interests do you wish you had more of at work?
- What part of your current job interests you most?
- If you could create the perfect job, what percentage of people, data, things, or xideas would be in it?
- How have your interests changed over the last five years?

Values
- What are your most prized values?
- Describe each value you selected and what it means for you?
- Would your best friend/family have guessed that you would have select those values?
- What would be at the bottom of your list, for example, values you wouldn't think of selecting?
- Which values does your present job truly deliver on?
- How have your values changed?
- Which values are not possible given your current job? Why do you see it this way?

Transferability can occur in one of three ways: (1) A specific skill—such as typing, budgeting, programming, or organizing—can be transferred from one job to another; (2) a knowledge area—such as accounting, consumer credit, sales, or data processing—can be transferred; or (3) an entire activity or array of skills—such as supervising operations procedures, analyzing customer needs, or interviewing prospective candidates—can also be transferred. Each of these can be used in many parts of any one organization. Each can also be transferred from organization to organization.

A variety of approaches can be used to help employees describe their transferable skills, identify alternative uses for those skills, and determine how those alternatives relate to other jobs within the organization. Exercises could include determining skills and then naming other places in the organization where those skills would be used, whether or not one wanted to move in that direction.

VERIFYING VALUES

While it is essential that an individual base career choices on appropriate skills, it is equally important to mesh career considerations with the personal values that shape life preferences. Values are those esteemed ideals and concepts that are expressed in our everyday behavior and our long-term priorities. Because of their influence on behavior and priority-setting, values affect satisfaction and determine effectiveness on the job. For a person to be productive and happy, a fit must exist between the job and the employee's personal values.

An individual who places high value on personal freedom, for example, may need to work independently, unhampered by restrictions imposed by others. Those who value a sense of accomplishment require strong feedback in response to their endeavors. Security is a high priority for some people, who may feel the work doesn't have to be exciting or challenging as long as there is little fear of losing the job.

Practitioners need to build a repertoire of exercises to help employees identify values. Most values assessments suggest various values and ask respondents to prioritize or rate their importance. Table 9 lists typical work values that can affect career decisions.

These work values are clearly related to general life values, such as a stable and loving family life, rewarding friendships, time for leisure activities, good health, and a secure future. Individuals must establish a fit between their values for working and their

TABLE 9

WORK VALUES

Achievement	Prestige
Authority	Security
Autonomy	Self-esteem
Continued learning	Social contact
Creativity	Social contribution
Esteem of others	Spirituality
Monetary rewards	Variety
Opportunity for advancement	Workplace environment

overall life values, in order that each contributes to and builds upon the other. Career decisions that take values into account are more likely to result in satisfying and rewarding job achievement.

THE RIGHT CONTEXT

The context of the job is the psychological and physical setting in which work is performed. Context preferences closely reflect personal values. A job that requires a great deal of travel, for example, might be considered desirable or undesirable, depending on individual values and lifestyle. Comfort with work requiring selling, persuading, or directing interaction with other people reflects other values. The degree of stress involved in a job is part of its context. Even the nature of an organization, or an entire industry—conservative, progressive, or in-between—sets the tone of the work context and helps determine how individuals will fit with it. Product lines and the primary customers are also important in considering individual value systems. For instance, a person who highly values peace and nonviolence could hardly be happy working in a defense- or nuclear-related industry, the products of which are used in armaments.

Often it is these job characteristics that are responsible for an employee's sense of job satisfaction. If the profiling process is intended to lead to setting realistic goals, it is important that an employee's profile include an examination of the contextual factors that contribute to their sense of job satisfaction, as well as those factors leading to stress or dissatisfaction.

Exercises and dialogue can bring these preferences into the open and make them a vital part of the career profile. Some job factors that may be considered include:

Its environmental context:

- The "look" of physical surroundings (such as furniture and lighting)
- Mobility (ability to move about to perform tasks)
- Location (such as urban or suburban, indoor or outdoor)
- Privacy (space from or closeness to others)
- Communication (face-to-face, written, telephone)

Its interactional context:

- Degree of supervision
- Degree of contact with peers
- Degree of contact with clients
- Degree of friendliness in relations with others
- Degree of and frequency of feedback about performance

Its functional context:

- Degree of challenge in work
- Degree of certainty about scheduling and duties
- Opportunities for learning
- Type of work (technical, supervisory, policymaking)
- Work hours
- Degree of control (formal procedures, rules)
- Pay and benefits

Employees can be guided through a review of these factors, asking themselves, "What do I feel I need in each of these areas?" Those who go through this process will be better equipped to select career opportunities that have the greatest personal fit and are most likely to lead to satisfaction.

Resources for Identification

Very few individuals are capable of conducting the in-depth self-exploration necessary for effective profiling. Therefore, guidance is needed at this point. The charge for the career development practitioner is (1) to provide broad-based support for a number of people in a manner that recognizes their unique, individual needs, and (2) to determine who in the system is most appropriate to deliver these services to employees.

A variety of proven tools and techniques exist, which can be drawn upon to guide employees through the identification process. They can be delivered by the practitioner, or by leaders, career counselors/advisors, or members of the training staff. Computer-based programs often allow the employees to work through the first part of the identification process on their own, producing their own individualized development plan that they can discuss with the practitioner or their leader. Two categories of instruments that can facilitate profiling are self-assessment exercises and scored surveys.

Self-assessment exercises generally call for individual creativity and internal brainstorming. They ask open-ended questions that give respondents the latitude to develop answers out of their own experience and self-knowledge. Such inventories may ask a respondent to create a composite of the ideal work setting, to prioritize a list of value statements, or to select key words from a list of personal adjectives. The results are examined by the participant and may be discussed with others in order to add to the composite developed at the Profiling Stage.

Scored surveys are paper-and-pencil tests geared to previously determined measures, which indicate vocational interests, aptitudes, motivations, values, and other personal characteristics. Generally, they ask a number of close-ended questions (answers limited to yes or no, true or false) and lead to scores that connote different degrees of skills or preferences for different jobs or job characteristics. For example, individuals can determine if their strengths lie in working with concepts or working with numbers, or if their preferences are for leading the team or following the lead of others. Often practitioners have these surveys available on their shelf or in their database but overlook their usefulness at the identification phase of the Profiling Stage.

Each of these aids may be delivered individually, by using self-scored tests in workbooks that contain scoring interpretations, or through group activities, such as workshops in which participants share results and assist one another in interpretation. An effective way is to combine both methods, by first administering individual exercises and then using the results as a basis for group workshop activities. Participants can thus gain information that relates to their unique characteristics, but they can be motivated and assisted by others in analyzing that information in relation to the career development process.

Many organizations combine these methods through computer-based approaches that include everything from self-assessments of an individual's interests, to career decision planning tools, to how to write a resume and choose the right profession. These computer-based programs offer a highly individualized approach, allowing employees to produce their own career development plans in only a few hours. The flexibility of this approach allows a maximization of training time, since individuals can do a lot of preliminary work on their own, thus using the trainer's time and resources more effectively. Another important advantage is that their plans can be tested against both career development theory and the specific organization's reality. The individual is able to get immediate scoring results, to search both public and organizational databases for information on development programs and job options, and to customize content, interface, and databases.

Computer-based approaches to career development are evolving ever more rapidly. Among the features and activities currently offered on computer-based systems are *Holland's Self-Directed Search,* which helps individuals identify their interests and how they relate to their job, the *Myers-Briggs Type Indicator®,* which defines an individual's personality type and personal preferences, and 360-degree feedback instruments, which can combine feedback on individuals' skills from multiple sources, both inside and outside of the organization.

Whether the process is computer based or not, workshops should be led by skilled facilitators who can draw from individuals the information and interpretations that may not readily come to mind. A group setting adds to the profiling process because of the motivational impact of peer assistance. Individuals discover that they are not alone as they move into the more difficult aspects of profiling. In addition, the power of group interaction during a workshop can lead participants to more in-depth discussion about their skills and job preferences than might be possible when they work alone.

Both kinds of interventions, self-assessment exercises and scored surveys, stimulate the identification process. The selection of activities best suited to a particular group depends upon the nature of the group and the skill level of the professionals administering the activity. To assist practitioners in making the most informed choices, a detailed description of the two categories of instruments follows.

SELF-ASSESSMENT EXERCISES

Because they are designed to maximize creative thinking and internal brainstorming, self-assessment exercises leave substantial latitude for individual interpretation (unlike scored tests in which interpretation is predetermined for various numerical results). This interpretive latitude places particular emphasis on how the exercise is used by the individual administering it as well as several other factors that contribute to interpretation, such as:

- Setting—individual, small group, or large group
- Opportunities for sharing individual results
- Opportunities for peer-to-peer feedback and advice
- Probing questions by the facilitator
- Interpretive assistance by the facilitator

Self-assessment exercises rarely end with the respondent completing a form and putting down the pen. Generally, additional prodding is necessary to generate ideas that do not readily come to mind. Quite often some discussion of responses is useful to inspire in-depth interpretation of results. While the design of the exercise itself is important, the format in which it is used is often the key to its success as a profiling tool. Books containing self-assessment exercises proliferate the marketplace. They contain many exercises that help individuals define their skills. Generally these approaches start with a design for listing skills or related personal qualities and continue through a format for further probing and interpretation. A careful analysis of the wide variety of exercises available is necessary before selecting those to be offered to employees.

The *Search* technique helps participants define a wide range of skills, by naming a primary technical or conceptual skill used on the job and then brainstorming related subskills that it entails. The primary skill is written in the center of a piece of paper, with subskills placed, like branches, on arrows leading into it, giving participants a visual aid to prod their thinking. The technical skill of "editing" may actually involve a great range of subskills that may be difficult for the individual to think of (such as "interviewing," "organizing," "researching," "rewriting," "decision making," "creating," "planning") or that the individual may well take for granted. An example of a "search" appears in Figure 2.

This process can be enhanced by a facilitator verbally probing what other skills one would use to accomplish the central skill, by sharing new ideas that come to mind, and by providing lists of

FIGURE 2

The Skill "Search"

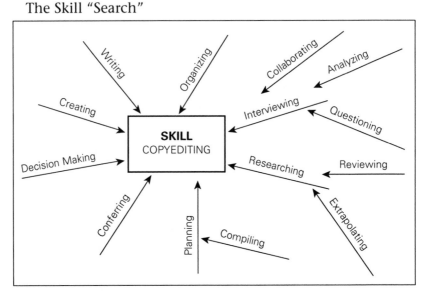

other skills to which participants may refer when they run out of ideas. Search can be done by a leader or career advisor in a personalized setting, or in a workshop setting where participants are encouraged to assist one another and learn, from the searches done by their colleagues, more about their own unacknowledged skills. The payoff of this technique lies in participants' realizations that their skills far exceed frequent characterizations, such as "I'm only a secretary" or "All I do is edit copy."

Success Stories, one of the oldest and most widely used profiling techniques, helps individuals recognize the personal skills that they may have demonstrated in the past, may not be using on their current jobs, may take for granted, or may have completely forgotten about. If a workshop setting is selected, each person in a small group would relate a past experience in which he or she felt successful. Group members then assist each other in developing a list of the skills demonstrated in the story. This exercise can also be used in a one-to-one discussion between leader and employee or between career advisor and employee.

The excitement generated by this exercise can break through old mental blocks such as "I don't have any particular skills" or " I can't think of anything I'm good at." Employees find that past achievements demonstrate abilities in planning, organizing, public speaking, negotiating, fund-raising, delegating, and so on. These may be skills that can be reactivated and used toward achieving specific career goals.

Another way to use success stories is to center on a person's accomplishments over the past twelve to eighteen months on the job. Employees are asked to think of examples of success stories that characterize such things as decision making, problem solving, or interpersonal style. Employees find themselves becoming more specific about their current skills as a result of this exercise. It can be especially useful when the success stories being told relate to specific behavior to be evaluated in performance appraisals. Individuals can use the information gleaned from this exercise to more effectively prepare for an employee-initiated dialogue during the performance appraisal.

A similar exercise, *Career History,* asks employees to describe the progression of their work life. Group members listen for skills that have been demonstrated, particularly those that have reappeared time and time again. Individual values and work context preferences may also be revealed. This exercise serves as an excellent warm-up activity and can easily be done in either a one-to-one or group setting.

The *Typical Day* exercise seeks to identify currently used skills that may be overlooked or taken for granted. A facilitator uses guided imagery to move the individual through a typical work day. Prodding the memory for exactly what happens hour-by-hour helps individuals to elaborate about daily activities, so that they can begin to note the variety of skills practiced each day.

A great many books on the market contain exercises useful in eliciting skills from participants. The problem is not so much in finding exercises or designing them as in determining which ones offer the right combinations for a particular group of employees. The materials available on the market can be weighed against program needs in a manner such as the one shown in Table 10.

SCORED SURVEYS

The objectives of scored surveys are similar to those of self-assessment exercises—to aid individuals in discovering abilities, job interests, values, and other factors that can help shape an appropriate match between the individual and the job. Scored surveys, however, accomplish this through a tangible bottom line,

TABLE 10

SKILL IDENTIFICATION TECHNIQUES

Technique	Objective	Format	Outcome
Search	Determine numerous skills emanating from one central skill	Individuals brainstorm their associated skills with help of others	Going beyond using immediate descriptor of job at hand as only skill definition
Success Story	Understand how past achievements contribute to to personal skills inventory and identify preference patterns leading to successful feelings	Individuals relate past successes to to others who draw out skill definitions	Discovering skills that may be forgotten or taken for granted
Career History	Develop a complete list of skills indicated by job experiences, and identify preference patterns for types of work and contexts	Individuals relate career history to others who suggest skills that have been used	Naming a wide variety of skills that have been evidenced throughout an array of work experiences
Typical Day	Determine variety of skills that are used on current job	Individuals are asked to relate typical day and skills used throughout	Discovering skills that are frequently used, but may be taken for granted as routine

the score, which indicates exactly how test results are to be interpreted.

For many individuals these concrete results are preferable to self-assessment information, which is really left to the vagaries of individual interpretation. Others, however, feel constrained by the narrow categories into which test results may fall, and question the validity of test construction. It is valuable to offer a mix of self-assessment exercises and scored surveys, so that varied profiling methods appropriate to different individuals can be presented. Variety also offers a cross-check on results.

Scored surveys can also be used as the basis for interaction in group settings, significantly enriching the potential use of these instruments at the Profiling Stage. As with self-assessment exercises, a workshop setting can encourage the sharing of conclusions and the discussion of general questions pertaining to each individual's results.

Tested and validated survey instruments are available from numerous sources, including universities, training and consulting firms, and publishing companies. Generally they are aimed at extracting information about interests, styles, and work/life values.

These surveys can assist individuals in acquiring self-knowledge in different areas of their personal and professional lives. However, it is still up to the individual to pull the pieces together into a single, coherent view.

Occupational Interests

Interest inventories are designed to help individuals translate their likes and dislikes into specific work preferences. They can provide information that helps in determining occupational choices, as well as in identifying sources of job dissatisfaction. However, it must be emphasized that they are not tests of aptitudes, but rather of interests in and possible satisfaction with a range of occupations.

Working with interest inventories is best done by career counselors, advisors, or trained facilitators within a workshop setting. Line managers and team leaders may not be as effective in using these, unless they have had a great deal of experience and find themselves sincerely interested in the inventory.

Personal Styles

Surveys aimed at helping people become aware of their personalities and styles of interpersonal behavior can provide useful information for the profile and additional insight toward helping the individual work more effectively with others, a key to career success.

Such surveys generally ask respondents to build a self-portrait by choosing from a variety of descriptive adjectives, or by answering questions about how they behave in a number of different situations.

The primary value from any identification inventory lies in the self-insight provided to employees embarking on a career development program. Whether they deal with job contexts and the expectations that individuals seek to fulfill in the work environment, or with behavior and motivations one takes into that context, surveys and inventories provide basic information that must be validated in other contexts and with other individuals before it can be used in setting goals.

Reality-Testing: Taking a Second Look

To acquire serious personal validity, identification information needs to be supported by additional data available from immediate experience. Such information provides the basis for the second phase of profiling. Reality-testing can be generated from two major sources: (1) the perceptions of individuals who can be called upon to supply candid impressions of the employee's strengths and weaknesses, and (2) the existing programs and policies in the organization that serve as additional support for career development at this stage. The reality-testing process, then, can be viewed as a means of tapping external information sources in order to verify the new information that has been developed, mostly by individuals themselves.

PEOPLE PERCEPTIONS

Reality-testing must include discussions with individuals who have some knowledge of the employee developing a profile. This is the most informal, but generally most difficult, aspect of the profiling process, and it is often difficult for both the giver and the receiver of feedback. The likelihood of discomfort can be decreased, and the possibility of honest interchange can be increased, if certain norms or principles are followed. Employees need to be familiarized with these before they engage in reality-testing.

Soliciting Feedback

The first norm concerns the notion of respect. Individuals must respect the views, knowledge, and capabilities of the person offering assessment. If the individual does not value and trust the other person's opinion, reality-testing input will have little effect. Trust develops partly from the feeling that the other person's input will be sincere and helpful. Employees receiving feedback must also be convinced that assessments offered are intended to be in their best interests.

The second norm is privacy. Employees should have a feeling of safety with those selected for this process. They must be convinced that anything revealed will remain confidential and will not be misused.

Openness is the third norm, and this involves a willingness on the part of the assessor to be frank. Openness is two-sided—the employee must also be willing to hear frank statements and must not become defensive when information is provided. The employee must be willing to listen closely, but must also be encouraged to reflect on what has been said. The idea is not merely to hear the feedback, but also to put it to use.

Often employees need a formula to follow to help them solicit data. For individuals who aren't used to being proactive about this, a step-by-step approach may improve their comfort as well as their effectiveness. One approach, devised by the author and consultant Beverly Bernstein (1991) suggests that there are five distinct steps that are necessary in order to get straight and effective feedback:

- **Step 1:** *Decide what* you want feedback on.
- **Step 2:** *Determine who* can give you that feedback.
- **Step 3:** *Determine where* you ask for it.
- **Step 4:** *Decide when* is the best time to ask for it.
- **Step 5:** *Decide how* to ask for it.

There are many reasons for soliciting specific feedback from a variety of sources: (1) It is important to clarify marketable skills. It can be helpful to get input from people we have worked with and worked for over the years. Their perspective will help us see ourselves in a new light. (2) Many of us are blind to our strongest skills. Other people can sometimes see them more clearly, and they're less likely to take them for granted. We may be humble about our own skills, because we were taught from an early age not to brag or blow our own horn. (3) Straight, honest feedback helps to focus on areas in which development is needed. No matter how good one is at a specific task or skill, there is always room for improvement. Exercise 5 provides specific steps for soliciting feedback.

Giving Feedback

Those providing reality-testing information should recognize that they have a vital role as well. They are not trying to make another individual more like themselves. The assessor is concerned with providing perceptive information, not with correcting faults or shaping personalities and behavior more compatible with their own beliefs.

When employees in most organizations are asked what they would like more of from their managers, their first response is usually "feedback." People want to know where they stand—they want to know if their manager's perception of their performance is the same as their own.

A manager's role is to provide candid, constructive feedback about performance and behavior to help employees grow and develop in their current job, and beyond. Many managers are uncomfortable giving feedback, either positive or negative, because they don't always know how to do it simply and effectively. Giving feedback so that it can be heard nondefensively is key: Managers need to be specific and to share feelings as well. Precisely how managers phrase their feedback will determine the effectiveness of a reality-testing conversation. The following points are critical:

- *Use specific examples:* The more relevant the examples, the greater the possibility the employee will understand.
- *Disclose feelings/impact:* This makes it easier to take feedback seriously.
- *Discuss their perspective:* This keeps the feedback from being unilateral or heavy-handed.
- *Develop suggestions for growth:* Particularly with negative feedback, having ways to improve provides direction and hope.
- *Decide on follow-up agenda:* It is always helpful for people to know what will happen next.

EXERCISE 5
Soliciting Feedback

Step 1

The first step in the process is to determine exactly **WHAT** you would like to receive feedback on. Be as *specific* as possible; asking a broad question like "Am I doing a good job?" will not elicit a response that can help you. You might ask for feedback on a specific skill or a behavior. Determine not only what skill or behavior is involved, but give a definite incident so that your question is clearly understood. Select one skill, behavior, or attitude on which you want feedback.

Step 2

Now determine **WHO** can give you the feedback based on **WHAT** you want to learn. The person you select should be somebody you work with who has seen you demonstrate the skill or behavior in question. Remember, it may be a co-worker as well as a supervisor. Based on what you want feedback on, select the person(s) you intend to talk to.

Step 3

Next determine **WHERE** the best place might be to ask for feedback from your selected person. A busy hallway immediately after an important meeting may not be the right place. Try to find an office or meeting room that affords privacy, or a lunch place where you can be alone. The key element is that it is a place where you will have the full attention of the person whom you are asking. Select one of the people from Step 2 and pick the best place for a productive conversation to occur.

Step 4

Now determine **WHEN** the best time to ask for feedback might be in the same manner in which you selected the WHERE. An ideal time may be when you have just finished a project, or are about to begin or request a new assignment. In addition, don't pick a time when your selected person is late rushing to a meeting; arrange for a period when you can be assured of the time you will need. Using the same person from Step 3, select the right moment.

Step 5

The most important question to be asked is **HOW**. Asking for feedback so that it will be given to you honestly and directly is the goal of this workshop. Precisely how you phrase your request for information will determine the quality of the response. In addition to being specific, it is best to also disclose your own perception of the behavior or skill. Using the five steps listed here and on page 93, write a brief script that will prepare you to ask for feedback. Check with others to see if your script is specific and if it promotes honesty from the giver of the feedback.

EXERCISE 6

Giving Feedback

Step 1

WHO should receive it? The person you select should be someone you work with and have seen demonstrate a skill or behavior on which you can offer feedback. Although a direct report may be the most obvious choice, it may be a colleague, team member, or interface from another area who will profit from your feedback.

Step 2

Now determine **WHAT** should be heard by your selected person. Pick a specific skill or personal attribute that is essential to the person's job; be as specific as possible, and use timely examples. Remember, the feedback can be on something positive—people can never hear too many good things about their performance. Based on whom you have selected, pick skills and attributes on which you want to give feedback.

Step 3

The next step is to choose **WHERE** the best place might be to give the feedback to your selected person. A busy hallway immediately after an important meeting may not be the right place. Try to find an office or meeting room that affords privacy, or another private place. The key element is that it be a place where you will have the full attention of the person to whom you are giving feedback. Then select one skill or attribute from Step 2 and pick the right place(s) to give feedback.

Step 4

Next determine **WHEN** the best time to give feedback might be. An ideal time may be when your selected person has just finished a project, or when you're unable to offer a desired assignment. In addition, arrange for a period when you can be assured of the time you will need. List several ideas for the right moment.

Bernstein (1991) suggests four preliminary questions that must also be answered:

- Who should receive it?
- What needs to be heard?
- Where can it be given?
- When is it appropriate?

Exercise 6 provides some steps for giving feedback.

360-Degree Feedback

One popular and effective method of reality-testing is the 360-degree feedback, or multirater, approach. This approach relies on input from those who have a variety of different relationships to a learner, such as leaders, colleagues, subordinates, or customers. Because input is sought from multiple sources, the outcome is a wide range of perspectives on performance and evaluation.

Technology has also allowed 360-degree feedback to become much more user-friendly than in the past. Now it is possible to collect the data and it data much more readily than previously. It is easy to ask follow-up questions that will provide a greater depth of information. Furthermore, this additional data offers a chance to break through the common defense scripts of learners. For example, a learner may defend a negative rating by stating, "but at least I know I have improved that in the past year." Technology would allow the practitioner or feedback facilitator to quickly access data that would either support or negate the learner's hypothesis. For example, the data might show that raters feel the learner has not improved, or has even changed for the worse on a particular competency.

Ideally, the outcome of the 360-degree feedback will be focused on development rather than judgment. In a personal consversation, Gary Schuman, management consultant, said an especially effective approach to identifying areas for growth and improvement is to produce a *Skills Map*. As presented in Table 11, feedback from various sources provides valuable comparison and contrast of the different views of the individual's skills and performance and how those relate to the organization's needs.

Employees can go beyond the immediate job setting for reality-testing information. While peers, leaders, subordinates, and customers can give important feedback about task performance and interaction on the job, family and friends can assist in exploring essential information priorities. Furthermore, sharing profiling information with family and friends at this stage in the career development process enables employees to generate personal support and understanding that will be valuable as career changes are being contemplated or implemented later on.

STRUCTURAL SUPPORTS

It is important to remember that every organization has ongoing systems and procedures that, if fully used and linked with the

---

TABLE 11

SKILLS MAP APPROACH

The *Skills Map* approach produces a graphical comparison and contrast of the feedback sources' level of agreement or disagreement on:

- The skills necessary in the learner's current position
- The skills necessary for success in that position
- The learner's strengths and skills already possessed
- The skills that most need improvement
- The learner's current level of performance

Adapted from Gary Schuman, 1995

career development program, can enrich individual career development activities and contribute to organizational objectives. When taken into account during the planning of career development efforts, they provide valuable structural support for its activities.

Several of these structural support programs are particularly relevant to the Profiling Stage, because of their ability to aid in identification and in providing information for reality-testing. Three programs that can make major contributions are job descriptions (often including job analysis and performance standards), performance appraisals, and skills inventories.

A Job Well Defined

Although many organizations still exist and function quite well without any kind of job descriptions, most organizations find benefits and value in having some documentation that describes jobs and positions within the organization. In order to meet the increasing pressures to be more flexible and resilient, many organizations are reframing their job descriptions. Some delineate key competencies required by specific jobs, others delegate to the group levels, and still others delegate key performance results, leaving specifics to groups and leaders.

Job descriptions are sometimes supplemented by written performance standards related to goals to be accomplished over a set period of time. Performance standards state what is to be done, as well as how much and how well it is to be done. In general, performance standards need review and revision at least annually and should be arrived at through mutual agreement between employee and leader. Job descriptions support not only employee profiling activities, but also human resource planning, orientation, recruiting and screening, training and development, hiring and placement, and the development of organizational career paths.

Employees can use the job description to see whether or not the skills identified earlier in this phase are required of them on the job.

Performance Appraisal

As described in the preceding chapter, performance appraisal systems and techniques are closely linked to all stages of a career development program. During the Profiling Stage, however, performance appraisals help supply employees with an opportunity to candidly reality-test their skills with leaders. And if it is to enhance the profiling process, a performance appraisal system must be more than a signed list of check-marked ratings slipped surreptitiously on employees' desks by their leaders while the employees are on a lunch break. It should involve face-to-face discussion that affords opportunities for:

- Description of performance strengths and suggestions for capitalizing on them
- Description of performance deficiencies and suggestions for correcting them
- Establishment of performance standards for the upcoming year in light of these strengths and weaknesses
- Exchange of mutual expectations and needs for interaction between leader and employees

Performance appraisals are commonly given only at prescribed times and, even then, under conditions of formality and discomfort. However, feedback given regularly, appropriately, and soon after significant events helps the employees do a better job, provides valuable information for their profiles, and makes the leader-employee interface easier.

In order to be effective, reality-testing feedback from leaders should meet three criteria:

1. The employee should understand what the leader is saying.
2. The employee should be willing and able to accept what is being said as constructive.
3. The employee should be able to use the feedback as a basis for action or change.

CASE 12

*Performance Appraisal Training
for Both Managers and Employees*

A large department store chain has initiated an approach to performance appraisal training for both leaders and employees. They use a set of workbooks that are customized to their industry and that provide exercises and instruments to assist both parties in preparing for the appraisal process. Exercises for leaders help them to carefully consider the strengths and weaknesses of employees. Exercises also help employees develop strength profiles, which can be used as the basis of exchanges with the manager during the performance appraisal process.

Feedback that is focused on behavior rather than on personality, that is based on observations rather than opinions, that is descriptive rather than judgmental, that involves the sharing of ideas and information, that is specific about situations, and that is given at the appropriate time will be effective as a reality-test of the employee's own perceptions.

Thus, adequate performance appraisal is not just a rating activity to provide data for HR files. It is one of the best means of providing employees and leaders with in-depth information about their work skills and abilities. If both parties prepare for the process and are conscious of their common need for this information, it can add to the self-awareness of the Profiling Stage. These conditions can make performance appraisals a WIN-WIN situation to be anticipated, rather than a drudgery to be feared. All but the most cursory written appraisals are generally difficult and undesirable tasks for leaders. Special training, close accountability, and attractive incentives will probably be required to motivate more meaningful appraisals. Attempts have been made to provide this training through workshops, counseling sessions, and workbooks. Active identification of skills at the Profiling Stage is one of the best ways to prepare employees to effectively use the appraisal process.

Assessment Centers

Another structure that can contribute to profiling is the assessment center, either in-house or at an outside location. By providing evaluation in a variety of group and individual settings, assessment centers offer objective off-the-job evaluation of abilities, potential, strengths, weaknesses, and motivation. Most organizations currently using assessment centers do so to identify and evaluate potential for advancement or even initial selection, usually at leadership and managerial levels, rather than to provide profiling information. However, when individual results are provided to employees at the end of an assessment center session, participants are exposed to vital information they can readily apply to their self-profiles.

The assessment center, which has grown increasingly popular in recent years, is generally two days to one week in duration, with six to twelve participants observed by a team of assessors. Participants are evaluated in a variety of group role-playing sessions, which simulate leadership and leaderless situations in decision-making settings. The sessions also generally include individual interviews and may require one or more pen-and-paper tests. It is important that the assessing organization determine beforehand the skills and characteristics being evaluated, which typically include:

leadership	motivation
oral communication	decisiveness
planning	personal impact on others
work under pressure	teamwork
response to stress	organization
energy	analysis

Self-awareness in the above skill areas contributes much to the identification process and, because those skills are witnessed by an impartial observer, the assessment contributes to reality-testing.

When used as a selection tool, the results of the assessment center's feedback would normally be sent to a leader several levels above the participant in the participant's organization. The material may, of course, be sent to the assessee's direct leader. When the feedback is employed as a profiling tool, the report would go to participants themselves, giving them the opportunity to ask questions and to choose whether or not to share the data with anyone else.

CASE 13

Assessment Centers

Assessment Centers have been used at a manufacturing firm for some selection decisions, but the majority have been used for developmental purposes. The first-line field supervisory positions within the company have major administrative requirements but are filled most often by people of proven technical competence who may be unfamiliar with supervisory tasks. The Assessment Center provides employees the chance to experience, through simulation, some of the administrative problems of the job. Because the employees get feedback on their assessment-center performance, they can make informed decisions about how best to develop their career. At the same time, the company identifies a pool of employees with the required administrative skills for consideration when vacancies occur.

Organizations that have assessment center technology available to them are beginning to recognize its usefulness as a profiling vehicle and as a selection and developmental tool.

Skills Inventories

The skills inventory serves the vital purpose of documenting the profile developed, so that the organization can utilize that information further. The ability to have skills inventories available in most firms of any size allows better use of employee skills. Talents are also more easily identified, which benefits both the organization and the employee. Overall efficiency can be increased, and employee morale can be improved.

A skills inventory data bank might include these items about individuals:

- Title
- Department
- Grade/job classification
- Salary
- Current work experience
- Past work experience
- Foreign language proficiency
- Willingness to relocate/geographic preference

CASE 14

*Using a Computerized Matching Skill Inventory
System to Recruit from Within*

A simplified but highly effective inventory system has been developed by a large bank for matching job vacancies with candidates inside the organization. The computerized matching system relies on two major sets of information: (1) a profile of tasks required on the job (and frequency with which they will be performed) and (2) a profile of tasks that the employee has performed satisfactorily (and performance frequency).

The tasks related to the job are determined by the supervisor, who selects from a list of seventy-four task descriptions and ascribes frequencies to them. The employee specifies tasks satisfactorily performed from the same list of seventy-four descriptions and verifies this with an HR interviewer. In addition, this system allows employees to indicate on a preference scale the degree to which they desire to perform the various tasks on their next job. The system can be initiated by a request to find a candidate who can fit an available position or to find a position that fits a candidate seeking a change. A match is run prior to attempting outside recruitment to assure that no qualified internal candidates have been overlooked.

- Career interests
- Education
- Professional designations, certificates, licenses
- Training courses completed
- Professional organization memberships

This information should be updated at least annually; and, depending on the capabilities of the HR information system, it should be revised as often as necessary to reflect new training, new professional memberships, or other changes.

Annual updates could be completed by leaders and employees jointly agreeing on new information before it is submitted to the system and, in this way, providing valuable face-to-face feedback for profile development.

Skills inventories, especially those that are computerized and cover thousands of employees, have been particularly valuable to organizations committed to employee development and recruit-

CASE 15

*Using a Skill Inventory
as an Organizational Database*

A large oil company developed a skills inventory that became a database of vital organizational information. Its structure permitted immediate retrieval of almost any desired item or combination of items of employee related information. The database is quite different from many so-called skills inventories; yet all of the information needed only amounts to two sides of one page for each employee.

The skills inventory can be thought of as a giant honeycomb containing over 600,000 individual items of factual, cross-referenced information about employees—information such as "John Doe has a bachelor's degree in chemical engineering" or "Jane Roe was manager of corporate accounting in 1979." The database also contains some information about employees' skills, career interests, and activities not related to their jobs, but the emphasis is on demonstrable fact versus what employees say about themselves.

Each employee annually corrects and updates his or her profile, thus enabling the company to fulfill one of the basic requirements of governmental "right to privacy" legislation, namely, that the data are correct. Operation of the database meets other regulatory requirements as well.

ment from within. Not only do they make it possible to locate individuals with existing skills, they also identify deficiencies (which can be addressed at later stages in the career development cycle). As selection devices they quickly narrow the field to a manageable number of candidates. Many leaders are surprised to find qualified individuals within their own organizations who can fill vacancies without expensive recruitment campaigns. A negative attitude not only denies employees visibility and possible advancement, but also denies the organization the benefit of using human resources to their fullest potential. It is important that leaders be required to use the skills inventory.

Profiling, then, is not just a matter of arranging a series of workshops or using an array of instruments. To be effective, profiling must be supported by ongoing policies and procedures that shape it and ensure that the assessment and validation processes continue, even if the workshops and counseling sessions do not.

RESPONSIBILITIES FOR EVERYONE

The Profiling Stage is primarily the responsibility of the employees who are creating their own profiles. It is each employee's responsibility to review the past, draw inferences from the present, and project a mental picture of the future. Profiling requires employees to undertake exercises in self-insight that may seem laborious and tedious and to exhibit a great deal of motivation to complete the process. Career development practitioners and leaders throughout the organization also have responsibility for the profiling process.

The Practitioner of Many Hats

During the Profiling Stage, the practitioners are called upon to play a number of roles. Depending on the attention and importance the company is placing on career development, these roles could include:

1. *Innovator* Knowing that different profiling techniques are necessary for different people, the practitioner must creatively seek out and experiment with a multitude of for mats for use in a variety of settings. While many tools and techniques already exist for profiling uses, the practitioner must be innovative in adapting these to immediate needs, as well as in designing others as required.

2. *Support generator* It is essential that the practitioner generate support, especially from leaders, career advisors, or trainers, before the profiling process begins. This means making the process visible and introducing the rationale, benefits, approach, and technology of the process. Building commitment will help facilitate support for the entire career development effort.

3. *Information channel* The practitioner must work toward ensuring that the information generated during profiling is fully used by the individuals and the organization. This entails clarifying the link between profiling and setting goals. It means ensuring that, where possible, profiling results are used in skills inventories and performance appraisals, and that leaders seek ways to use employees' profiling information as a guide in making decisions about human resources.

4. *Support giver* The practitioner must give support to employees and their leaders during profiling. This can include verbally encouraging them, scheduling workshops, administering batteries of tests, and accommodating special needs.

The Supportive Leader

During the Profiling Stage, as elsewhere during the career development effort, the leader plays a never-ending role of providing encouragement and guidance. The leader, if actively involved in the process, should personally discuss profiles with employees and assist them in translating profiling information to on-the-job concerns. The leader must also be willing to allow the employee the time necessary (often taken out of working hours) to pursue the exercises vital to this stage.

Even leaders with the best of intentions often do not realize the dramatic impact they can exert by being a role model or by providing guidance to employees seeking new paths to career satisfaction. Managers can sabotage the career development process by doing nothing when supporting and advancing the process requires only a little effort.

Practitioners, then, must build a partnership between employees, leaders, and themselves, if the Profiling Stage is to be a success. They must make each of the players understand the benefits of profiling and the successes that can be attained if all participate.

Though this effort may seem monumental, it is essential that it be accomplished at this point to set the stage for the continued sharing of responsibility during the Targeting Stage.

| 4 |

Optimizing Options

THE TARGETING STAGE

*"When one door closes another opens,
but we often look so long and so regretfully
upon the closed door that we do not see
the one which has opened to us."*
—ALEXANDER GRAHAM BELL

For the employees, targeting means exploring possibilities and specifying goals. For the organization, targeting entails providing the guidance that will keep employees' exploration efforts pointed in a direction consonant with the organization. For the leaders and practitioners, the Targeting Stage will be filled with challenges and opportunities to make exploration an opening of possibilities and goal-setting a realistic and profitable exercise.

This stage often makes managers nervous. Perhaps what leadership most fears about a career development effort is that it will raise unrealistic expectations. Employees might believe they are more mobile in the organization than they ever can be. In line with this concern is the fear that the career development effort will cause rapid promotion or transfer of master performers, leaving the supervisor to continually train new staff members. Because of these concerns, many managers are reluctant to encourage the institution of career development efforts.

But, if well executed, the process of targeting can prevent employees from setting unrealistic goals and actually encourage them to look closer at their present work environments in seeking job satisfaction. Setting effective career goals helps ensure that employees undertake appropriate action, and it helps minimize the aimless groping that does not benefit the individual or the organization.

There is no single way for a person to move as a result of a career development effort. Targeting will often show that a current job can be enriched to provide satisfaction; or that a lateral move, either within one's own group or to another related one, may be the ideal direction for a worker. Sometimes a move downward can be the first step toward accomplishing a long-term goal. Moving on in one's career may also mean leaving the organization. This occurs when the work no longer matches the individual's skills, interests, or values, or when the individual sees that the organization will be rightsizing or restructuring and decides to find a more viable match.

Just as an architect does not simply look at a construction site and insert a window here and a door there (there is a well-designed plan for the building process), employees too need an organized method for approaching the goal-setting process. And just as the builder does not start with the roof, the person selecting and specifying career goals must not begin with "the job." Yet, unfortunately, this is just the place where most begin—by singling out a job title or functional area that sounds appealing, without ever getting a feel for the realities of the organization and larger environment in which they operate. Without the careful analysis, planning, and examination of options that comprise the targeting process, the career goal is not likely to be built—or, if built, it is not likely to withstand the passage of time. The major phases of the Targeting Stage are directed at (1) assisting employees in *exploring* the trends affecting the organization and the world of work, and based on that information, (2) *specifying* action-oriented career goals.

Exploration

The process of targeting requires ongoing interaction between the individual and the organization. The employee needs assistance in translating skill profiles into desirable and realistic career goals. Without the knowledge of skills, personal values, and contextual preferences defined during the Profiling Stage, individuals have neither the self-insight nor the self-confidence to select appropriate goals. Similarly, without knowledge of company business plans, individuals do not have the necessary information to set personal career goals that link with organizational realities.

There is a great deal of information about the organization, the environment, the job, the industry, and the profession that the employee must know before beginning a targeting effort. While knowing their own values and abilities is key for employees, if they don't have an understanding and overview of the world of work, their career development effort may be severely hampered. Being a player means you must know the game, its rules, and the playing field. Caela Farren (1996) recommends that the individual consider four main areas: the profession, the industry, the organization, and the job. These areas are constantly in motion, they are interdependent, and they react to changes in other areas as well as the environment.

Profession categories are critical. They may be broad, they may evolve, but at the core they are stable over time. In order to stay current on the important issues, Farren suggests that individuals keep an eye on their professional leaders, as well as current journals and books that are key to the profession. They must also be aware of and follow important trends in the profession.

One's profession may not directly dictate which industry one operates in. A communications specialist may work in media, telecommunications, or education. An electrical engineer may work in aerospace or the automotive industry, while a human resource specialist may work in any of the above industries. Individuals can stay current on industry issues through membership in industry associations, industry publications, and networking. Knowing industry leaders and being aware of industry trends helps employees understand how their own work in their current organization may be affected.

Information about the organization's human resource plans, performance requirements, career paths, projected openings, and current job titles and tasks are all additionally helpful. Most employees do not have access to this information or know how to find it. Leaders and practitioners can provide invaluable assistance by discussing organizational long-range plans and staffing requirements. Peers also play a major role in providing support and information about the organization by sharing their personal experiences, even their own grapevine information.

Attempting to build a successful career development goal without access to organizational data is similar to attempting to paint a picture in a dark room. Certain things—the canvas, the palette, the brushes, and the paint tubes—can be identified by feel, but

FIGURE 3

A Targeting Model

even a skilled artist must be able to see in order to develop the colors, composition, and image. The employee who has limited information may have some feel for what must be done in career planning, but the light can only be provided by the organization and leadership. Although the employee may be able to create something in the dark, the result may not be in the best interests of either the individual or the organization. With information about where and how the organization is changing, employees can more effectively voice their own ideas regarding that fit, thereby minimizing surprises on both sides. The process can be summarized as shown in Figure 3.

TARGETING TRENDS OF TODAY

John Naisbitt showed the importance of overarching trends in his 1982 book, *Megatrends* (as well as his 1990 work, *Megatrends 2000*, and his 1996 edition of *Megatrends Asia*). Naisbitt asserted that our industries, institutions, companies, and careers are overshadowed by these global forces. Effective career development efforts must not only consider trends, but anticipate and plan for them (1996).

Since Naisbitt's original publication, a growing list of writers, consultants, and academics have penned many lists of the newest trends predicted to affect business and the world of work. Yet, as the number of trend lists has increased, our clarity about the future has not always grown sharper. In fact, many trend lists written a decade ago are now the object of humor on late-night television.

The purpose of this section is not to create another trend list, but rather to summarize the trends for which there is overall consensus among experts. This section also presents practical ways practitioners, leaders, and employees can stay abreast of emerging trends, and shows how individuals can draw specific career development implications once these trends are identified.

Globalization

The business scene of the postwar world—in which the United States and major European countries dominated industry and trade—has been replaced by a new model in which labor, manufacturing, and markets are global. With advances in information flow and more relaxed trading laws among industrialized and developing countries, even smaller businesses can now span borders and continents. The result is a business environment that both is more competitive and also offers more opportunity to those companies and individuals willing to expand to new markets. In terms of career development, people and companies now think beyond national borders—expatriate assignments are more common than ever, candidates for top management positions often need a greater global awareness, and career development practitioners must plan ways of developing an increasingly diverse workforce to service increasingly international markets.

Work Redesign

More than a decade ago, American business became fascinated by Total Quality Management (TQM), a movement that had helped Japanese industry rebound from World War II and become a giant in technology and manufacturing. In the years since TQM's introduction, business process reengineering has helped to reduce cycle time, decrease defect rates, cut work-in-progress inventories, and increase overall profitability in many companies. Work redesign, which includes changes in a company's core processes, is having a dramatic change effect on career development. Specific changes include the flattening of organizations, resulting in fewer management jobs; greater span of control for the management jobs that remain; traditional oversight responsibilities often delegated to self-managed teams; and more jobs requiring generalist backgrounds.

Communications Technology

While companies once relied on more conventional ways of doing business—like TV ads, direct mail, and chain-store retailing—today businesses are reinventing themselves to take advantage of newer methods of communication. Even communication industries—like long-distance telecommunication, cable TV, and online service providers—are using newer technologies to cooperate rather than compete. Career development is being transformed by these new technologies in several ways. First, newer and more advanced computerized career development tools are now available packaged and online. Second, researching and applying for jobs over the Internet is now commonplace; some firms even allow for online interviewing, electronic employment offers, and online chat sessions in lieu of formal orientation meetings. And third, an entirely new type of employment—work in "virtual companies," in which the leaders and employees have only met over electronic communication—is now a serious option for some people.

Increased Organizational Flexibility

Organizations today are faced with increased competitive pressure, resulting in the need to constantly refocus on shifting markets. The result is that many companies are downsizing certain areas, while at the same time they are hiring new employees in other areas. Career development in this context can be difficult, since practitioners and leaders must balance organizational concerns that aren't as predictable as in prior years. This trend makes establishing career paths difficult. And the challenge for employees is also great. With companies and careers changing so quickly, employees are often frustrated in trying to figure out which new skills to learn, which industries to target, and how to stay competitive in the world of work that keeps changing.

TARGETING TRENDS OF TOMORROW

These trends are creating new challenges and opportunities for leaders, practitioners, and employees throughout the new economy. People need to not only know what trends are emerging today but also be prepared to learn about the trends of tomorrow.

Organizations have a great deal of information about trends, yet often this information isn't tapped by practitioners and leaders involved in career development. There are several ways the organization can utilize the information it already has—in the minds of leaders, practitioners, and employees.

First, trends can be explored within staff meetings or workshop settings. One effective method several companies use is to bring in newspaper headlines and, working together, draw implications about trends from these clippings.

Second, leaders can bring in articles from industry or professional journals and talk with their staff members about how these articles relate to careers within the field. In one organization, before staff meetings began, each person had to bring in an amazing statistic or quotation. These statistics were used as a way of brainstorming about how trends are shaping industries and companies.

A third way trends can be explored is that senior industry leaders can dialogue in open forums or within a career development workshop. Many companies have found that employees greatly desire this interaction and are grateful for opportunities to engage experts.

The fourth approach is more creative. It involves asking people to close their eyes and imagine how their industry or company will be different several years from now, and then to share their thoughts with each other. These exercises are all designed to help individuals discover what they already know about trends from each other, their reading, and common sense. This discovery process gives them a feeling that the future is indeed not quite so elusive as one might think. If individuals can be convinced to be continual trend watchers, and if a chance for them to dialogue about these trends could be provided, individuals would indeed feel more able to self-manage their careers.

Specification

The organization can reap substantial benefits from encouraging employees' commitment to well-defined career goals. Setting specific goals encourages the motivation to pursue purposeful personal development and job achievement, rather than aimless movement from job to job. Jobs have less meaning for individuals and the organization if they are not perceived as a step in a particular direction. The specification of goals provides a vital link to using human resources productively. Job satisfaction results from employees feeling that they are a part of the team. If the organization translates its own plans and goals to employees, they can then weigh their own desires and directions against those of the organization to determine the degree to which they support one another.

The *specification phase* is the point at which goals evolve from vague generalities to precise statements of objective. But how many employees know how to make the transition from the general to the specific? How many employees know how to effectively develop step-by-step procedures that will make goals attainable? The practitioner or leader can provide instruction in how to write and test goal statements that will ensure clear action. Failure to complete this component of the Targeting Stage results in goals that can be easily and conveniently overlooked in the hurly-burly of one's daily routine. Vague goals do not act as a reminder of plans that have not been executed. They do not generate an imperative to act.

Goals committed to paper help motivate individuals to assess their efforts toward attaining them, while there is still time to act. Individuals with goals clearly in mind are much more alert to opportunities to move toward them and are much more likely to act on those opportunities. Targeting information helps employees learn the essential steps for specifying goals and provides a means of sharing and reality-testing statements.

During the first phase of targeting, which involves exploring alternatives, employees are assisted in understanding that career development goals may relate to a wide range of options beyond the usual notion of upward advancement. The practitioner will need to help individuals explore possible career paths that include:

- *Enrichment*—growing in place
- *Vertical*—moving up
- *Lateral*—moving across
- *Realignment*—moving down
- *Relocation*—moving out
- *Exploratory*—investigating possibilities

It is important that the practitioner help employees understand the value of considering goals in each of these areas. The concept of selecting multiple career goals is particularly relevant in today's rapidly changing job market. Leaders and practitioners should encourage employees to select at least one possible goal in each category and to pursue multiple and simultaneous goals. This multifaceted approach allows the employee to remain ready for, and open to, any changes that may occur within the system, whether they reflect the opening of new opportunities or the foreclosure of existing ones. Multiple goals allow employees to perceive themselves as more in control of their future and less at the mercy of outside forces. Should the desired direction become blocked, one has at least begun to think in terms of other options. The following discussion of career path possibilities may help show employees the range of alternatives.

GROWING IN PLACE—ENRICHMENT

Systems Analyst.................Part-time Trainer of Systems Analysts

One of the most viable options today involves growth in one's current job. Indeed, the actions that are often easiest to enact and quickest to show results are those directed at an employee's present environment.

In our current world of work, flexibility is high on the list of required attributes. To meet this demand, the resourceful individual must seek opportunities for enrichment. Furthermore, employees who recognize that numerous opportunities exist right within their current jobs are more likely to be avid continual learners. The job enrichment option, clearly presented as a viable option, can win over leaders who fear that career development means losing valuable employees.

Enrichment that builds flexibility works especially well with teams. When teams require members to be able to take on each other's roles, flexibility is key. Enrichment assignments that broaden the members' competencies, developing the versatility of their skills, will benefit the whole team. Exercise 7 focuses on the motivation potential of enrichment goals.

Job enrichment is a way of increasing the challenge and meaningfulness of a job by changing the job and its responsibilities. It means recognizing the job tasks or functions that the employee finds personally stimulating and rewarding, and working to dis-

EXERCISE 7

Enrichment Goal Exercise

Once a specific enrichment goal has been selected, questions addressing three different areas should be asked in order to check the motivating potential of that goal:

What's in it for you?

- How will it increase your marketability in your profession?
- How will it increase your reputation as a specialist or generalist?
- How will it enable you to gain more confidence and competence in your current position?

What's in it for your work group?

- How will it enable you to work more effectively with your current team?
- How will it increase/enhance your contribution to your work group or department?
- How does it build new collaborations or extend your network?

What's in it for the organization?

- How will it increase your value to the organization?
- How does it contribute to current organizational mission, strategy, or goals?
- How does it address a current relevant business need?

cover a way to more strongly build those tasks or functions into the job. This does not mean simply adding more tasks in the hope that greater variety will lead to greater meaningfulness. Job enrichment provides developmental opportunities without employees leaving their present positions.

One way to distinguish between job enrichment and job enlargement is to think of how responsibilities would be expanded. Additional responsibilities that are piled on vertically and simply increase the time and pressure required to carry them out cause job enlargement. However, the addition of duties and responsibilities that expand the scope, visibility, attractiveness, and learning potential of the job result in job enrichment. With new experiences, employees add to their own portfolios of strengths and gain more marketable skills. Often a job can be enriched by simply giving the employee the authority to sign or approve certain items that had previously required approval by another. Similarly, job

---

CASE 16

Job Enrichment by Refining and Implementing Employees' Enrichment Goals

A large oil company fostered the power of job enrichment by focusing on enrichment goals. As part of the process, each employee in their career development program was required to set at least two enrichment goals. Those goals were presented to a planning committee who helped the employees refine and implement their plans. The planning committee was often able to effect changes and switches just between the enrichment goals brought to them by each group of employees.

---

enlargement might occur if an additional responsibility is given to an employee, but the authority to carry out that responsibility is withheld.

Examples of job enrichment goals include developing and implementing a particular procedure, task, or project on the job; learning computer programming, in order to be able to respond to internal software needs; becoming a member of a special task force; and achieving greater responsibility and autonomy on the job.

Accountants who take on responsibility for orienting others to a new accounting system and enjoy this mentoring role are enriching their jobs. Similarly job enrichment occurs when a secretary not only word processes but also drafts letters in response to inquiries, or when a management trainee is given full authority over management of a new project.

The development effort should stimulate employees to consider their present jobs as potential candidates for job enrichment before, or while, looking elsewhere, and to encourage support for such efforts from supervisors and the system as a whole.

Richard Hackman (Hackman and Suttle, 1977), some twenty years ago, suggested that the key concepts underlying job enrichment are perceiving the work as meaningful, feeling a sense of responsibility, and being able to determine outcomes. He showed that certain job characteristics can contribute to the creation of these three psychological states. These characteristics include:

- *Skill variety*—increasing the number and variety of skills and talents used in carrying out a job
- *Task completion*—being assigned an identifiable unit of work to complete (doing a job from beginning to end)
- *Task significance*—understanding the type and degree of impact a particular job has on the lives and work of other people in the organization or on the organization as a whole
- *Autonomy*—increasing responsibility, independence, and discretion in determining work procedures
- *Feedback*—establishing opportunities for feedback intrinsic in the job itself, as well as for feedback from peers and leaders
- *Interpersonal relationships*—providing employees with opportunities to work more closely with clients, or with people in other parts of the organization, in addition to other members of the work unit
- *Training*—providing opportunities for growth through on-the-job training, special seminars, and courses

Employees can often develop ideas for enriching their own jobs, but they typically need assistance in beginning the process. The practitioner can help employees recognize a variety of starting points to aid them in building job enrichment goals, which encompass the characteristics mentioned above. One way in which this might be done is to suggest that employees select short-term projects that meet these job enrichment criteria. Projects could involve designing new systems for the organization, the department, or the division of which the employee is a member. Projects could be designed to encourage taking on personal assignments that, during their course, cause employees to be recognized in the organization as having skills. (A description of a program using the notion of project assignment is included in the next chapter.) A rating form such as the one in Exercise 8 could be used by the practitioner as a check for job enrichment capacity.

Another exercise individuals might use to identify the potential for job enrichment in their present positions is to list their job duties on a typical day. Working from the list of job enrichment possibilities, employees write out and discuss how each duty could be modified to use a variety of skills, to complete a task in its entirety, to provide more autonomy, or to provide more feedback from or contact with others. The list can also be used for employees to explore the importance of a particular task to others. The resulting data provides an excellent starting point for individuals

EXERCISE 8

A Worksheet for Rating Job Enrichment Potential

Does the project fulfill the following requirements of potential job enrichment?

1. **Skill Variety**   Yes   No

   Will the project increase the number and variety of skills and talents used in carrying out the job?

2. **Task Completion**   Yes   No

   Will the project provide an opportunity to complete a particular task from beginning to end?

3. **Task Significance**   Yes   No

   Will the project help the individual to understand the degree of impact that the project has on the lives and work of other people in the organization?

4. **Autonomy**   Yes   No

   Will the project assist the individual in exploring ways to increase independence and discretion in determining work procedures?

5. **Feedback**   Yes   No

   Does the project provide opportunities for feedback from the project itself, as well as from co-workers and supervisors?

6. **Interpersonal Relationships**   Yes   No

   Does the project provide opportunities to work more closely with clients, or with people in other parts of the organization, in addition to other members of the work unit?

7. **Training**   Yes   No

   Does the project provide an opportunity for growth through on-the-job training, especially seminars?

Adapted from Hackman, 1977

to apply their own problem-solving skills to discovering job enrichment opportunities. The employee could, for example, rank the possibilities on the list in order of importance and ease of attainability. Those changes that would be easiest to implement and that are of greatest import would represent the first job enrichment efforts.

If successful, implementation of job enrichment offers rewards that are twofold. First, employees will have created one psychological success upon which future successes may be built. Second, the odds are high that a supervisor, who may have previously been reluctant to support the individual's hopes for growth or change, will become a supporter. Thus, efforts on the present job can enhance opportunities for attaining other career goals.

For those whose present position is unchanged, job enrichment still offers the opportunity to encourage the supervisor to become a supporter and salesperson for the individual, especially with regard to future moves. In addition, employees who learn to look upon their present job as an opportunity to showcase their present skills and to help develop new ones will be rewarded with increased job satisfaction.

It is essential that practitioners gain managers' commitment to the notion of job enrichment. Those leaders who see development of subordinates as one of their responsibilities or who feel rewarded for developing employees should become immediate and enthusiastic supporters. Others may have to be encouraged to support job enrichment on the basis of the improved job commitment it provides.

UP, UP, AND AWAY—VERTICAL MOVES

Assistant Director of HR

Manager of Compensation

Traditionally, vertical mobility was considered the only acceptable and rewarding way to develop in a career. Vertical mobility meant that one climbed the hierarchical ladder, gaining more status, responsibility, remuneration, and authority along the way. Movement up meant success; all other movement did not count—or counted against the individual. Much of the past literature on career mobility concerned itself with moving vertically within the organization. Despite drastic changes in the business world, old assumptions are hard to shake. Although in many organizations and industries the "corporate ladder" has become the "corporate step stool," a common assumption is still that *up* is the best and only direction in which an individual should desire to move; for example, accountants are encouraged to become managers of the financial division; product designers are encouraged to become product managers; and machinists are encouraged to aim toward plant management.

Prompted by the limited opportunities in most organizations today, and by shifts in cultural values vis-à-vis the work ethic, this belief is beginning to change. Both individuals and organizations now place a higher value on depth and breadth of experience than on the speed with which one can climb the corporate ladder. More and more workers are being encouraged to become generalists rather than specialists. Today some employees look to the present job for personal growth, evaluating new job opportunities (including vertical moves) in light of how they may conflict with personal values, and sometimes declining the new opportunities because of that conflict. Others still define personal success as upward career movement and remain interested in vertical goals. Employees often need assistance in determining what the next logical hierarchical move should be, as well as in assessing the abilities and experience required to make such a move.

Several major factors should be considered when setting a vertical career goal. The larger the organization, the greater will be the competition for the increasingly limited positions available as one moves upward in an organization. If everyone in the hierarchy wants to move upward, the competition for those limited jobs can be fierce. Too often employees see only the desirable status, authority, and money enjoyed by those at higher levels. They fail to realize that a price is attached to those benefits: stress. Some organizations have higher stress levels than others and some people have a higher tolerance for stress than others. Practitioners should help employees investigate this area of concern before a final decision to move upward is made.

Personal values are also important to consider before setting goals. The increased responsibility carried at upper levels in an organization often makes demands on family, leisure time, and ability to pursue non-job-related interests. The practitioner must help employees investigate those demands and their own ability to make value adaptations before they begin exploring upward mobility goals.

Collapsing Ladders

In the rapidly changing world of work, career ladders are becoming quite rickety and starting to collapse. For example, high-technology organizations have a special problem in trying to provide vertical mobility for technical professionals, such as engineers and computer specialists. The most competent of these employees soon reach the top title and salary available in their technical specialty, and the only advancement option is a switch to the management hierarchy. Yet, these individuals may not want to leave their laboratories and computers, or may not be suited for the human relations skills and political maneuvering required of managers. Still, they may desire an increase in status and pay, as well as greater influence over company policymaking.

This is only one example of the problem with career ladders. The whole premise on which the career ladders of the past were based is falling apart today. Career ladders were based on (1) specific positions—but today positions keep changing, evolving, or are eliminated very rapidly; (2) years and decades of tenure at a company—yet today the average worker stays only about four years with each company; (3) a linear ascension of levels or "rungs"—today's structures are flatter, and functional units and teams have replaced the hierarchy; (4) a linear increase in pay to go along with steps up the ladder—today, however, compensation is more linked to developing competencies; and (5) valuing and rewarding seniority in and of itself—whereas today, organizations are moving toward pay for performance, rewarding achievements over time served.

MOVING ACROSS—LATERAL MOVES

Team Leader, Planning Division ⟶ Team Leader, Marketing Division

Lateral moves involve a change in function and responsibility, but not necessarily a change in status or remuneration. Once considered a way of shelving "dead wood," lateral moves have become a way for employees to broaden existing skills, learn about other areas of the organization, develop new talents, demonstrate versatility, and prepare for future vertical moves. Such movement is also a method through which organizations with slow internal job markets can continue to challenge their highly motivated employees. In fact, in many organizations lateral movement is a sign of recognized potential and promotability, as individuals are groomed for higher positions by broadening their base of knowledge across functional lines. Unfortunately, the reverse is also sometimes true. A great many organizations have policies that make lateral movements exceedingly difficult. The feeling is that lateral movement encourages interdivisional pirating of promising employees. Practitioners should thoroughly investigate organizational policy regarding this option. The "silo" mentality is a difficult mind-set and structure to change.

It is important to stress the degree to which lateral moves reflect and demonstrate the concept of transferable skills and job knowledge. An employee who has a background in production and who has been successfully selling production proposals to top management may be qualified to consider a lateral move to a position in marketing, by virtue of that concept.

There is an increasing need for lifelong learning, to keep acquiring new and transferable competencies. Employees can build skills and gain valuable expertise and self-confidence through lateral movement. Similarly, a lateral move in a high-technology organization may mean moving from one systems group to another— transferring a number of technical, functional, and personal skills to the new assignment and gaining new ones in the process. Human relations skills and conceptual skills may be added to existing technical skills.

One of the first steps the practitioner could undertake to present this as a viable option is to evaluate the attitudes within the organization toward such movement. In many companies lateral moves occur frequently and are seen as part of routine training and development. Job rotation programs are common and are designed to prevent overspecialization and to encourage understanding of the unique demands of each function within the organization. Where such movement is commonplace, it is possible to identify typical crossover points, to catalogue logical cross-functional moves that will provide the greatest depth of experience, to determine entry requirements into job rotation programs, and to otherwise identify information that employees may need in order to pursue lateral mobility. This information should be widely disseminated in order to encourage considering lateral movement when setting goals.

Where lateral movement is infrequent or seen as a sign of probable failure, the practitioner must determine whether and how lateral mobility can be legitimized. The practitioner may need only to review mobility patterns of the past six to twelve months and point out that the frequency of such moves is actually greater than generally perceived. Such a process is certainly made easier if a computerized human resource data system is available for retaining historical job classification data. However, a simplified version can be compiled by hand. For even greater impact, some of this

---

CASE 17

Legitimizing Lateral Moves
When Employees Take a Pay Cut

Recognizing that financial considerations can be a major obstacle to employees who contemplate lateral moves, a large insurance company has instituted a lateral movement policy that removes the financial burden from this career option. If an employee wants to make a lateral move involving a job with a lower salary range, the company will continue to treat the employee as though he or she were in the higher salary level for a year.

---

information can be compiled in internal publications that present the abbreviated work histories of several successful people who have benefited from lateral moves.

A job posting/transfer system can encourage lateral moves, when jobs are publicized as providing opportunities to transfer skills to new work environments and to learn about other parts of the organization. Job rotation programs encourage employees to experiment with transferring their present skills to jobs at similar levels in other functional areas.

In addition, an approach might be designed for making and processing transfer requests without unnecessary red tape. Primarily it is the practitioner's responsibility to ensure that the organization is open to lateral mobility and is doing all it can to make such opportunities available, and to help employees recognize the benefits of broadening their experiential base through lateral moves. Basic to such an approach is the necessity of convincing managers within the organization that lateral movements are beneficial to the whole organization, even though they may pose some hardships within its component parts.

DOWN THE ORGANIZATION—REALIGNMENT

IS Manager

↓

Senior Systems Analyst

CASE 18

Promoting Downshifting: A Matter of Choice

A s part of its career development program, a financial services company encouraged realignment moves as a viable option. This option allowed employees more freedom to make choices based on their personal situations and career goals. One way the organization promoted this option was to maintain the employees' previous compensation level for a specified period of time.

Realignment moves involve downward shifts in the hierarchy, often from a managerial position back to one as an individual contributor. Although a downward transfer is not a common career development option, practitioners who recognize it as a viable alternative will be able to help employees expand their range of choices. Through a downward move an individual may be able to acquire the competencies and skills necessary for the redirection of his or her long-term career goal. It is not unusual that some employees find themselves selected for job levels that do not suit them and need assistance in making a career move back down the hierarchy. Other employees may simply decide that they can personally benefit from jobs that entail less pressure and responsibility, fewer overtime hours, and more day-to-day certainty than the ones they now hold.

Today many individuals choose to realign due to a desire to facilitate personal growth and development, or to change from one field of endeavor into another. Individuals who wish to change their routine and expand their knowledge of future options often find that their accrued salary and benefits have effectively priced them out of the market for learning opportunities or new starts. The organization, unwilling to pay the higher rate while waiting for the person to become productive in the new area, closes the door on personal growth involving such a major change. Only two choices remain open: stay on the present job and seek other ways of growing and developing; or trade income, benefits, and status for the opportunity presented by a realignment move.

While downshifting may be losing its stigma as the kiss of death, the organization and the practitioner must be aware of a key determinant in its potential success as a career strategy. That determinant is *choice*. Over a decade of massive downsizing has shown that when employees were forced into choosing between being laid off or demoted, morale invariable suffered. Downshifting must be a choice, made by the employee, as a part of his or her career planning effort.

Another type of realignment move involves returning to a previous position, in which an employee performed better or was more satisfied. An example of a realignment career move of this type can be seen when managers decide to return to their former positions as technical specialists, or when supervisors return to a clerical position they previously held. Realignment, if handled appropriately, can offer a satisfactory solution to the dilemma of having promoted the best worker, only to discover that the individual is not suited to managerial or supervisorial responsibilities. Similar situations occur when an employee in a promote-from-within training program moves into a supervisory position and finds that it is less attractive or more demanding than anticipated. By developing options for returning to a less demanding position without the stigma of demotion, organizations can retain their good employees in positions where they can be effective producers.

Developing plans and programs to handle realignments will challenge the creative and human relations skills of the practitioner. Several options and considerations follow, which may be useful in developing plans.

Some organizations have prepared in advance for this type of occurrence by creating fallback positions, which reduce the risk involved in granting or accepting a promotion by guaranteeing each promoted employee the opportunity to return to a position equal in status and pay to the old job, if the new one does not work out as intended. This guarantee encourages an individual to accept the risk of moving into a different department or function, and benefits the organization by opening up blocked pathways for newer and possibly more talented employees.

Realignment is often chosen to relieve job-related stress. As the definition of compensable occupational injuries is evolving to include psychological damage induced by stress inherent in a job, companies are faced with a potential new financial burden, in terms of actual transfer payments made and days spent on medical leave. And individuals are beginning to believe that their personal health is more important than having a prestigious job. Accordingly the downward transfer is an important alternative. Employees could be encouraged to consider this type of career movement, even on a temporary basis, and the system could be encouraged to treat it as a viable career option, rather than a form of punishment.

Practitioners should recognize that realignment moves have been shown to have a positive effect on individuals at lower levels in the organization. When a more senior person chooses realignment, junior employees are afforded closer contact with an individual in an excellent position to coach and advise them as a mentor. In addition, organizational communication is improved when individuals moving downward bring with them the information sources and communication channels they enjoyed in their previous organizational roles.

Nevertheless, a strong norm still exists in many companies against moving downward. If the realigned individuals happen to be women or members of minority groups who were, perhaps, promoted too quickly or placed above their level of capability, there will be a different pressure—one of having let down the rest of the group or of having justified the mistrust of those who did not want to see the person promoted in the first place. This will often happen even if the women or minority individuals functioned beautifully in the assignment, but simply found it not to their liking. Choosing to realign carries with it the implied warning, "we gave you a chance and you let us down." Leaders and practitioners might confront some of these cultural norms that support organizational resistance to downward transfers, so that such reactions are no longer typical and realignment moves are legitimized as normal career options available to all individuals.

To encourage employees to seriously consider this option and to alleviate possible anxiety about downward transfers, they could be provided with information from the media about the increasing number of people who are choosing realignment. Internal publicity about individuals who have given up higher level jobs to learn other functions and who, perhaps, have now regained their former rank level can be an effective device. Practitioners could also review compensation policies to determine if fallback positions can be established, or if minimum salary or other job security measures can be enacted to foster effective realignment.

OUTWARD BOUND—RELOCATION

Trainer, XYZ Corporation ⟶ Consultant, Entrepreneur

The primary job of the organizational career development practitioner is to help the organization and its people change and develop. However, there are times and situations in which the person-to-organization mismatch is so great that it would be to the decided advantage of both if the employee were to seek growth opportunities elsewhere. This option is most frequently invoked when retirement is imminent, when layoffs are frequent, when individuals feel they are at a dead end in the organization, when entrepreneurial ventures attract employees, or when personal and organizational goals are in conflict.

After serious introspection, some individuals may find that their present occupation, industry, profession, or firm does not meet their needs and may opt to relocate. Employees whose needs could be satisfied by the company must be able to recognize this fact, while others, better suited elsewhere, should not be discouraged from leaving jobs in which they are only marginally productive or marginally satisfied.

Employees must think through various alternatives and follow up on those that seem most appropriate. The assumption in some organizations is that employees will not think of relocation on their own, and the belief is that the organization should not encourage it. More and more organizations have chosen to offer outplacement services to assist employees in obtaining positions with other firms, although this aid is generally used when the organization decides to terminate the employee.

Organizations that openly discuss this option in their career development approach gain a distinct advantage. Employees of these organizations are encouraged to identify relocation as one of their potential goals; they are then prepared for potential situations in which movement out of the organization is the best way to go. This approach enhances the organization's credibility, and employees feel that the career development program is not intended only to serve the expediency of the company. Interestingly enough, this approach encourages loyalty and commitment to the organization.

The organization must understand that employees who are mismatched with their present jobs or company are likely to be less productive than those whose needs are being satisfied by the job.

Allowing an individual to leave, therefore, creates opportunities for others. In addition to potentially improved productivity and the increased promotion opportunities when relocation information is available, resources that might have been spent in trying to motivate, train, or develop the former employee can be redirected to those who have identified a desire for such work and development.

Outplacement services encourage individuals to look at broader options or creative alternatives. A relocation goal may involve changing fields, not just changing organizations. Employees who have the desire to teach, for example, but cannot find the opportunity to do so within the present organization might find that returning to the formal education system or moving to a larger company, more oriented toward training, in the same industry will more directly meet their needs.

CASTING ABOUT—EXPLORATORY RESEARCH PROJECTS

Customer Service Representative...............Research About Marketing

Often employees feel vaguely discontent with their present jobs but have difficulty selecting alternative career paths. It is important that they be shown how to undertake an experimentation process that involves researching, interviewing, and testing ideas and opportunities within or outside the organization, so they can eventually decide about another field of interest. By encouraging employees to set research goals, practitioners can help them overcome the frustration of feeling they have no choices. The practitioner uses this option most effectively by encouraging employees to select one area of interest and to research possibilities associated with it. Research goals should include a detailed statement about areas of possible interest and a structured plan for researching those areas. As a result, employees should gather enough information to enable themselves to make a sound decision about whether or not moving into another area would be desirable.

Employees in the accounting department, for example, might research a variety of jobs within the HR division in order to understand more about why they might wish to move into a particular area of human resource development, rather than simply claiming that they "like people." A research goal of this type could involve interviewing various department members to learn about the scope and variety of jobs within the department; investigating job availability; attending meetings of affiliated professional societies;

and reading selected journals, books, or articles. At the end of a predetermined research period, the employee might elect to continue exploring in one particular area of human resources (for example, training and development); decide that the HR function is, in fact, no longer appealing; or reframe the goal to a specific lateral or vertical move to the area of HR that is of interest.

Practitioners can help employees recognize that vertical and lateral goals may be based on unfounded assumptions made as a result of work experience in other areas. Research goals replace fantasizing with structured, goal-oriented behavior and ensure that potential goals are tested against reality. Research goals require effort but can be easily pursued in tandem with other goals. When discussing the concept of research goals with employees, the practitioner must not get co-opted into letting the employees think that the work will be done for them. Research goals are individual projects. The practitioner may assist and offer guidance, but the work must be done by the person concerned. Exercise 9 provides a sample exploratory worksheet to be completed by the individual.

The practitioner could facilitate the exploration process by identifying key contact people in various functional areas who would be willing to act as information resources for employees conducting research, and who could set aside time to be interviewed. Formal presentation by representatives of various units to describe their unit's functional responsibilities can also be arranged. Alternatively, supervisors or career counselors can be trained to field questions about other functional areas. Special interest articles concerning work in various units can be published in the company paper or newsletter.

Another important but complementary task is encouraging employees to contact peer-level people in other parts of the organization for informal discussions. Even an existing job posting system, an existing transfer system, or descriptions of job responsibilities in recruitment publications can serve as the foundation for developing informational brochures about work within various organizational components.

These are just a few of the potential sources of information that might be provided. It is likely that the organization already has such systems but is simply not using them in this manner. The more support the practitioner can offer in terms of information resources, the more employees will be helped to see that the orga-

EXERCISE 9

Exploratory Research Worksheet

To assist employees in establishing research goals, develop interview and report-back forms that contain standard questions pertaining to the department(s) being explored. The forms could include questions about the purpose of the functional area as a whole, the function of any subunit being explored, and the nature of specific jobs at the employee's own level. Questions about behavioral job demands, skill requirements, working conditions, and the like should also be included. Entries made by employees could note the different people interviewed, the method used to contact them, their level in the organization, and the insights they shared with the employee. An employee could arrange to follow up by reporting back (to a supervisor, counselor, workshop teammate, or other persons) at a specified time after having conducted the research.

Position/unit being researched: _____

1. Who can tell me about the position?
2. What other information sources about the position are available?
3. What are the duties and responsibilities involved in this position?
4. What appeals to me about the position?
5. What might I dislike about the position?
6. Will the position develop me for future advancement?
7. What kind of ability, experience, and training is necessary in order to obtain this position?

nization is in itself a labor market with multiple opportunities for career growth and development.

THE ROAD TO RESULTS

When first stated, most career goals lack the clarity and specificity necessary to inspire action. While individuals may have been urged to set goals for themselves, it is unlikely that they have been instructed in the nuances of setting realistic goals. Exercise 10 poses some specific actions that employees can consider to gain more information about each of the goals.

In order to assist employees in specifying goals, the practitioner must be both instructor and motivator, instructing employees in how to write clear goals that lead to action plans and results, and motivating them to make a commitment to those goals by putting them in writing and discussing them with others.

Career Choices

Job Enrichment

- List two skills that would make you a more valued contributor in your current job.
- Name a task or project in which you can develop those two skills.

Vertical Movement

- Discuss with a higher-level employee the new learning requirements of his or her job.
- Identify two future trends that could help or hinder your promotional opportunities.

Lateral Movement

- List three of your skills that are most transferable.
- Discuss with a colleague three ways your lateral move could reposition you for the future.

Realignment

- Consult with someone who has made a downward move to find out the benefits.
- List two benefits of a downward move that your current position doesn't provide.

Relocation

- Join a professional association that would expand your professional network.
- Name a local organization with whose core you think your profession would fit.

Exploration

- Conduct an informational interview to learn about the most desirable new skills in your profession.
- Volunteer for a project that offers opportunities to learn from people who are pacesetters in your profession.

Specifying goals requires a step-by-step process of writing, testing, and revising goal statements. And it requires that goals be tangible and action oriented. Employees will need encouragement and assistance in articulating goals that meet those criteria. The following questions (Career Systems International, 1994) regarding goal statements may identify conceptual or strategic flaws:

- Will your team leader/manager be likely to support this option?
- Are you ready to take on the necessary work and time commitment to prepare yourself for this option?
- Do you have the experience and qualifications necessary for this option?
- Is this option going to fit the organization's strategic plan?
- Will you be able to accomplish your goal within the next eighteen months?
- Is this option congruent with your personal values?
- How does this option take the possibility of downsizing into consideration?
- Do you have access to the training necessary for this option?
- Will this option enhance your employability and the marketability of your skills?

Adequate organizational support systems must be in place to supply individuals with the necessary information to specify realistic goals. Structural supports such as job posting and information about career paths provide data for stimulating goal ideas and testing goal relevance.

THE GOAL STATEMENT

Goal statements move individuals from the intangible to the tangible. To lead to concrete action, they must be SMART:

Specific—name the competency, project, position you want to accomplish

Measurable—yardsticks for assessing success are clear; you will know when you succeed

Attainable—the goal is relatively within your grasp, yet provides an opportunity for growth

Relevant—the goal is in sync with the organization, industry, and profession trends

Time-bound—time frames and deadlines are stated and specific

The practitioner is now charged with guiding employees to understand the preceding characteristics and to assess their goals in light of them. Each of those characteristics is essential in moving from goal formulation to goal achievement and is half the battle of achievement. The Goal Matrix in Exercise 11 can be used by employees to check whether their goals include all categories of movement and have all necessary characteristics.

EXERCISE 11

Goal Matrix

	S Specific	M Mea- surable	A Attainable	R Relevant	T Time- Bound
ENRICHMENT					
VERTICAL					
LATERAL					
REALIGNMENT					
RELOCATION					
EXPLORATORY					

"Can't You Be More Specific?"

Career goals should be expressed in specific terms that hold the same meaning for the employee, the supervisor, and others who review or hear of them. Formulating specific goal statements means explicitly stating as many details as possible of the position being aimed at. Specificity can be achieved by identifying aspects such as job title, job category, grade level, functions and tasks involved, and location or division.

When designing exploratory career goals, the employee should include the specific departments or divisions to be explored, job categories of interest, and specific questions to which the employee is seeking answers. Job enrichment goals should specify the job enrichment project being considered, the portion of the job to be affected by the job enrichment intervention, new or changed activities, and expected outcomes.

The biggest problem that may be encountered at this point results from employees' lack of familiarity with their organization. It is difficult for them to be as specific as necessary if they do not have enough information about the organization to intelligently identify and define job titles, job categories, grade levels, and functions. Practitioners will often find it necessary to provide assistance in obtaining this information.

One possible approach is to create a marketing survey form that will allow employees to research their organization as if it were a market in which they wished to introduce a new product—them-

EXERCISE 12

Marketing Survey Form

Primary skills to be marketed:_____

_____

Consumer number one:_____
(Department, division)

Specific user of skill:_____
(Specific group, office, and location)

Name of position:_____
(Job title, category, level)

Skills, functions, tasks required:_____

_____

Consumer number two:_____
(Department, division)

Specific user of skill:_____
(Specific group, office, and location)

Name of position:_____
(Job title, category, level)

Skills, functions, tasks required:_____

_____

selves. This survey form could fit the format of Exercise 12, or it could be developed by the practitioner and employees in a workshop session.

Any number of approaches may be useful in helping employees to learn more about the organization. Group projects, tours, guest speakers, and orientation sessions might provide the needed information.

Practitioners may find that they and their staff can compile specific information available into a book. Organizations that have computerized human resource accounting systems may be able to provide a readout of jobs, titles, levels, and codes. All means should be investigated.

■ ACTION PROVOKING QUESTIONS

EVALUATING GOALS

- Is the goal statement readily understandable and identifiable to a supervisor? To colleagues? To employees of another organization?
- Is there any way to clarify this statement further?
- Are the title, function, and division correct?
- Are the specific kinds of projects for exploratory or enrichment goals clear?

Once specific goals have been set, practitioners or managers could ask employees whether their goal statement specifically agrees with the skills, values, and contexts identified during the Profiling Stage. The more the goal builds upon identified strengths, the better. To evaluate the goals, the practitioner might ask the Action Provoking Questions above.

An example of a goal statement that meets the specificity requirement is "I plan to move from store manager, East City (grade 15), to assistant regional operations manager for the Eastern Region (grade 15) within the next six months." A *specific* enrichment goal would be "I plan to design a new bonus system for the department and take over responsibilities for initial drafting of the annual budget."

Measuring Milestones

Measurement involves assessing progress at a series of checkpoints along the way. These checkpoints help measure the relative success or failure experienced by the individual while in pursuit of the goal. Checkpoints should be inserted at intervals that permit corrections in defining the target. This allows individuals to test the accuracy of their self-assessments, the accuracy of their original assumptions about time parameters and attainability, and the accuracy of their perceptions about the evolving environment, throughout the career development process. Specifying desired outcomes for comparison with actual outcomes at designated points introduces an ongoing reality-testing mechanism. At this stage, the practitioner could ask the Action Provoking Questions on page 137.

■ **ACTION PROVOKING QUESTIONS**

EVALUATING CHECKPOINTS

- How will you know whether or not you are on the right track?
- Can the goal be broken down into a series of subgoals that can be monitored to assure that you are moving in the desired direction?
- What are the signs to look for that would signal adjustments in the goal?
- What contingency plans can be made to adjust the goal?

TABLE 12

MEASURABLE EXPLORATORY GOALS

I plan to explore job opportunities within the human resource department by:

Studying the department's organization chart	June 1
Reading a book on organizing the HR function	June 15
Reading the last two issues of *Personnel Report*	June 5
Interviewing Thora Christensen, management recruiter	June 8
Interviewing Dave Logan, HR specialist	June 10
Interviewing Sharon Evans, department head	June 18
Attending a Personnel Association meeting	June 9

Table 12 presents an example of an exploratory goal that meets the requirements for measurability.

Aiming for Attainability

Attainability suggests that the goal be within the employee's present competence, or that it represents a reasonable learning and development experience. It should provide strong motivation to stretch beyond current levels or functions, but it should not be an impossible dream.

Like relevance, attainability should be questioned from the viewpoint of an individual's skills and abilities and from that of the organization's structure and constraints. If the reality-testing component of profiling has been effectively accomplished, employees

---

■ ACTION PROVOKING QUESTIONS

EVALUATING ATTAINABILITY

- Is this a logical next step from the present position and salary grade?
- Will this move require crossing a job category threshold, and is that significant?
- Is this a typical job progression step that others have taken?
- Is the salary too high or too low to make this move?
- Is there likely to be an opening in that position?
- What is the competition likely to look like (qualifications and numbers)?
- Are the qualifications for the job presently possessed? Can qualifications be attained within the time frame specified?
- How will the employee's qualifications compare with those of the competition?

---

should be able to accurately calculate the attainability of their goals within the organizational framework. They should consider how reasonable their actions are in light of their present positions, normal organizational rates of movement, prerequisites for jobs, training opportunities, and availability of information about various segments of the organization.

Helpful input could include career progression charts, information about thresholds between job categories, job grouping by salary grade, and other data about current and future opportunities. One organization found it useful to prepare a graphic representation showing the number of employees at each salary grade level. Employees could then estimate the number of other people at similar grade levels who were competing for higher grade level jobs. The same graph provided them with an estimate of how many such jobs existed within the organization. Such information demonstrates that the number of positions in each higher grade level declines quickly after a certain point, and it helps employees understand the structure of the organization and the competition they face. At this stage, the practitioner might raise the Action Provoking Questions above.

If these questions can be answered satisfactorily, the following vertical goal statement will meet the attainability requirement: "I plan to move from junior buyer to senior buyer within twelve months."

While it is difficult to precisely measure goal attainment, these steps consist of specific verifiable activities or events that, when completed, should logically lead to accomplishing the career goal.

CASE 19

Keeping Goals Relevant: Naming Industry Trends

At a large bank, workshop participants are encouraged to test the relevancy of their career development goals by generating lists of changes that are likely to affect the bank over the next ten years. Workshop participants then prioritize ten trends that will affect banking and consider how they will affect jobs and goals. Examples of the trends named include:

- National and international branching
- Simplified forms; reduced legal jargon
- Internal automation
- Automated bill payment
- Electronic funds transfer
- Online banking

Lists such as this can then be discussed by practitioners to help participants see how changes will impact on individual careers.

Reasonable Relevance

Career goals must be relevant to current and future employee and organizational needs if they are to amount to more than fantasies. Emphasis on their comparison with profiling information will help employees determine if they have or can readily obtain the skills, traits, and experience necessary to reach the goal. The goal should be congruent with the employee's preferences for work environments, values, and job behavioral demands.

To meet the relevance requirement, individuals must know that the organization has or will have a need for the functions and positions to which they aspire. Goals should not conflict with current policies or projections of future trends. Organizational and individual goals should be viewed as interrelated components for achieving company purpose. Without compatible individual goals, the organization will suffer from lack of full human resource effectiveness; without compatible organizational goals, the individual will lack opportunity and sense of accomplishment.

While employees have few problems seeing the importance of their own goals and career plans, they often have a limited concept of the organization's needs and plans. This is not because infor-

---

■ ACTION PROVOKING QUESTIONS

EVALUATING RELEVANCE

- Is the goal in sync with present position, skills, and abilities?
- Does the goal match future expectations?
- Is the goal a step in the right direction?
- Is the goal congruent with the organization's present position?
- Is the goal congruent with the organization's future needs and policies?

---

mation is unavailable; it is often that employees do not know how to access it. The more the organization can make employees and leaders privy to such information as organizational long-range strategic and short-range plans, future product or organizational changes being contemplated, and shifts in direction, the more employees will be able to set their goals in sync with where the organization is going.

Publications such as annual reports, internal newsletters, trade magazines, workforce projection documents, and industry trend reports can provide valuable indications of future directions if other company documents are considered too confidential to distribute. By instructing employees to consider every document or conversation as a potential source of information for career development, practitioners can assist them in concretely assessing the relevance of their goals. The practitioner should be asking the Action Provoking Questions above regarding relevance.

For example, a relocation goal might say, "I plan to relocate to XYZ Computer Software Company, where I will be able to move out of systems programming and into software sales." If the employee could show that the sales opportunity is closed within the present organization, that XYZ Company could provide that opportunity, that the goal meets with the employee's current abilities, and that it is compatible with future plans of the employee and of the industry, then the relevance requirement would be met.

Well-Timed Goals

Time frames for career goals can be set to establish the number of weeks, months, or years within which the goal will be actualized. Exploratory goals should specify research completion dates (for example, "to complete my exploration of the job prospects in

■ ACTION PROVOKING QUESTIONS

EVALUATING TIME FRAMES

- Is the time limit reasonable, given the typical rate of movement in the organization?
- Is it reasonable, given current skill development and frequency with which openings occur?
- Is the time limit reasonable, given the length of time on the present job?
- Is it reasonable, given the employee's normal rate of progression from job to job?
- Is the position likely to be needed by the organization by the time one moves into it?

---

the accounting department by March 31"); whereas vertical, lateral, and realignment goals may be more appropriately framed within a given number of weeks, months, or years (for example, "to become corporate controller within eighteen months"). Job enrichment goals should have time parameters in order to encourage immediate implementation upon return to the job. They may consist of incremental job enrichment steps, each of which may have its own time parameter. The nature of relocation goals, on the other hand, may make them more long term.

Target dates strengthen the goal statement by providing milestones against which to measure progress. It is helpful to keep career goals within a three-year range, whenever possible. Setting long-term future goals does not place the same important pressures on the individual as shorter-term goals do. Most effective short-term career planning goals will focus on a six- to eighteen-month period. The strength of establishing a time frame lies in forcing the individual to consider contingency plans if the goal is not achieved within the specified time frame. Checkpoints along the way also provide the individual with ways of measuring progress. Practitioners should recognize that time frames must sometimes be extended, since it is not always possible to complete a goal within the initially defined time period. The employee should also be wary of setting unrealistic time frames. A time frame that is too long will remove any sense of urgency about the goal. A time frame that is too short will make the goal unattainable and may be simply an excuse for failure. The Action Provoking Questions above are useful in establishing the validity of employees' time frames.

FIGURE 4

The Four Steps of Goal Development

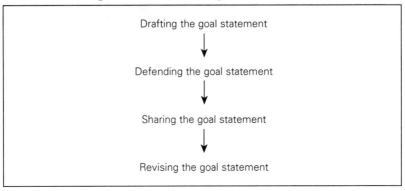

Drafting the goal statement

↓

Defending the goal statement

↓

Sharing the goal statement

↓

Revising the goal statement

The following realignment goal meets the requirement for time framing: "I plan to realign from manager of technical support to senior network analyst by June 15."

GETTING IT DOWN

Once employees understand the required characteristics of effective goals, the practitioner can offer assistance in actually drafting goal statements. A workshop setting can encourage employees to develop initial drafts individually, to share them with others, and to receive advice from peers and workshop staff concerning any necessary changes. Counseling sessions are another alternative, but they should be supplemented by employees exchanging their goal statements with others outside the individual sessions. No matter which vehicle is selected, the practitioner will need to support employees in the four distinct activities as depicted in Figure 4.

Drafting

For most employees, the most difficult part of setting goals is facing a blank sheet of paper. Practitioners can help by defining and clarifying the six career option categories and by strongly suggesting that goals in each category be established. The Goal Matrix described in Exercise 11 can provide a framework for generating ideas.

TABLE 13

DEFENDING SMART GOALS

- How does this goal incorporate my profiling information?
- Is the goal as specific as I can make it?
  —Am I able to specify a job title?
  —Am I able to name departments or divisions?
  —Am I able to define concrete actions indicated by the goal?
- Is the goal attainable?
  —Does such a job exist?
  —Is it a reasonable move for me?
  —Do I compare favorably with the competition?
  —Can I obtain additional skills I will need?
- Is the goal relevant?
  —Does the goal match the future I want and expect?
  —Is the goal in tune with information I have about the organization?
- Is the goal time-bound and relatively short term (six to eighteen months)?

Employees should be urged to review their personal profiling information as well as data gained about the organization as they set about drafting goals. And they should ask themselves if their statements meet all characteristics of action-oriented goals discussed in this chapter. Goal statements should be continually challenged with questions such as "Is this goal specific enough, in terms of the job title, salary/grade, and duties to which I aspire?" and "Is this goal relevant to the skills I now have or could easily develop?"

Goal statements should reflect a match between the realities of the organization and the individual's skills and aspirations. Conflicts, if any, should receive close attention and may warrant rewriting the goal statement.

Defending

During the defense of goal statements, employees explain why this goal is appropriate for them at this time. They should be able to write or verbalize a defense statement ensuring that their goals are SMART based on the questions asked in Table 13.

The defense step can be carried out with a counselor, a supervisor, or peers. It may be executed one-on-one, in small groups, or in a workshop setting. In a workshop setting, groups of two or three can take turns critiquing one another, using the SMART format.

Sharing

While goal statements have already been shared with other individuals during the defense step, employees should be encouraged to think of additional persons with whom they might discuss career goals. Goals are more likely to be acted upon if they are shared with those who can provide encouragement and with those who can open doors that may eventually lead to their attainment. Employees should view peers, supervisors, family, and friends as personal resources who can assist in a variety of tangible and intangible ways.

Employees should share their goal statements with as many members of the organization as possible—supervisors, co-workers, human resource staff—as makes political sense. Often (but not always) the more individuals in an organization who are aware of an employee's specific goals, the more assistance is available. If individuals feel reluctant to share goals with organization members, it is all the more important that the practitioner encourage them to convey their goals to family, friends, and peers.

In some companies visibility is promoted through using developmental reviews that ask employees to state career goals and to define abilities they wish to develop over the coming year. And in some, career goals are part of performance reviews.

Revising

As new information is obtained, or as assumptions prove to be in error, the goal statement should be modified. In some cases, the new information may be significant enough to require that the individual return to the first step and draft a new goal statement. In others, only minor adjustments may be needed.

Employees should remember that not all assumptions must be or can be tested immediately. Few career decisions are made with all the information on hand. The important point is to make the goal statement as precise and appropriate as possible with whatever information is at hand, to begin actively working toward goals, and to resist the rationalization that "I can't really go after that goal because I'm not sure I'd achieve it anyway."

By the end of the Targeting Stage, employees should have developed realistic career-planning goals that have high probability for success. At this point, practitioners could ask the Action Provoking Questions below.

■ **ACTION PROVOKING QUESTIONS**

EVALUATING GOALS' PROBABILITY OF SUCCESS

- Do you have adequate information about the organization's current activities and future plans to select personal career goals?
- How can you get the additional information you need?
- Have you considered all available pathways in selecting your goal options?
- Do the options you have generated adequately cover a variety of circumstances that may occur in the organization and in specific job areas?
- Should you select more goal options than you now have?
- Do your goals realistically reflect profiling information?
- Are your goals compatible with organizational goals and plans?
- Are your goal statements oriented toward a specific action?
- Are your goals stated in such a way that their progress can easily be checked along the way?

STRUCTURAL SUPPORTS FOR TARGETING

Thus far, practitioners have been invited to design career workshops and counseling sessions necessary to assist employees in exploring and specifying career goals. They have been advised to use vital organizational information to aid employees in making their goal statements more realistic and in sync with the organization's overall goals. The organization has a variety of processes that are part of its structure and that can greatly assist in the targeting process. It is the practitioner's job to learn and understand these processes and to translate them for use at the Targeting Stage. The organizational policy and practice areas described in the following section can serve as a guide, but practitioners must consider their own organization and how its policies might be further tied to the career development process at the Targeting Stage.

Organizational Planning

Most organizations, regardless of size, have several different types of planning processes. These might be broken down into two general types: the longer-term strategic plans and the shorter-term operational, or tactical, plans.

Strategic plans are those long-term schemes that deal with projected changes in direction, growth efforts and velocities, and environmental adaptations. They normally involve major commitments of resources and affect how an organization will proceed with its business in the long run and how fundamental questions of policy and organizational mission will be addressed.

Operational or tactical plans are those that deal with the step-by-step objectives along the route toward strategic goals. These plans may be looked upon as the milestones for measuring progress along the strategic path.

Suppose that an employee, as a result of a career development plan, establishes a goal of becoming a marketing manager in a particular product area. Suppose also that the organization's strategic plans call for the termination of that product line in a certain number of years. The employee develops the goal, and the leader or practitioner, just as ignorant of the long-term plans as the employee, endorses that goal. Three-quarters of the way through the plan to reach the career goal, however, the employee suddenly finds that the career path is a dead end, that acquired skills are inapplicable, and that a return to the start position is the only logical choice. In such a case, employees feel that they have been led astray and that valuable time and effort has been wasted. Practitioners and leaders find themselves less trusted, the career development effort suffers, and the organization feels that dollars have been wasted. In the end, the organization may lose an employee who could have been quite valuable.

To avoid this type of LOSE-LOSE-LOSE situation, it is imperative that practitioners have access to organizational planning information and develop the skills necessary to translate and disseminate it. Toward this end, the practitioner will have to convince those in authority of the vital importance of sharing with employees as much of this information as possible. Existing documents such as annual reports, company newspapers, industrial trend reports, and current media reports about environmental, cultural, political, and legal changes can be used effectively at the Targeting Stage. In other instances, it may be necessary to actually gather raw data that pertains to upcoming corporate changes in technology, product, and market strategy and prepare it for employee consumption.

CASE 20

Keeping Goals Relevant:
Organizational Strategic Planning

At a manufacturing company, the strategic planning department publishes an online newsletter that projects changes that will affect the industry. Employees can "subscribe" electronically to the newsletter and remain up-to-date on the current trends in manufacturing and affiliated industries. For many who attend the career seminars, this valuable informative item is first introduced to them when the Targeting Stage is presented, and becomes a valuable asset for their continuing career futures.

The practitioner can develop files of such information or assign employee task forces to gather it for their departments and present it at group meetings or workshops.

Charts and Titles

Much of the information that can provide a base for targeting is assumed to be common knowledge in most organizations, though in fact it is not widely disseminated throughout the organization. Organizational charts and lists of titles and grades are often considered to be of value only to human resource staff. Some organizations keep these charts confidential. However, these charts (although changing frequently) can assist all employees in setting more specific goals for movement within the organization.

When specific job titles, grades, or qualifications are not readily available to employees, practitioners might consider preparing special career information reports that contain as much of this data as can be gathered and easily understood. Job titles and classification listings can be categorized into job families and task groups for easy identification of functions and skills. Career path examples can demonstrate grade level clusters and major thresholds between categories, such as nonexempt and exempt, exempt and managerial, and managerial and executive levels.

Organizational charts can assist employees in understanding reporting relationships between individuals and between divisions

CASE 21

Using an Online Development Matrix

A finance organization designed a development matrix for all participants in the career development target group. Matrix information was offered on paper as well as online, and described the competencies needed for each position, the various pathways into a position, and the particular capabilities that were essential for success. The matrix helped participants fine tune their career goals and gain a more realistic assessment of what was truly possible in the organization and what was not.

The development matrix product had three objectives:

- To provide employees information about the similarities among the requirements for the jobs covered in the matrix, to help guide their exploration of career options within the organization
- To give employees a preview of the responsibilities and skills required to perform specific jobs
- To provide employees with general information about what skills they might have to acquire or enhance in order to move from one job to another

and units. These charts present visually a great deal of information that may not be as easily understood if presented verbally. This information will be of particular benefit to those who have research goals but who do not realize the expanse of the various organizational units (for example, that HR includes placement, training and development, employee relations, compensation, job analysis, employment, benefits, and research).

A great many organizations are now putting together organizational charts that display pictures of key staff members. These can be valuable to employees in identifying those within the organization who may be contacted to gather more information about the viability of a particular goal.

Company Goals and Trends

To ensure the integration of company and personal goals, individuals must understand overall business objectives before formulating their personal plans. Since the success of the organization requires that each of its employees be working toward achieving company objectives, employees must be aware of overall organizational goals and must understand them in order to be committed to the role they are expected to play in achieving those goals.

A great many organizations have facilitated this process through Management by Objectives (MBO) programs, which not only clarify organizational goals but also provide a mechanism through which individual goals can be coordinated with organizational goals. Ideally, MBO programs provide for the formulation and promulgation of clear, concisely stated objectives from which action plans are developed. These action plans can be monitored and their progress measured because they are quantitatively stated and give a time frame. MBO plans also provide for taking corrective actions to keep efforts on track.

Ideally, an MBO program provides for a series of objectives that relate to goals down through the organization, so that individual employees, regardless of level, can determine exactly what must be accomplished and by when.

Organizational objectives define certain desired results in each major area of the organizational hierarchy. Each division addresses those objectives through a series of statements about specific actions. Each department takes those objectives that relate to it and determines what actions will be necessary to accomplish those objectives, along with any others that its management may desire to pursue. The process continues to filter down through groups and subdepartments and, finally, to individuals who determine what part of their group's objectives they can accomplish.

There is a recurring fear that MBO imposes objectives and schedules, rather than letting the organization's individual units and employees determine what they wish to accomplish. This is somewhat true, but MBO does provide a means by which organization-wide objectives can be stated and coordinated. Some organizations have experimented, with varying degrees of success, with bottom-up MBO, wherein objectives begin at the individual employee level and work their way up to the organizational level.

Practitioners who work in either top-down or bottom-up MBO organizations will find that coordinating personal career development goals with organizational objectives is easy. Information is easier to come by than in most other organizations, and employees have a better understanding of organizational directions and trends.

Job Posting

In addition to their use in internal job placement, bulletins announcing job openings can give employees a sense of the types of employment available and of the changes taking place. Employees who keep informed about potential jobs—even those for which they do not intend to apply—will begin to see company trends in employment and trends in growth or decline of certain functional areas. For example, they may get their first clue about expansion of a branch office by noting the number of jobs posted for that site. Or they may note that while many jobs are opening in the Marketing Division, they tend to be clustered at the lower levels, with little turnover at the top. Simply seeing the variety of jobs that become available can generate ideas for goal options that employees may not have previously considered.

To be effective, a job posting system must include all openings and must be part of an honest effort to objectively select from among applicants. In many cases, however, job posting is simply a routine that is followed because of regulations, when in fact a candidate has already been selected. Since this practice is not likely to change dramatically, the practitioner may need to candidly caution employees to be realistic in their expectations. Some organizations make it a policy to at least have a face-to-face discussion with applicants from within—explaining selection procedures and reasons—rather than simply sending them the same form letter that others may receive.

Job announcements should be posted where all employees will see them (for best effect, in a number of locations) and should display as much information as possible about the job. This includes title, salary, experience and education requirements, and major duties. Also useful is an enumeration of how many persons have held the position over the past five to ten years and a description of the potential career ladder(s) that could result from the job.

This information can be supplemented by compiling statistics on who has moved where over the past several years. Table 14 shows examples of career tracking data. Furthermore, offering the information in a workshop setting can help employees to be more realistic in their attempts to set goals.

Succession Planning

Generally used to plan and clarify progression in managerial ranks, succession planning assists the organization in training backup staff members who are likely to fill certain positions.

TABLE 14

CAREER TRACK DATA

- HR Analyst III (1975–77). HR Supervisor (1977–79). Assistant for Labor-Management Relations (1980).
- Secretary, Marketing (II) (1974–76). Office Manager (1976–79). Assistant Account Supervisor (1980).
- Supply Clerk, Public Relations (1975–77). Assistant Office Manager (1977–80).

Often these succession plans are made behind closed doors; individuals are not cognizant of the specific targets being developed for them. As a result, individuals often end up determining several specific targets, while the organization has designed a radically different game plan. One result of this approach can be that the heir apparent, not knowing of the secret selection, begins looking elsewhere for opportunity. The first that the employee knows of management's plans and the first that management knows of the employee's disgruntlement is when the employee tenders a resignation, citing a lack of opportunity. By then it can be too late to rectify the situation. The organization's intent is usually to keep all options open, but the new opportunities finally offered to the employee are often turned down or met with mixed emotions.

One method of succession planning involves the incumbents naming and training their successors. This gives the successor direct contact with and instruction from the predecessor as well as visibility among others in the unit. However, this practice can result in questionable selection criteria if incumbents are allowed to be the sole judge in replacing themselves.

A more formal method of succession planning is a team selection approach, whereby a team of managers evaluate potential candidates, generally nominated by their own supervisors or identified through a testing procedure, for higher positions. Those who prove to be superior performers are then placed in a fast-track development program, designed to give them extensive experience and training in preparation for advancement. They continue to be evaluated in order to determine their specific placement in the organization. This system relies heavily on training or job rotation to develop multifunctional employees who have potential for management.

CASE 22

New Approaches to Succession Planning

A t a large energy company, recruitment forecasting and succession planning provide both the company and employees with a valuable database for decision making and planning. The programs are backed by information from the company's extensive skills inventory (with cross-referenced information on employee education, experience, skills, and interests) and its organizational change model (a mathematical simulation that tracks demographic distribution, functions, employee ages, departures, status, and new recruits).

The organizational change model supplies estimated attrition rates, which along with the company's human resource needs, forecasting, and other data, provide the basis for development of a companywide recruiting forecast. This forecast, in turn, becomes valuable input for the succession planning process.

A managerial needs forecast is used by succession planning groups in each unit who apply personal knowledge and skills inventory information to determine potential candidates for key managerial positions that will come open. The candidates' preparation is linked to an individual development plan, designed to help them ready themselves for advancement. Responsibility for seeing that the plan is carried out—including deadlines for specific developmental activities—rests with each candidate's manager.

If practitioners could make succession plans available to individuals during this stage, individuals would have enough time to contemplate their option and consider whether or not the organization's plan meets with their own career goals. The more thought that individuals have given to their skills and desires during the Profiling Stage, the better they will be prepared to actively pursue the next step of their career development needs. Clearly the practitioner and the organization need to give serious thought to the succession planning issue and to sharing that information with employees at the Targeting Stage.

SHARED RESPONSIBILITIES

It is apparent that the Targeting Stage requires a partnership of individual employees, practitioners, and the organization as a whole. Individuals can set goals for themselves, but they cannot do so in a vacuum. The organization must be prepared to share information that is necessary in generating goals, and the practitioner must develop ways to translate that information into usable, meaningful terms.

During the Targeting Stage, managers and supervisors must be prepared to help employees push toward their goals. Managers and supervisors can set targets for subordinates and challenge them to meet those targets. They must give honest performance evaluation to their subordinates and help them to increase their skills. And finally, they must be sensitive to their subordinates, to the work environment, and to how individual goals mesh with those of the organization. Practitioners must be prepared to help managers and supervisors fulfill these responsibilities.

The practitioner, thus, is an intermediary who may need to prod top management to provide information and may need to encourage and instruct employees to use it in setting goals. Where necessary, the practitioner may need to guide employees to sources of information about career opportunities outside the organization. The practitioner may also become involved in designing programs to assist employees in setting goals.

Once career plans have been identified and tested against the realities of organizational life, employees will be ready to begin designing the action plans that will enable them to pursue their goals in an organized manner. During the Strategizing Stage, employees work to make their goals operational.

Making Maps

THE STRATEGIZING STAGE

*"The people who get on in this world
are people who get up and look for
the circumstances they want, and,
if they can't find them, make them."*
—GEORGE BERNARD SHAW

Once goals have been established, the next stage in the career development cycle is formulating a comprehensive strategy to accomplish them. All too often the career development process moves along to the point of individual goals being set, and it is assumed that employees will be able to function on their own.

Goals alone do not stimulate action. Action results from a carefully thought out and well-structured plan that describes how a goal is to be accomplished. Employees must develop those plans to discover potential problems, and to give thought to a means of overcoming the problems en route to accomplishing their goals. To do this they must thoroughly understand the culture and norms in their organizations and develop workable plans to achieve their goals, by effectively synthesizing that information into an achievable course of action. This two-part process takes planning out of a vacuum and makes the goal statements and the process of their achievement come alive.

Surmountable Obstacles

The strategizing process is not easy. The first obstacle is resistance to change. Strategizing confronts individuals and pushes them to name specific actions and events that they may encounter imme-diately. This new concern often brings with it a sudden realization that lives could really change. Understanding the change process will be particularly useful at this stage.

Change is particularly difficult for people who aren't sure where they are going. Whatever aspect of a person's life causes the need to reassess, forays into the unknown are often followed by hasty retreats to a more stable condition. Sometimes a work situation must become physically unbearable before a person is willing to risk even minor movement. At the Strategizing Stage, individuals can counter fears of change by learning how to plan for change. The whole purpose of strategizing is to gain control over the changes in one's career and develop the flexibility to manage those changes. Employees need to develop skills in analyzing organizational reali-ties, in assessing alternative paths toward achieving goals, and in developing a realistic plan for what to do and how to do it.

It is often simple to ignore the importance of strategizing. The goal-setting process results in such a tidy end product that it is dif-ficult to recognize it as only the beginning. People need to realize that nothing can happen without continued work and commit-ment. Goals that have been established require follow-up to bring them to fruition.

Understanding the System

Organizations are composed of more than just structures, rules, procedures, and policies. Not only is there the formal, established, traditional organization; in addition, a host of informal norms appear in response to the social and personal needs of the people involved. In order for effective action planning to take place, it is important to understand both the formal and the informal orga-nization. An employee who attempts to achieve a career develop-ment goal based upon a plan that considers only the formal orga-nization will encounter difficulties as that plan moves into areas influenced by the informal system.

FORMALITY AND INFORMALITY

The structure of the formal organization is based upon the jobs to be performed by the organization as a whole as well as by its individual component parts. Although there may be some overlap of functions within an organization, each department, group, or division has its own hierarchy of managers, supervisors, and executives. The formal organization is established by rules and regulations designed to facilitate the fulfillment of organizational requirements. Informal organizations, on the other hand, spring up without planning or overt intention and are aimed at meeting the personal needs of individual members.

The formal organization is maintained by a system designed to promote order and focus efforts toward organizational goals. Informal organizations tend to exist only so long as personal needs are being met by and for their memberships. When members have new or changed needs that the informal organization cannot satisfy, they will move on to join or form another group more capable of meeting them.

Formal organizations are established for accomplishing specific purposes, and as long as those purposes are being accomplished the organizations will continue to exist. Informal organizations may be temporary, lasting for only a few days, or permanent, lasting the entire lifetimes of their members. The deciding factor in determining the length of an informal organization's life span is based on the strengths of the associations formed and the needs being fulfilled.

Later research has shown that for every function or system that operates within a formal organization, parallel or shadow functions of systems operate within the related informal organizations. It is imperative, therefore, that the practitioner understand these functions and systems in order to assist career development program participants in understanding them. To aid the practitioner with the process of organizational analysis, eight separate functions or systems will be identified and described. Most organizations will have these functions or systems operating within them. Understanding the system means knowing about:

- Relationships: Formal and informal
- Influence
- Politics
- Technology
- Support: Mentors, networks, and task groups
- Information and communications
- Culture
- Values

In most formal organizations, relationships are work oriented, system imposed, and hierarchical. An employee has a function that has been established as necessary in order to accomplish certain organizational goals and objectives. The employee is situated in the workplace around other employees who have specific functions and jobs. All employees within a common workplace have a supervisor, appointed by the organization. That supervisor works for another supervisor, who, in turn, works for another supervisor, and so on up the chain of command.

In the informal organization, on the other hand, relationships are socially oriented, are established by the group and its individual members, and are sociometrically based. Regardless of their functions within the organization, members make individual decisions about their associations. Though members of the informal group may be friendly with all others in the organization, certain close ties will be formed with certain individuals more than with others. These relationships all affect the action plans developed by individuals as they pursue career goals.

Suppose, for example, that a machinist set a lateral career goal of moving into quality assurance. The machinist would need to understand not only the formal organizational relationships of the quality assurance group, but the system of informal relationships existing there as well. Machinists would in this case have to examine their own needs for special relationships and determine if those needs would be fulfilled in and by the new group. Current friendships could certainly be affected. Barriers could also be encountered in such a change of relationships—some internal to the individual making the move, and some within the group to be joined. The machinist would need to consider how those barriers might be overcome or effectively neutralized.

THE POWER OF INFLUENCE

One skill needed to deal with both the formal and informal system is the skill of influence. Influence, in the context of career development, means the ability to cause others to take desired actions that assist in the pursuit of a career goal. Importantly, however, it means doing this in a way that maintains effective relationships.

The importance of influence skills is tied directly to the notion that career development requires a proactive stance on the part of employees—making things happen, rather than waiting for them to happen. Although leaders and practitioners can encourage and coach, it is up to the individual employee to act—to discover and seize opportunities, to walk through doors that are open and open those that are not, and to work with and through others who can help make career development happen.

Much, if not most, of this proactivity requires some involvement of others, and these others frequently need to be influenced to various degrees (for example, from giving advice to granting permission). In some cases, an individual will only need to influence someone to take the time to discuss an idea or provide information. In other cases, influence might extend to putting a new item in the budget or changing a job description. Whatever the degree of influence involved, it is difficult to imagine that individuals can be proactive in pursuit of their own career development without ability in this area.

Influence becomes even more important as employees go beyond the self-assessment at profiling and career goal setting at targeting. It is vital as individuals prepare for career change. Whether that change means taking on new responsibilities in the current position or seeking new projects, employees will find they are in a competitive arena where they need to determinedly "go after" what they want. The ability to influence others on their own behalf is a crucial strategy in a tight marketplace.

Fortunately, influence has a way of snowballing for people who learn to use it in furthering career development goals. An individual who is able to influence others generally becomes visible in the workplace as favorable consequences start to happen for that person. That visibility quickly translates to being viewed as an "influential person"—someone whose opinions are worth hearing and whose ideas are worth trying. With that attention comes, of course, still greater influence. The influence skills practiced in just a few circumstances have ramifications well beyond.

A Learned Skill

Too often, influence is viewed as something we either come by naturally or simply do not have at all. Those that have it are lucky, and the rest simply have to work harder in other ways. That view tends to represent influence as a birthright rather than a skill. Yet, there are individuals in nearly every work setting who have increased their influence over time. Experience and practice—and maybe even some valuable advice—have enabled them to *learn* how to influence. Indeed, influence is a skill that can be taught, practiced, learned, and adapted.

One model, developed by Kim Barnes (1994), is particularly useful in understanding and subsequently becoming more skillful at influence. The model identifies eight types of influence behavior and recognizes that a variety of actions can be influential in a variety of situations. The eight influence "styles," comprising sixteen influence behaviors, can be identified through participation in and discussions of business cases and through the use of a 360-degree feedback instrument. Participants in "Exercising Influence" workshops learn the effective use of behavioral influence skills, how to build long-term influence relationships, and how to establish clear influence goals, all within the context of current organizational issues.

The Career Connection

It is perhaps easiest to understand the connection between influence and career development by first thinking of specific instances in which influence can be valuable. Typical of the many occasions for influence are:

- Influencing colleagues and managers to spend time reviewing work accomplishments in order to help identify areas of strength and weakness
- Influencing a boss to grant time away from the workplace to attend professional meetings and conferences
- Influencing a boss to assign some new and more challenging work opportunities
- Influencing a colleague to provide information and on-the-job experience needed to learn a new skill
- Influencing a manager to include budget items for tuition reimbursement and off-site workshops
- Influencing a high-level colleague to spend time as a mentor

Although the need for influence is perhaps most obvious when an individual begins planning actions to achieve his or her goals, a good understanding of influence and personal styles of influence, as well as skills in the use of influence, can help individuals work their way through each of the crucial stages in the career development process.

■ ACTION PROVOKING QUESTIONS

DEVELOPMENT MOXIE: AN INFLUENCE AUDIT

Practitioners can check the influence-ability of their employee popula-tion by asking themselves, or employee groups the following questions:

- Do employees in our organization easily access their peers for input and feedback regarding skills and abilities?
- Do employees possess the strength to speak up for themselves when feedback is inappropriate?
- Do employees query their own managers for feedback about skills and abilities other than during performance appraisals?
- Do managers feel comfortable giving straight feedback to employees?
- Are managers able to impress on their direct reports the link between performance and potential?
- Do employees regularly seek information about the direction of the business from others higher in the chain of command?
- Are employees proactive about initiating contacts with individuals in other business units about the state of the business?
- Do employees take charge of building their own networks and con-tacts in ways other than those structured through education programs?
- Do managers request information not normally available to provide their direct reports with a wider point of view?
- Do employees initiate requests for placement on company-wide task forces or committees?
- Do managers request unique development opportunities that go beyond their own turf, in their efforts to grow their people?

Influence During Profiling

An understanding of one's skill level in influence and of one's style of influence can be a valuable part of one's own self-profile. For example, in identifying weaknesses or deficiencies in the area, an individual who discovers he or she has only very limited influ-ence skills will be able to use that information to plan some future developmental strategies. Likewise, the individual who finds his or her influence approach confined to only one style may begin to see why there are some situations in which attempts to influence fail. It is important to develop flexibility that enables various responses to a variety of circumstances. The Action Provoking Questions above provide a way for practitioners to check the influ-ence-ability of their employee population.

Individuals who learn about their influence abilities and styles at the Profiling Stage will be able to use the information in three particularly important ways: first, by beginning to immediately develop and practice influence skills in areas of weakness they have identified; second, by using newly acquired skills as they continue through the remaining stages of the career development process; and third, by drawing upon the styles that represent particular areas of strength as information that can help determine appropriate career goals and action steps.

The ability to influence can also be especially valuable when reality-testing. Managers and others who can provide this are often too busy or do not understand and value the process. Those asking for feedback need to be prepared to use their influence appropriately to gain the information they need . . . and deserve.

Individuals who have solicited feedback may also need to influence the process—although not the substance—in order to keep it focused on behavior rather than personality and on specific observations rather than opinions. Giving feedback that is useful for career development planning requires a great deal of caring and candor. If these are not already present, the individual asking for feedback may need to use influence skills to attain them.

Influence During Targeting

A key to goal-setting in career development is knowing and understanding all possible options. Unfortunately, this information is really not readily available in any one place in most organizations. Rather, the individual has to "ferret it out" by asking questions, reading and interpreting company documents, and observing. The process is facilitated by good "connectedness" in the organization—knowing something about the political environment and knowing who to ask about what. The ability to influence is particularly useful as individuals seek to establish that connectedness. The skills of influence also enable the individual to draw out key information that will be helpful to his or her career.

Influence is also necessary when one is involved in setting goals for positions or activities that represent a departure from what currently exits in the organization. Some very innovative individuals set their sights on a job that has not yet been created, but that might be if the right individuals were convinced it was good idea. Others may set a goal that relates to the expansion or enrichment of their current job. In either case, it takes a good deal of influence to move others toward change. The directness of the expressive influence behaviors and the drawing out of information or ideas of the receptive influence behaviors described by Kim Barnes (1994) can be particularly useful in these situations.

Influence During Strategizing and Implementing

The occasions for using influence skills are perhaps most apparent when planning specific strategies for reaching one's goals. Typically, these strategies require something from the organization (for example, tuition reimbursement, on-site training, creative learning assignments) or from the manager (for example, time off to attend training, on-the-job development, time for serving on committees or attending conferences, new projects not included in current scope of work). These activities are more likely to occur if influence is skillfully used in requesting them.

Influence is one of the most important components of a strategic career plan. Individuals should ask themselves, "Who do I need to influence to make this happen?" and "How can I best influence the appropriate person(s)?" This also provides somewhat of a check on reality of the action plan. For example, if a strategy requires more influence than an individual can realistically develop, then perhaps a different strategy should be explored.

Influence, to many individuals, may seem a bit too intangible to consider in terms of being a specific learnable skill. By its very nature, influence sounds more like something that should just seep into our consciousness and happen or not happen without any deliberate forethought. Unfortunately, however, without deliberate forethought, opportunities for using influence will be missed by those still waiting for the "seeping" process to occur. Learning to influence is crucial to taking charge of one's career.

POLITICS COUNT

Another area with which the practitioner must be familiar is that of organizational politics. While books on this subject flood the marketplace, individuals are still at a loss to understand the meaning of politics, and many still see it as a dirty word. Even though employees know that something besides long-term goals and hierarchical structure influences what happens within an organization, they are often reluctant to admit that their organization, like every other, is rife with political influence. This myopic view can hinder the progress of those who are strategizing to achieve career goals. Only by recognizing, studying, and understanding the internal political system can they fully structure their plans to deal with the barriers it presents and take advantage of the opportunities it affords.

It takes a great deal of effort to get organizational politics out of the closet. Even though most people in formal organizations pride themselves on their discretionary use of power, they find it difficult to admit that this use of power is the basis for well-planned and executed political maneuvers. While it is considered an organizational taboo to play office politics, everyone admires the skilled artist who is able to obtain the impossible, soothe ruffled feathers, and get ahead in the competition for scarce resources. Practicing organizational politics means skillfully balancing power, saving the work group's face in bad situations, bartering and horse trading where necessary, working out compromises and keeping intergroup relationships harmonious, being able to think on one's feet in tough situations, and exercising tact and diplomacy.

Politics have become an accepted part of informal organizations. As politics become more overt, great skill is required to practice them. Informal group politics are almost an art form. Politically it would be the kiss of death to ignore another member of the group. The glue that holds together most informal groups is the mutual satisfaction of needs. Common sense tells the members of the informal group that to admit that one does not wish to satisfy another member's needs would be destructive to the group, so group members engage in compromise, tact, diplomacy, and power balancing. Politics become the life blood of the informal group.

Practitioners may be able to help individuals recognize that the system of organizational politics (formal and informal) is largely a matter of relationships between people and the influence of those relationships on how decisions are made. It is a subtle set of activities and information for sharing, building reputations, and gathering influence that usually happens outside formal channels. Politics often shape organizational decisions by answering questions such as "Who will win or lose if we do this?" and "Whose opinion really counts the most?" Appointments of committee chairpersons may be based as much on their ability to get the attention of top management as on their expertise in the subject matter at hand. A decision to reorganize part of a company may be influenced by the opportunity to give more control to likable rather than knowledgeable people. Those who excel at playing office politics put themselves in a position to gather inside information and to get the attention of those with organizational influence.

There are a variety of clear approaches to thinking politically. Such thinking may involve:

- *Visibility*—making sure that accomplishments become well known, by sending memos, circulating reports, and making presentations at meetings
- *Attention*—getting the ear of people who are in positions of influence and power
- *Association*—forming friendships and networks with valuable contact people at lunches, coffee breaks, and conferences
- *Information*—gathering inside information from such diverse sources as secretaries, mail clerks, auditors, and managers
- *Aspirations*—making career advancement ambitions known to those who can assist
- *Demonstration*—finding opportunities to demonstrate abilities by volunteering for committee assignments, special projects, and oral presentations

Employees can learn a lot about internal politics by learning to observe (1) *Internal periodicals of the organization:* What individuals and departments consistently get most play? What types of programs and activities seem to get most mention? (2) *Memos and reports:* Who sends documents to whom? Who is on the internal routing list and in what order? How does the follow-up on reports occur? (3) *Information flow:* Who seems to know everything that goes on? Where is information exchanged (formal meetings, coffee breaks, lunches)? Why is some information shared and other information withheld? (4) *Power success:* Who has the best offices and furnishings? Who spends time with the top brass? Whose subordinates get promoted? Who were the big winners in the last reorganization? Who is responsible for major human resource changes?

Once participants thoroughly understand the relationships, power, and political systems, they will already begin to have some knowledge about how people within the organization assist each other and provide support to one another.

SYSTEMS THAT SUPPORT

When informal groups and organizations were initially recognized as operating within formal organizations, many managers and organizational leaders saw them as potentially dangerous and counterproductive to the goals of the formal organization. In some cases that assumption was valid, but for the most part, informal groups and organizations are valuable support adjuncts to the formal organization. For this reason, employees strategizing to accomplish career development goals should understand the informal groups within the organization and the other support systems operating there.

All organizations, formal and informal, have two specific informal systems that provide support for their members: (1) networks, and (2) mentors. It is interesting to note that in recent years many organizations have sought to capture the power of these informal systems by formalizing them and educating employees about how to proactively pursue each. The following sections highlight some of these more formalized approaches.

Networking

Once seen as a questionable activity, networking is now seen as essential for anyone seriously interested in developing his or her career. The practice has received recognition and official sanction as a means of providing support for those at all levels of formal organizations.

Some networks are organized to solve specific problems, while others are designed to meet specific needs of certain interest groups. Practitioners can provide invaluable aid to those seeking to accomplish their career development goals by helping program participants join those networks or initiate them with some specific goal in mind. Informal support networks within an organization can be especially valuable to women, minority-group members, the physically handicapped, and those contemplating a major job area shift. Those who have blazed the trails are often willing to help others avoid the pitfalls they have encountered.

Many networks are now being established outside organizations. Practitioners might investigate these and make information about them available to participants for use during the Strategizing Stage.

Beverly Bernstein (Bernstein and Kaye, 1990) researched the subject with the author and delineated five distinct steps in the networking process.

1. *Know what you want.* The concept of networking has been around for a long time, but few people build and use their networks effectively. Knowing a number of people is not enough. Successful networking requires that valuable time and resources be productively directed.

CASE 23

"Walking Books":
Networking Inside Today's Organizations

It became abundantly clear that a large aerospace organization's technical library could not keep up with the phenomenal rate of technological change being experienced. Material could not be written, printed, and distributed fast enough to make certain of its availability to those who might need it. It was known, however, that within the organization there were a great many people working on projects, or having recent experience in certain areas, that were among those progressing with the greatest rapidity. A farseeing director of technology carefully researched and indexed every field and subject in which his division of the company was working. He then requested that every person within the company who had worked on these areas, or projects related to them, make themselves known to the technical librarians and, through the librarians, available to others who might be seeking help in a job related to that particular expertise. The network worked beautifully. In effect, he established a walking, breathing library of human books and created a technical expertise network. Now, when a particular question comes up, in any field, two lists are checked at the technical library: the printed books available and the walking books in the network. Research delays have been cut significantly.

2. *Know who's out there.* A collection of contacts needs continual updating since it is the centerpiece of networking. Gathering and organizing the names of people from a variety of situations helps define one's network.

3. *Know how others can help.* People can help in a variety of ways. There are six key networking functions: (a) advise, (b) sponsor, (c) inform, (d) teach, (e) nurture, (f) connect. It is essential to identify the functions of the people in one's network. At different times in a career some of these functions will become more important than others.

4. *Know the odds.* Successful networking doesn't just happen. It takes effort. It is important to decide how much time, money, and energy can be expended. The more effort put into networking, the greater the chances of success.

5. *Know what you have to offer.* All serious networking is recip-rocal. People who devote time and energy deserve some-thing in return. Individuals on the receiving end need to find ways to give back.

Bernstein elaborates further on the importance of knowing what you want by suggesting that individuals always approach others with a clear idea of what they hope to get from them. This can include information, support, more visibility, feedback, or con-nections. Without a clear sense of purpose, mistakes like the fol-lowing are easily made:

- Asking for too much: "Can you tell me all about the field of . . ." This can alienate the receiver, requiring too much of his or her time. Because this request is so vague, the receiver has no clear reference point from which to start.
- Missing opportunities that present themselves. If you do not get specific, you may not recognize a connection if you fall over it.
- Wasting everybody's time. Without a specific agenda and desired outcome, conversations may miss the mark, go on forever, and leave all parties frustrated.

Before embarking on networking, she warns about the need to clarify both long- and short-term objectives. Networking actions will consequently be in harmony with goals. Answering the state-ments in Exercise 13 may help clarify your networking purpose.

Mentoring

There is no substitute for personal advice, assistance, and sup-port from somebody who knows the ropes and is in a position to help others up the ladder. One-on-one mentor-protégé relation-ships are a major component for individuals aspiring to achieve career goals. The design of effective strategizing activities should include helping employees to initiate one or more mentor rela-tionships and to plan how to best use those relationships to reach goals. Mentors are important throughout the career development model described in this book; however, they carry slightly different responsibilities at each stage.

At strategizing mentors can (1) actively prepare the individual for new responsibilities and higher positions (suggesting opportu-nities for relevant experience and training); (2) coach the individ-ual in using the informal system (including appropriate associa-tions, behavior, and dress); (3) provide specific advice on career

EXERCISE 13

Networking Purpose

- I want help with gaining more visibility and exposure in my company.   Yes   No
- I want help to do my current job better, faster, or more efficiently.   Yes   No
- I want help with building skills and competencies for the future.   Yes   No
- I want to look for key people who can evolve into real mentors over time.   Yes   No
- I want help to look for contacts inside or outside my company who can supply me with current industry information.   Yes   No
- I want to have someone who will support me emotionally by listening to my frustrations, fears, successes, etc.   Yes   No
- I want to have someone who will give me advice and feedback about my work.   Yes   No
- Other ideas:_____

Bernstein and Kaye, 1996

plans; and (4) protect the individual's interests in the organization (suggest specific ways to become visible, to be considered for good assignments, and to obtain developmental opportunities).

Practitioners might advise the employee to look for mentors who have done substantial overt career planning of their own and have experienced obstacles and successes in moving toward career goals. Such an individual can help test the validity of the action plan developed by the employee, suggest alternative actions, and present ideas for working around obstacles. In addition, he or she can teach the workings of the informal system, share information generated from the informal system, and advise on ways to best use it. A number of studies of successful executives have verified that those who have had mentors do, in fact, earn more money at a younger age, are better educated, are more likely to follow a carefully delineated career plan, and also mentor others. The practitioner may wish to organize a formal mentoring system that establishes these relationships, knowing that the payoff is considerable.

The practitioner has several alternatives for increasing the possibility that mentor relationships will form during the Strategizing

Stage. These include soliciting interest in mentoring from mature, experienced employees (a good job enrichment idea too!) and directing them to specific individuals whom they might take under their tutelage. The alternatives can also involve designing activities that simply make these potential mentors more visible to individuals who are actively participating in the career development effort. This might involve sponsoring one or more discussion groups where specific topics can be addressed and where potential linking can occur on a less formal basis.

After strategizing, the career development participant will need somewhat different resources from a mentor, who may or may not be the same individual sought for strategizing assistance. The mentor should be someone who can provide not only support and guidance, but also active assistance in removing obstacles to implementing the plan. This may be an individual who can nominate an employee for tuition reimbursement programs or provide the employee with a rotational assignment in the employee's own or another unit.

One way that practitioners might attract prospective mentors to participate is to point out that the mentor-protégé relationship is not a one-way street—mentors also stand to gain much from it. Some people become mentors simply out of goodwill, often seeing themselves in the younger or junior person they are helping. Others recognize that they, too, have much to gain from the relationship. Fast-track employees, for example, can lend credibility to mentors or assist them by preparing special reports, undertaking new projects, and sharing valuable information that may not be accessible to the mentors.

Mentor programs do offer things other career development programs don't—primarily individual attention. In a complex organization, it is particularly beneficial for an individual to learn how the system operates from someone who is better educated or more experienced than him or herself. It's also worth noting that when a mentor relationship works, it's the easiest way for an organization to support career development because, once in place, it usually no longer requires much involvement from the company. Still, for all these advantages, formal mentor programs are not easy to establish. One reason, perhaps, is that both people may find themselves committed before they really know one another or know what to expect from the program.

Practitioners can augment the formal one-on-one process by working closely with both mentors and mentees. Suggested questions to consider in a session with prospective mentors include:

- What are your expectations of your mentees in this program? What do mentees need to do or try in order to keep your commitment going and make your involvement in the mentoring program worth your time?
- What do you feel you have to offer a mentee?
- What might indicate success in each of the following areas: technical skills, interpersonal skills, political skills, managerial skills?
- What are the problems you see yourself encountering in the mentoring process?
- What do you, as the mentor, expect to get out of this program to make the experience mutually rewarding?

Suggested questions that might be useful in a meeting with prospective mentees:

- What do you feel you need or want from a mentor?
- What do you have to offer in the mentoring relationship?
- What do you think indicates success in this program?
- What skills or commitments do you feel you need in a mentor?
- What do you think the mentor should expect to get out of this program to make the experience mutually rewarding?

Questions such as these can go a long way toward preparing both mentor and mentee for their roles and responsibilities in the process.

Mentoring in Groups

Recently, some companies have given up on trying to duplicate mentoring systems that worked well in the informal organization. The reasons are varied. Many formal one-on-one mentoring programs have trouble tapping into the subtle, but essential, personal chemistry found in successful informal mentor relationships. Few organizational reward systems support the process. And one-on-one relationships can actually narrow the opportunities for employees whose development requires diverse networks—including peer support. Another trouble spot is a lack of potential mentors. In many organizations, there just aren't enough mentors to go around.

In an effort to deal with these issues, Betsy Jacobson and the author (Kaye and Jacobson, 1995) have experimented with a variety of group mentoring approaches. In the past, the approach for developing mentoring programs or participating in informal mentoring relationships reduced the issue to a one-on-one experience between mentor and protégé. The new approach expands the idea of mentor/mentee development to groups of employees (learning groups) led by organizational veterans (learning leaders) who are networked together so that nontraditional learning occurs.

Unlike one-on-one mentor relationships, this is a group experience. One-on-one relationships that are often built between mentors and mentees may not develop in the same way in this new setting. The responsibilities of the learning leader will center more on the creation of group learning experiences as opposed to individual learning experiences. In this role, leaders help a group of people function as a support system.

The individuals in the learning group are high-performing learners whose capacity and potential enables them to grow through the learning group experience. Learning leaders will be teaching them about the informal system, helping them to better understand the organization, debriefing ideas, and supporting them in their efforts to grow their own careers. Much of what takes place at the learning meetings will evolve naturally from the group and their particular needs. Frequently conversations center on the learnings that individuals feel they are getting from their assignments and what they are learning in the process. As these conversations take place, the learning leader helps individuals explore *what* they are learning and *how* they are learning along with the support of their learning group.

Mentoring programs are not the cure-all for career development programs, but they provide a strong conduit for the teachings of the informal system. A strong mentoring effort can make the practitioner's job considerably easier and can provide a wealth of information for the participant.

Channels to Information and Communication

Many organizations and the people within them still operate on the premise that knowledge is power. When this is the case, the information flow and communication networks are closed and closely guarded. Information is made available only to those with a

EXERCISE 14

Information Flow

To help determine the nature of the formal organization, practitioners can suggest that participants investigate:

The general attitude toward sharing, holding, and withholding information

- Is there a free flow of information?
- If not, is information held until a need to know is established, or is information withheld as a means of establishing power and control?

The general nature of communications

- Is information spread verbally in order to avoid putting things in writing, or just because this has been established as an effective informal means of passing data?
- Are memoranda carefully drafted so that only necessary information is circulated, or are memoranda casual, containing full details of projects, problems, and plans?
- Who can sign memoranda?

The flow of information

- Is information passed vertically or vertically *and* horizontally?
- Is there a two-way flow of information, or are orders and questions passed downward and answers upward?

Two of the preceding questions ("Who can sign memoranda?" and "Is information passed vertically or vertically *and* horizontally?") can give participants and practitioners a great deal of insight into the nature of the political and cultural systems of the organization.

demonstrated need to know, and communications are highly structured and closely screened to make certain there never is too much information released. Practitioners and participants operating in such organizations will find gathering data, analyzing it, understanding the system, and building successful action plans difficult.

Closed formal organizations usually result in relatively closed informal organizations operating within them. The intragroup information flow may be fairly open, but intergroup communications or those with outsiders may be quite closed. Exercise 14 will aid participants in understanding the nature of the information flow within their organization.

However, even the fact that information is difficult to obtain can be of value. Participants who are operating in or come into contact with closed organizations will need much more detailed action plans and more time for accomplishing their plans than those who are dealing with open systems.

A sure sign of a closed organization in which politics is a major factor is when only managers and supervisors are allowed to sign communications going out of the work group. This might be done for two reasons: (1) Managers and supervisors must approve any and all information going into or out of the organization or work group to give assurance that data is controlled. (2) Those in non-supervisory positions are kept in relative obscurity with low levels of visibility.

Conversely, of course, open organizations will allow subordinates to sign memos going out of their work groups. It will be much easier to investigate, develop plans for, and make decisions about the desirability of these organizations.

Similar indications can be gleaned from the flow of information and communications in an organization. If all information must go upward to the supervisor or manager before going to other working levels within the organization, the group is probably fairly closed. On the other hand, those organizations in which communications are freely passed between horizontal levels are more likely to be open and will be ones in which gathering data is easier.

As was stated earlier, informal organizations will often follow the model of the formal one of which they are a part. A closed formal organization in which only approved information is passed will very often have cliquish informal groups operating within it that do not share information with others. Open organizations normally give birth to a system of informal groups that exchange information with ease.

There are times, of course, when informal groups operating within the environment of a closed formal organization will react in a totally opposite manner. Sometimes when this occurs an "us against them" attitude develops, and there is an open and free exchange of information horizontally while everything possible is kept from the boss(es).

Employees can experience culture shock if they have been working in an open organization and suddenly find that the assumed Utopia of their career development goal is closed or greatly different than they had imagined.

The communication networks, politics, power distribution, relationships, and support systems of formal and informal organizations are factors that help determine the culture of groups within the organization. For this reason the issue of organizational cultures must be examined carefully.

A Not-So-Foreign Culture

The culture of an organization has its roots in formal and informal systems, written and unwritten rules, and spoken and unspoken approval or disapproval of individual behavior. The culture is influenced by the organization's origins and history, by the type of work in which the organization is engaged, by the kinds of employees the organization attracts, and by the organization's physical surroundings and geographic location. All this distinguishes each organization as a unique entity. And within each organization there are subcultures among departments and divisions, which have unique identities of their own.

Like human cultures, any given organization operates with a set of assumptions that signal acceptable conduct and activities within its culture. It is essential to clarify these assumptions as part of the Strategizing Stage, in order to ensure that plans fit with the realities of existing norms. For example, if administrative leave to attend a year of special study is totally counter to organizational tradition, the employee will want to consider the repercussions of planning such a leave. If it is an acceptable organizational norm to substitute experience for a college degree in order to obtain a certain position in the organization, then employees can examine how this has been done in the past so that they can determine proper strategies.

It may be helpful to build a normative profile of the organization and of departments and divisions. Employees could review this profile with their own managers or with a member of the career development staff in order to determine the fit between their plans and current organizational norms. A number of exercises, such as Exercise 15, can be built around such a profile, which asks for input in several categories, listed in Table 15.

Exploring norms at this point in the career development effort develops an important awareness. While employees work within the culture every day, they rarely take time to consider how it affects their mobility. If they don't take time for such exploration, they may find out too late that cultural realities present insur-

EXERCISE 15

Building an Organizational Profile

An exercise useful in building such a profile might consist of the following steps:

1. A group in a workshop setting answers the questions listed in Table 15 pertaining to organization-wide norms.
2. Subgroups (by units within the organization) answer the same questions about their units.
3. Each individual reviews the lists of answers and asks which norms could create problems for reaching his or her career goals and why.
4. Small groups (three or four people) exchange individual information and assist one another in identifying ways to alleviate the problems they have identified, or in selecting new routes to career goals.
5. Small groups report highlights of their discussions and what they have learned.
6. Groups discuss the general influence of norms on strategizing efforts.

mountable obstacles to attaining their career goals. If this becomes apparent early, they may be able to adjust their goals, select alternative methods for pursuing their goals, or look for other departments or organizations with cultures more amenable to their aspirations.

Employees can use their knowledge of organizational norms to their advantage in working toward goals. They may determine that adhering to certain norms of conduct and appearance can help them. Or, if they discover that certain personal associations and professional memberships are within the norm of the job they want, they may find it beneficial to initiate and maintain those relationships. Understanding the organization as a culture gives employees another informational tool for successful career planning.

The Value of Values

Just as conflicts between cultures can cause shock and disturb employees' goals, differences between organizational values and the personal values of employees can represent a primary cause of employee dissatisfaction and low productivity. Employees who move into areas where values differ greatly from their own do themselves no favors. However, understanding and weighing this factor can improve overall organizational and individual effectiveness.

TABLE 15

ORGANIZATIONAL PROFILE

Performance

- Is there a standard of excellence, or is mediocrity acceptable?
- How is exceptional performance encouraged and rewarded?
- Is quality or quantity more important to decision makers and policy-makers?

Teamwork

- Are cooperation and communication highly valued?
- Do people get ahead by being team leaders and members or by being individual entrepreneurs?

Leadership

- Are supervisors rewarded for skills in working with subordinates or for controlling subordinates?
- Are supervisors concerned more with production or with people or with both?
- How important is it for supervisors to ensure that subordinates adhere to written rules and regulations at all times?

Creativity

- Are new ideas encouraged and rewarded?
- Do people feel it is risky to do things differently than they have been done in the past?
- Are people promoted and hired because they fit a traditional mold or because they contribute something new and different?

Employee Development

- Are adequate resources committed to training and development?
- Are individuals personally encouraged to seek developmental opportunities?
- Are jobs and tasks structured to provide opportunities for learning and new experiences?

Open Communication

- Are people afraid to share opinions with one another?
- Is negative feedback about operations discouraged?
- Does anyone listen?

Cost-Effectiveness

- Are employees encouraged to find means of increasing productivity?
- Does management consider cost-effectiveness in decision making?

The value systems of formal organizations develop from a number of sources. They may originate with organizational founders and may be tempered by a succession of inputs from organizational leaders, boards of directors, stockholders, major customers, and environmental factors. An organization, for instance, that was founded by a person who was creative, innovative, and adventurous might have retained those characteristics through the years. However, a succession of organizational leaders who placed high value on sound business judgment, judicious expansion, and fiscal restraints might cause the company to shift emphasis from innovative exploration and research to research designed to meet established, low-risk customer needs. If the organization served customers who placed high value on product reliability and economy, the organizational values could again be altered so that producing high quality goods at the lowest possible price could become the priority.

Informal organizations are often an amalgam of their individual members. People with similar values will generally group themselves together. Minor differences in values will be resolved through compromise or through ignoring those differences. People with major differences in values seldom form close groupings. The good-time crew hardly ever hangs around with the workaholics, and the three-martini lunch bunch contains few members of the health food crowd.

Certain employees can adjust their values with little or no trouble. Some may be able to understand and cope with the relationships; the networks of power, politics, and communications; and the cultural systems within their target groups without difficulty. However, the last system to be analyzed and understood, the technological system, may pose a gap that cannot be bridged.

Technology Troubles

A short true case study helps to explain the problems often encountered when investigating the technological system:

Bob H. was a brilliant young business administration major who, after receiving his bachelor's degree, took a job in the shipping department of a large manufacturing firm. His goal was clear. Bob intended to use the shipping department position as an entree into the company. As soon as an opening occurred in the organization's accounting department, he intended to make his move into his chosen field.

Bob did most of his strategizing well. He studied the formal and informal organizations of the accounting department thoroughly. He understood the relationships, power structures, political atmosphere, support systems, and the flow of information and communications. He found that the culture and values systems of the accounting department were in complete agreement with his own. He felt that he was ready to make the move as a position opened.

Shortly after completing his research, Bob learned of an opening in the accounting department, and he immediately applied. He was interviewed by several supervisors and managers within the accounting department and felt that everything went well. He settled back to await his transfer.

When the job was filled, however, it went to someone from outside the organization. It was not until then that Bob realized that he had failed to consider an important aspect of his targeted job. The computer system used in the accounting department was totally different from that with which Bob was familiar. Even though Bob seemed perfect in every other respect, the accounting department management had decided that they could not afford the time necessary to train him in their system. It was easier, they reasoned, to train an outsider who was already familiar with the computers about company policy than vice versa.

How could such an error occur? Easily. Very often assumptions about technology are made that make both the employee and the boss believe that there is a natural fit. Had Bob considered all aspects of the strategy necessary to move toward that particular career goal, he might have detected the difference between the technological system and his expertise, and this would have helped him develop a plan to bridge that gap.

It may sound elementary, but organizations are littered with Bob H.'s, people who lacked the technical skill to move up but did not realize it until too late. Practitioners must be alert to employees' technological deficiencies and not only help them to overcome their shortcomings but, very often, develop programs aimed at correcting the deficiencies. Effective career development plans must provide for technical skill evaluations that look at (1) requirements, (2) personal skills available, (3) skills to be developed, and (4) methods for attaining those skills.

Informal groups often form around technical skill areas. Research and development people, for instance, will form social groups based on their common technical interests. Members of

TABLE 16

STRATEGIC MATRIX

System	Formal Organization	Informal Organization
Relationships	Work oriented Imposed by organizational structure Hierarchical	Specially oriented Voluntarily established May be hierarchical, but often tend toward sociometric alliances
Power	Structurally imposed, with emphasis on position, expertise, implied influence, actual coercive influence, applied pressure, and raw force	Tacitly established, with emphasis on charisma, implied influence, actual coercive influence, and applied pressure
Politics	Covert—based on power structures and on games within the organization; tied to the flow of information	Overt—based on charisma and power structures of influence; determines the flow of information
Support	Based on expertise 1. mentor 2. work group	Based on charisma and influence 1. mentor 2. networking
Information	Vertical flow Work related	Vertical and horizontal flow Social and work related
Orientation	May be that of task, role, power, or person, in either the people area or organizational area	Probably has people-area orientation only—but may be that of task, role, power, or person
Communication	Formal written or verbal	Grapevine approach—verbal or written

TABLE 16 (CONTINUED)

STRATEGIC MATRIX

System	Formal Organization	Informal Organization
Culture	Organizationally imposed, resulting from history and traditions	Usually composite of the culture of its members
Values	Established by organization, reflect organizational leadership traditions	Established by membership as a result of needs, cultures, and goals

technical groups may also belong to other informal groups that focus on athletic preferences, literary interests, or political persuasions, but at least a part of their social lives usually centers on technical expertise. A newcomer to a work group who demonstrates a lack of technical expertise will be excluded from the informal structure and will continue to be an outsider. Practitioners should recognize this and help prepare participants so that they can overcome those shortcomings.

Getting to know the organization includes considering and investigating a great many subsystems and functions during the Strategizing Stage. The ones discussed herein are not meant to be all-inclusive or the only ones that will be encountered. The individual must become as familiar as possible with the organizational system in order to help the employee to see the forest as well as the trees.

One way to undertake a more systematic analysis at this stage might be to develop a matrix, such as the one in Table 16, that addresses specifics of the various systems just discussed. This tool can be helpful to employees who are just beginning the strategizing process.

"TO MARKET, TO MARKET"

One final aid that may help employees to further understand the system is to present the organization as a marketplace for individual development and career advancement. In Exercise 16 the employee becomes a professional marketer who is concerned with product research and development, packaging, salesmanship, competition, economy, and all other marketplace features. This concept can help employees understand the reality of the environment in which their products (skills and experiences) must be marketed if their career goals are to be achieved. To adequately study the market, the employee needs to examine three major areas: the product, the market, and the competition.

Part of employees' strategy should be to improve their market position, which may mean enhancing their product or competitive position. The preceding questions can be used in a workshop setting, in a counseling situation, or in a workbook so that employees can ponder their meaning whenever they have the opportunity.

In this first phase of strategizing it is critical to understand the system. Unless they understand the system, with all its subtleties, employees will be hard pressed to come up with an effective plan to use that knowledge toward reaching a career goal.

Synthesizing Information

With a greater understanding of the system in which strategizing takes place, the employee is now ready to synthesize ideas and information and to frame a coherent plan of action. This phase includes considering opportunities and obstacles and drafting a developmental plan for pursuing each of the career goals determined during the Targeting Stage.

During the synthesizing phase, employees need tools and techniques that can help them analyze what they know and structure it into a planning format; and they need organizational information that might help them generate realistic analyses and plans. This helps employees to acquire the skill and the information necessary to complete the planning process.

ANALYSIS WITHOUT PARALYSIS

Analyzing all the data that employees have acquired about themselves and their organizations is the step that facilitates establishing relationships between the diverse pieces of information gathered. During this step, employees need to think back to past experiences and think forward to potential obstacles and opportunities.

A variety of techniques can be used to organize and coordinate this effort. They are all aimed at helping employees to structure

EXERCISE 16
Understanding the System

The Product

- What are key tasks you have successfully performed in past positions?
- What skills do you offer?
- What reputation do you have among others in the marketplace?
- What are the limits to what you'll be able to produce?
- Will others provide the support necessary for you to fully utilize your strengths?
- Will personal values and needs limit your ability to fully utilize your strengths?
- How is the product packaged? How do you present yourself and your skills to others?
- What can you do to improve the products you have to offer?

The Market

- Is there a market for your skills?
- Is the demand for your skills great or limited within that market?
- Is there a way to strengthen or expand the market?
- Are your strengths transferable to a variety of situations within the market?
- Who are the most likely customers for your product?
- How effective are you at selling your product to potential customers?
- How can you improve your marketing position?

The Competition

- Who is your competition?
- What does the competition offer?
- How are your skills and experiences distinct from those of the competition?
- What marketing strategies are the competition using?
- What advantages do you have? Does the competition have?

their thinking and to arrive at concrete results. They usually involve at least three steps:

1. Determining forces
2. Understanding obstacles
3. Assessing knowledge areas

Most of these techniques could be solo activities. However, sharing the strategizing process with others is likely to enhance it.

Workshops can be designed that enable employees to use the various techniques on their own and then share the results in small groups whose members exchange ideas and help one another test their viability.

Determining Forces

For every goal that employees set during targeting, there are circumstances, personal beliefs, and other factors that push them toward or away from that goal. Sometimes these factors are obvious, such as lack of training needed to perform a sought-after job. At other times the forces holding individuals back or propelling them forward are more subtle, such as lack of faith in personal ability, or strong personal ambition for greater challenges.

The contributing and restraining forces combine to hold a situation in a state of equilibrium, where it will remain until those forces somehow change. It is important that program participants have a thorough understanding of what they have working for them and what is going against them.

An excellent tool for helping participants to recognize their strengths, weaknesses, aids, and obstacles is a simple variation on the open-system map or relational planning model depicted in Figure 5.

This model may be used in either individual counseling or in group workshops. Each participant draws and labels as many factors as possible that might affect accomplishing a goal. If participants have conducted an organizational analysis similar to the one outlined in the first part of this chapter, a great many resources and obstacles will already have been identified.

Once the personal and environmental resources and obstacles have been identified, their actual effect on the career development goal(s) should be determined. Social scientist Kurt Lewin's Force Field Analysis model is an excellent tool for aiding participants in this process.

Personal and environmental resources, those factors which participants see as aiding them in accomplishing their goals, become driving forces in the Force Field. The obstacles, of course, are the restraining forces, those factors that are hindering achievement of goals.

Goal statements can be considered by looking at the driving and restraining forces in a format such as Exercise 17.

EXERCISE 17

Force Field Analysis

The statements from the open-system map are written on as many arrows as necessary to show the driving and restraining forces:

RESTRAINING FORCES
(inhibit, block movement)

Examples of restraining forces are:
"I don't have the required three years of experience."
"My spouse wouldn't like the long hours it requires."
"I'm not really confident I could succeed."

CONTRIBUTING FORCES
(facilitate, motivate, inspire movement)

Examples of contributing forces are:
"My boss has encouraged me to apply for the position."
"I need the additional money I would make in the new job."
"I feel the challenge would be stimulating to me."

FIGURE 5

Planning Map

SOME EXAMPLES OF OBSTACLES ARE:

Personal:
"I'm overworked."
"I prefer to work alone."

Environmental:
"I had to take a job because I didn't have money for college."
"I lost my last good job when the company went bankrupt."

Personal Obstacles	Environmental Obstacles
ME	
Personal Resources	Outside Resources

SOME EXAMPLES OF RESOURCES ARE:

Personal:
"I am good at listening to others' problems."
"I write well."

Outside:
"My spouse encourages me in my career."
"My subordinates really try to make me look good."

There are several ways of working on a Force Field once the forces have been defined and analyzed. One is to look at the tension between the forces to determine if one kind of force seems to override another. If forces are equal, no movement will occur, and participants should strive to have the contributing forces outweigh the restraining forces. Options are:

- Add to the list of contributing forces
- Increase the magnitude of existing contributing forces
- Remove restraining forces
- Decrease the magnitude of existing restraining forces
- Move restraining forces to the contributing side of the field

It is also important that employees examine their assumptions about the forces. The feelings of others or barriers created by the organization may be only assumed rather than real restraining forces.

Understanding Obstacles

The next step is to consider the obstacles to achieving goals and to determine whether or not these obstacles are real. Employees often make obstacles seem larger than they are or fail to recognize how obstacles can be related to resources and even neutralized by them.

To effectively deal with obstacles or restraining forces it is necessary to determine their sources. When initially listed, the obstacles were shown as originating from the individual or the environment. These sources may be more specifically identified by listing them as being:

- Self-imposed
- System imposed
- Boss imposed
- "Other" imposed

Now participants can make a similar determination about resources. Tie-ins will immediately emerge, and participants will get ideas for generating additional resources to remove obstacles. For each of their restraining forces, participants can be encouraged to ask such questions as:

- Is this obstacle something that others would see, or is it simply my own invention?
- Am I using this resource to my greatest benefit?

EXERCISE 18

Assessing Knowledge Areas

Job-related issues

- What is the relationship of this target job to other jobs in the organization?
- What technical and administrative skills are required?

Organization-related issues

- What specific organizational politics affect this job?
- What are this division's long-term goals?

Manager-related issues

- What are the actual span and the limits of my manager's job?
- How much concern does my manager really have for my development as an employee?

Assessing Knowledge Areas

A good check-back procedure before employees develop a plan of action is for them to ask themselves, "Do I really know all I need to know in order to strategize effectively?" In this way they can take one final look at the factors affecting career plans and ascertain whether or not they have acquired the essential information related to each. Managers who are involved in the process will want to test the employees' readiness to begin executing their career plans.

Areas that the employee should consider checking could relate to the job, the family, peers, subordinates, supervisors, or even the organizational structure. Individuals might test their knowledge in each of these areas by using a series of questions and rating their answers on a scale of one (I don't know anything of what I need to know) to five (I know all I need to know). Examples of questions that might be used are listed in Exercise 18.

Employees undertaking this exercise should be encouraged to develop as many check-back issues as possible.

FRAMING THE PLAN

When all available information about self and system—including developmental needs, organizational resources, and possible barriers—has been generated, employees are ready to frame a

---

CASE 24

The Employee Development Plan

A financial services company is experimenting with a development plan for all program participants. The plan directs
employees to state a development goal (discovered during
the workshop portion of the program) and to identify the (1) skills
the employee wants to develop, (2) activities that will help develop
those skills, and (3) sources of assistance in improving those skills.
Suggestions are made as to how employees can track their own
progress and measure their success in skill mastery. Mentors and
managers comment on the choice of development ideas and show
their concurrence by signing off on their employees' development
plans.

---

developmental plan for pursuing career goals. The developmental
plan (1) defines the specific actions that will be taken, (2) relates
them to needs and to specific skills and experiences, (3) pinpoints
the necessary resources, and (4) sets time frames for completion
actions.

The value of the developmental plan is that it sets forth a
detailed strategy that can easily be monitored for progress at each
step.

Needs and Desires

Determining needs and desires is directly linked to skill, knowledge, resource deficiencies, work values, and context preferences
that the employee identified at prior stages of the career development effort. The employee should now be able to state these needs
on a detailed developmental plan that makes each more specific.

The listing should include not only skills and knowledge to be
acquired, but also certain experiences and relationships with others, not necessarily directly related to work, that can facilitate
movement toward career goals. Examples of statements about
knowledge or skill areas are:

- To feel more at ease and present a positive image when
  addressing large groups
- To have experience in or exposure to at least two organization-wide task forces

- To understand how to effectively communicate through management reports to higher levels and how to verbally obtain information from all levels
- To become conversant with the goals of the sales management group so that I can effectively explain them to other groups within the organization
- To be confident about proposing and evaluating budgetary requirements in my own division
- To increase my skills in and knowledge of computer functions, policies, procedures, scheduling, and workload

The more detailed the description of need, the easier it will be to determine specific actions and resources to meet that need.

Actions

Actions that are specified in the plan are the tasks to be undertaken in pursuit of career goals, and they assist the employee in answering the question "What can I do to get where I want to go?"

It is important to emphasize two key elements that often cause problems in stating actions. First, action statements must often be divided into specific steps rather than one general task. For example, the action that is stated, "Complete the remaining requirements for my advanced university degree," may be better set forth as, "Apply for tuition reimbursement; apply for admission to courses X, Y, and Z; and complete my thesis."

Second, actions should be stated with a great deal of specificity, so that there is no doubt as to whether and when they have been completed. The action "Form mentor relationships with persons who have experience in the same career progression" can be more specifically stated as "Invite John Drakes to lunch to discuss his similar experience, and initiate an ongoing mentor relationship with him."

There are a number of opportunities for employees to discuss their goals with managers. The performance appraisal session or designated career discussion session are both good vehicles. Action plans can also be discussed in specially designated support groups, which meet to help group members brainstorm about actions they might take to reach specific goals. They can be shared in workshops through exercises carefully designed to help employees help themselves. Actions that should be considered are those to which the organization can readily respond, and that seem to have the greatest return on investment for both the individual and the organization.

Resources

Each plan should include a definition of resources that are needed to make the actions a reality. Major resources available include people, money, and time. When considering resources, employees should ask, "Are there others who can help?" "What financial assistance is available?" and "What time can be committed?"

There are, in fact, a myriad of resources available. Personal resources include the employee's family, friends, colleagues, boss, peers, professional associations, and community networks. Monetary resources can be found in the organization's tuition reimbursement program, the organization's bonus plan for special development, or the employee's own savings account! The precious resource of time might be discovered in an employee's accrued leave (to attend a training session) or in simply asking for and receiving four extra hours a week to take on a special project. Resources come from the individual as well as from the organization.

Resources provided by others often need special attention because many individuals are reluctant to call upon other people for assistance. However, giving such assistance is rarely considered a burden, and may require only that someone make a phone call, give occasional encouragement, or offer advice. Using outside resources can give employees a sense of support: "Others are pulling for me; I don't want to disappoint them." Resource listings of people in specific departments who are willing to help will put employees ahead of the game.

Deadlines

Finally, a complete plan includes specified times for completing each step. While deadlines must be realistic, they must also be demanding enough to stimulate continual movement toward goals. Deadlines may be set by working backward from a final deadline for goal attainment or by setting incremental time frames forward from the earliest step to be completed. Although it is likely that deadlines may need to be revised as various actions are taken, this practice should be discouraged except when it absolutely cannot be avoided.

Often employees do not know enough about their own limits and organizational red tape to be able to plan effectively at this point. Practitioners can play an important role by offering sound time management advice and helping the participants establish realistic deadlines. Practitioners who are uncertain about how to help the participants establish deadlines would be well advised to seek help from others within the organization who are experienced in this area. Nothing will destroy a plan or discourage a participant faster than unrealistic deadlines. It is imperative that time schedules be workable and well thought out and, at the same time, involve effort and challenge for employees.

STRUCTURAL SUPPORTS FROM WITHIN

Two ongoing human resource development activities that are particularly valuable in the Strategizing Stage are establishing career paths and specialized counseling. These provide the employee with guidance and assist the organization in planning for the future and using employees efficiently.

Employees should not strategize in a vacuum. Without organizational support mechanisms, their plans become pipe dreams that are unrelated to what the organization is able or willing to do. Employees need to know the organization's plans and objectives concerning the development of its workforces. They also need material support and encouragement from the organization for their strategizing efforts.

Career Paths

Information about career paths within the organization is useful for realistic action planning by an employee. A career path is a written projection of a logical job progression sequence that may realistically occur for an employee. The progression includes alternatives related to the experience being acquired in the job and may include lateral or downward movement or movement to jobs outside the current department or unit. It may state the specific skills and knowledge to be developed as a requirement for each job.

Yet employees and leaders must realize that a career path is at best an optimistic guess about how a career might develop, given assumptions about the company, the economy, the implementation of new technology, the needs of management, and so on. Part of the confusion for some employees and leaders stems from the fact that, decades ago, career paths referred to vertical growth progression projections that were more than just optimistic guesses.

This older notion of career path, which is better termed *career ladder*, is dead or dying in most organizations today. As the name implies, individuals ascended the "ladder" by means of promotion, through the tiers of increasing responsibility in their functional area, until they reached a summit dictated by the limits of their competence or desire.

Career ladders are less relevant today for a variety of reasons. The list includes the globalization of business, which results in a greatly expanded labor pool and new demands on managers; outsourcing, which transfers critical noncore responsibilities outside the organization; organizational flattening, which limits the number of management positions; and reengineering and TQM, which shift management responsibilities to self-managed teams. Yet it is exactly because of all these uncertainties that employees need some sense of how their careers might develop, and what actions they need to take. Taken with all the above in mind, career paths or career pattern charts may play a role in providing this direction.

Career paths can enable employees to see the skills needed for certain jobs and the steps that are possible within those jobs. Career paths allow employees to compare their own plans with the organization's maps for employee progression. This can result in developmental efforts that are a mutually beneficial joint endeavor. Establishing a career path system can require a substantial commitment to analyzing jobs, categorizing them into related job families, and determining logical progression alternatives.

Practitioners may themselves want to directly impart information about career paths, at meetings or in one-on-one discussions. Some practitioners feel that it is not good to put career path information in writing because it formalizes the system in a way that gives the practitioners and managers less flexibility, and holds implied promises for employees.

Many organizations, however, have produced handbooks that actually describe the skills needed for jobs and the steps possible within those jobs. Handbooks are useful in that the employees might turn to them on their own to see what kinds of jobs might be a better fit for them, and they might then be able to seek out experience and education toward their goal. Handbooks also help facilitate the dialogue between employer and employee about career opportunities, and they are especially useful in forming the developmental plan. Still another way to share career path information is to deliver it within a workshop itself. Career path information can be disseminated, for example, by delivering a short lecture on the numbers of people at nonexempt, exempt, and first-line manage-

---

CASE 25

The Career Options Handbook

A large insurance company recognizes that its employees could often work in isolation, unaware of the many other job possibilities that exist—possibilities that might better tap their own interest and skills. To improve the matching of people's talents to the jobs available, it provides a Career Options Handbook as a beginning step toward providing vital information. The Handbook is given to supervisors as a tool to help their employees choose individual development and training activities that will guide them along the road to further self-development.

The Career Options Handbook is designed to help employees gain a sense of where they want to go, through an understanding of what major directions are open to them. With the supervisor's help, a clear developmental plan for activities for the coming year can be stated.

---

ment levels in the organization and by providing statistics about the numbers of people who move from one level to another.

Practitioners must make the point that career paths are flexible and do change. Career paths should be seen as another tool to be used in the Strategizing Stage.

Counseling for Career Change

Although offered with less frequency (unless an organization is in the midst of downsizing), counseling services are made available to help employees understand their own strengths and weaknesses, assess organizational opportunities, set realistic goals, and develop plans for career progress. Individual counseling recognizes the unique situations and needs of each employee and complements individual planning activities and group workshops. One particular type of counseling that is often utilized in organizations, often at the Strategizing Stage, is outplacement counseling. This service, which has experienced increased use in organizations throughout the country, is generally aimed at individually assisting those who are being involuntarily separated from the organization. In some organizations it is also offered to those who voluntarily resign. Since strategizing about career options can sometimes lead to a decision on both sides that moving out of the organization is the most logical move, outplacement counseling can be a valuable support program, and practitioners may wish to develop the capacity to offer this service within the organization.

Typical objectives of outplacement counseling include:

- To reduce negative psychological impact on terminated employees
- To provide guidance in identifying new job opportunities
- To improve the employee's skills in job search and application
- To help employees place themselves elsewhere as quickly as possible
- To ultimately bring the best match between people and available jobs

Outplacement counseling may be provided by the career development practitioner, by designated members of the HR staff, or by skilled outside consultants. While the internal HR staff are exceedingly helpful, outside consultants add a greater sense of anonymity and objectivity. Outside consultants are also necessary if internal expertise is not available.

Most comprehensive outplacement services include:

- Information about organization policies (such as compensation and accrued leave)
- Job search strategy training
- Employment interview training
- Resume preparation assistance
- Office support service (for typing resumes and taking phone calls)
- Information about job leads
- Personal counseling
- Attitude awareness training
- Resource appraisal
- Salary negotiation practice

Organizations benefit in a number of ways from viewing outplacement as a responsibility and an ongoing HR activity. One obvious payoff is public relations a company might receive from becoming known as forward thinking and sensitive to employee needs. In this way an organization may be seen as an attractive potential employer. And heightened sensitivity affects not only the morale of terminated employees but also the attitudes of current employees toward their place of work.

Often, as a result of some initial thinking during the Targeting Stage and some additional planning at the Strategizing Stage, employees may recognize their own need to leave the organization and seek a job elsewhere; but they are reluctant to take such a step into the unknown until their current situation becomes unbearable. A good outplacement counseling program can encourage these employees to take action to find another job that better fits their career needs, before their own work and personal life suffer as a result.

ACTIVE SUPPORT—PRACTITIONER AND MANAGER

During the Strategizing Stage the practitioner must be prepared to act as a designer/facilitator by guiding employees in conceptualizing ideas, and as a generator of organizational interest by seeking continued support for career development programs. As designer/facilitator, the practitioner seeks to supply ideas and techniques that enable employees to assess their own situations, to size up the organizational environment, to identify potential obstacles, to determine appropriate alternatives, and to set forth a realistic developmental plan. This role includes responsibility for providing informational materials and perhaps organizing group workshops and counseling. While practitioners may not be directly involved in all of the design or conduct of such activities, they have primary responsibility for stimulating staff members to pay attention to the Strategizing Stage and to support its actualization.

In addition, the practitioner must develop a deliberate strategy for informing managers and motivating them to actively support the strategizing process. Managers should play an active role in providing the encouragement, information, and organizational support mechanisms that facilitate strategizing. They can help employees understand organizational expectations, opportunities, and limitations. If they are willing to spend extra time with individual employees, they can provide reality-testing assistance by reviewing plans with subordinates and suggesting alternatives or changes. They can also develop opportunities for on-the-job experiences that facilitate acquiring the experience and knowledge called for in specific developmental plans.

There is substantial payoff at the Strategizing Stage as employees continue to dynamically use their organizing and synthesizing skills. These skills can be drawn upon to assess situations in which individuals operate and to help them continually plan and replan in light of a changing environment. By internalizing the strategizing processes, individuals acquire the flexibility to maximize their efforts and successes under conditions of organizational or environmental change.

Strategizing can provide the organization with valuable information about its employees and their developmental needs. The more actively the organization supports this process, the more it enhances its utilization of existing workforce capabilities and its ability to plan future workforce needs.

Strategizing clearly lays out a detailed plan of what individuals must do in order to move toward their career goals or to enrich their present position in the organization. At the Implementing Stage, individuals follow their developmental plan to acquire the tools, skills, and knowledge that in the Strategizing Stage they discovered were necessary.

| 6 |

Pursuing Plans

THE IMPLEMENTING STAGE

*"Life consists not in holding good cards
but in playing those you do hold well."*
–JOSH BILLINGS

T he career development pro-
gram participants are now about to start moving toward their
career goals. They know what they want, and they have developed
strategies for achieving their goals. They can now begin acquiring
the skills, training, experience, and personal support systems necessary for moving ahead. During this stage, each player is asked to
participate in a specific way. Organizational involvement is essential and complex. Shared responsibility is essential.

Employees participate in activities aimed at acquiring new
skills; brushing up on old skills; acquiring new contacts for personal support, information, or instruction; and supplementing
professional or technical skills with growing capacities for leadership, communication, or group interaction.

At the same time, the organization is concerned with providing
opportunities for off-site education and training, developing
in-house training and development opportunities, structuring
on-the-job experiences to promote learning and development,
structuring and encouraging informal learning and support among
employees at various levels of the organization, and providing
access to information about available resources.

Leaders and managers will find that they must actively disseminate program information, encourage and support employees in
accomplishing their plans, provide the time needed by employees
to pursue their plans, acquire training and development, establish

FIGURE 6

Shared Responsibilities at the Implementing Stage

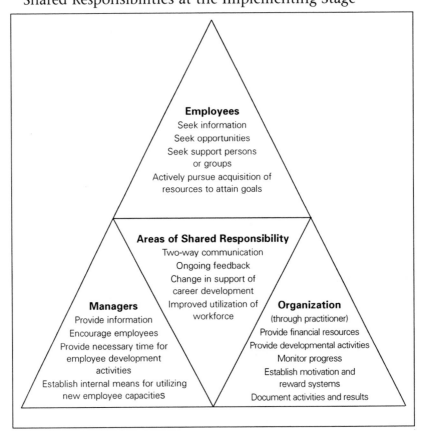

means by which the new skills can be practiced, and provide means of recognizing employees for their motivation and effort. Practitioners facilitate the fulfillment of organizational responsibilities; they make certain that the functions and programs developed are cost-effective, are based upon actual needs, and are focused on the goals to be accomplished. When displayed as a coordinated effort, these responsibilities and functions create the picture shown in Figure 6.

The Implementing Stage culminates in specific present and future benefits for the organization and the individual. These benefits include:

- Personal understanding and growth
- Skill development in the present job
- Increase in challenge and job interest
- Better understanding of the organization, other employees, and the informal structures within the system

These results are achieved through completing the two phases of implementing: (1) acquiring the resources necessary to attain a goal, and (2) demonstrating the new skills within the organization.

Resource Acquisition

Employees need a variety of skill building efforts and development opportunities in order to pursue career goals. Employees, leaders, as well as practitioners need to be well informed about five categories of resources: (1) *Training and education:* Programs conducted on-site or off-site, by internal or external training and development people, addressing technical skills, personal growth and development, and management training. (2) *Experience-based learning:* Experiences and efforts aimed at expanding skills through on-the-job learning, new job experiences, job rotation, and project or learning assignments in a variety of areas. (3) *Support-guided development:* Efforts that call upon the skills of others to provide growth and development, and include such resources as mentor arrangements, professional organizations, instructional groups and teams, and informal support groups. (4) *Computer-assisted development:* Tools to assist employees and managers to better understand their own strengths and weaknesses and to plan for career development; this includes computerized assessment tools, automated feedback models, "expert" computer assistance on which careers to consider, and online discussion forums with professional career counselors. (5) *Business simulations:* Tools that allow employees and managers to role-play situations involving business decisions, interpersonal problems at work, intercultural business scenarios, and situations requiring teamwork.

Not only is it important to be aware of the great variety of opportunities available for development outside of conventional institutional settings, it is also important for practitioners and leaders to be aware of the degree of openness to learning that exists within the participant population.

Openness to learning requires a degree of humility and self-acceptance. Perfectionists struggle with these issues because there is no final outcome. Learning takes place throughout one's entire life. Some questions to consider include:

- How hard is it to feel comfortable asking for help?
- How hard is it to depend on someone else who has more knowledge or experience?
- How hard is it to ask questions?
- How hard is it to experience the hurt pride and awkwardness that come with learning a new skill?
- How hard is it to accept the frustrations of learning?

Peter Vaill (1996) makes a point of warning practitioners that one of the best ways of approaching learning and the acquisition of new skills is by taking on the role of beginner, and feeling great comfort in that role. He warns that in our zeal for competence, we lose our ability to be truly open to learning.

TRAINING AND EDUCATION

Training and development efforts can be focused in at least four general areas: (1) *Technical training*: Technical skills to be acquired, improved, or expanded may range from operating new or different equipment, to using new methods of data processing or computer skills, to acquiring specialized knowledge through a university degree in a given area. The focus lies on broadening one's technical proficiency so that one's current job, or any future jobs, may be performed more effectively. (2) *Leadership/management training and development:* The skills, behavior, and attitudes that enhance individual capabilities in goal setting, problem solving, time management, employee motivation, report writing, and process flow analysis all fall into this category. These programs may be aimed at any or all organizational levels, though program content will vary at each level. (3) *Interpersonal development:* Programs in this area are designed to enhance and expand individual capabilities in the area of interpersonal relations, including communications, group leadership, teamwork, conflict management, and interpersonal problem solving. Development in this category may be necessary at all levels of the organization, with focus and design varying at each level. (4) *Organizational behavior development:* Skills in understanding the norms, values, and politics of the organization are generally acquired informally through others who can help provide awareness of the environment and knowledge of organiza-

■ ACTION PROVOKING QUESTIONS

EVALUATING TRAINING NEEDS

- What training programs have employees identified as needed?
- Are these programs currently available within the organization?
- If the answer to the question above is no: Is there sufficient need within the organization to merit the establishment of an internal program?
- If the answer to the question above is no: Are the programs available from external sources?
- Are training and education facilities within the organization sufficient to allow additional programs?
- Is the training and development budget sufficient to allow needed program expansion?
- How can additional resources be made available?
- How is our outside program tuition/educational reimbursement being administered? Are changes necessary? How can these changes be effected?

---

tional power and influence. Programs often contribute to the employee's knowledge of the organization, the industry, and the basic procedures pertinent to the job.

Employees must be aware of each of the categories so they can pursue opportunities beyond the traditionally perceived areas of training and development. Some of the opportunities will be available only outside of the organization, while others are best provided from within it.

The Inside Story

If the information acquired through the earlier career development stages is accurate and complete, it will have provided an excellent database for examining in-house training currently offered by the organization. If, for example, financial management training has always been offered but reviewing the career development plans set by employees during the Targeting Stage indicates that it is not needed, then this may be the time to question the efficacy of such a program. On the other hand, if many employees felt they needed to acquire systems planning skills, the organization may be able during the Implementing Stage to develop in-house training in this area. Clearly, the organization can use the information it has already acquired as a rich resource for guiding in-house training decisions before the organization seeks off-site programs to fill the gaps. Some basic questions to consider are presented in the Action Provoking Questions above.

The advantage of in-house training is that it can be specifically tailored to the organization. During training sessions, examples and experiences can be used that have immediate relevance to organizational tasks and structure. This often replaces theoretical subject matter with material that fits the context of the organization. An internal program, for example, is able to draw cases from the participating group that illustrate the same principles. These cases, then, become meaningful for participants. In addition, employees pursue their learning with others whom they are likely to work with or meet in the future. This provides an internal support system that can enhance their instructional experience and that may continue once the instruction ends.

Increased knowledge about team management and group dynamics are examples of development objectives that can be most effectively achieved through in-house training. They can be practiced with actual working groups, and problem solving and long-range planning can be related to existing issues. Participants who are also co-workers can begin to practice their newly acquired knowledge immediately, and they can provide each other with support for continuing to use it over time. Interpersonal skills such as open communication, candid feedback, and participatory problem solving often seem risky in practice and are more likely to be applied when several colleagues have been trained and have experienced them together.

In addition, in-house training can include the development and monitoring of follow-up activities to encourage transferring newly acquired knowledge to the job setting. This type of follow-up is especially important if the training involved business simulations, such as those currently popular on computer, which can seem less relevant to the workplace than more traditional modes of instruction.

The View from Outside

It is impossible to expect that any organization has enough resources to provide skill development programs sufficient to meet all of its employees' needs. It is essential that practitioners exercise discretion in incorporating outside programs into the training and education package.

Once again, information gathered from the earlier stages of this model can provide guidelines for determining what resources should be obtained from the outside. Practitioners should, therefore, review the data gathered during earlier stages to determine (1) needs to be addressed at each employee level within the already

CASE 26

A Self-Development Bank Account

The Educational Opportunities Plan at a large pharmaceutical company allows each employee an annual self-development allotment in a personal "bank account." The size of the allotment is tied to a formula based on the employee's performance rating, salary, self-development plan, and the company's earnings. It is scheduled such that lower-income employees are likely to receive higher allotments. Courses taken need not be directly job-related and can also include pursuing cultural interests; however, the vast majority of those selected by employees have been related to the immediate job or company business.

existing organization, (2) resources that already exist internally, (3) budget that is available, and (4) support from key decision makers. If this information makes apparent that the best resources in a particular area lie outside the organization, then that is where the practitioner should look. Whether training and education is off-site or in-house, it is essential that the organization consider ways to encourage, recognize, and reward its use. One way to do this is through providing rewards to managers who take an active interest in career development and begin to allow employees to undertake new projects that will apply their learning. A more formal approach to this problem is to include in official performance appraisals factors relating to the learning acquired, giving employees an opportunity to report on their recent training and development and how it is being applied to their jobs.

Educational Reimbursement

The methods and structures for administering financial assistance programs vary greatly from organization to organization in terms of who receives the assistance, who decides to whom it will be given, and how much assistance is made available. In fact, the trend has been toward less financial support and making the employee more accountable. Some organizations are continuing to reimburse employees for courses but are requiring that all courses be taken on employee time. Among those who continue to provide assistance, any number of options are available. Table 17 shows an example of an educational reimbursement decision guide.

TABLE 17

EDUCATIONAL REIMBURSEMENT DECISION GUIDE

Program Component	Program Options
Eligibility	■ All employees eligible (certain grace period) ■ Limited to certain levels of employees ■ Limited to employees in certain job categories ■ Cutoff number, with first come, first served
Dollar Amount	■ No set limits ■ Ceiling on individual amounts—same for each employee ■ Ceiling on individual amounts—adjusted for length of service and salary ■ Ceiling based on type of program—BA vs. MBA, under- vs. post-graduate
Decision About Who and How Much	■ Central unit (HR office) decides ■ Department heads decide ■ Immediate supervisors nominate or decide ■ Participants self-nominate
Program Delivery Mechanisms	■ All off-site learning programs eligible ■ Only accredited educational institutions eligible ■ Central unit develops roster of approved delivery institutions
Restrictions	■ Must complete courses satisfactorily for reimbursement ■ Must show job relatedness ■ Must show career relatedness ■ Must commit future amount of time for working for organization ■ No restrictions
Budget Structure	■ Central (HR office) budget for financial aid ■ Decentralized–from budget of each department ■ Each employee given personal annual budget for education and training

Particular care must be taken to ensure that decisions made about educational assistance are fair. Decisions should be made in the open, with employees clearly understanding what is available, how they may take advantage of it, and how it benefits the organization. If organizations decide what financial aid is available on a case-by-case basis, all employees do not have equal access to the system. And if departments or divisions are left to pull educational assistance resources from tight budgets, without having budgeted specifically for that purpose, it is likely that some will allow for no employee development while others allow for a great deal.

EXPERIENCE-BASED LEARNING

There are other ways to develop the necessary technical, personal, and management skills besides taking courses. A widely used approach is learning by doing, or experience-based learning, which provides employees the opportunity to observe, learn, and practice new techniques and skills in their current positions.

The workplace has often been called the ultimate classroom, and as such, on-the-job training has been the traditional mode for increasing technical skills, enhancing leadership and interpersonal abilities, and improving employees' capabilities for understanding the continual changes and challenges in organizational behavior.

Commonly used as a method for breaking in new workers, on-the-job training introduces employees to new tasks under the guidance of an individual who can instruct and coach. This provides employees with a chance to "learn the ropes" and gives supervisors an opportunity to observe and correct the performance of new employees.

This approach has broad applications for the more seasoned worker who suddenly finds it necessary to learn new skills related to changes in equipment, procedures, or business challenges. It can also be used as a means of cross-training to provide back-up support and to ensure that important functions will be covered in the event of temporary absences, or as a specific strategy used by organizations to increase their bench strength and prepare leaders for the future.

On-the-job training has now evolved into a more sophisticated development strategy. This strategy suggests that deliberate or intentional assignments can be devised by the employee, leader, or practitioner that provide an immediate opportunity to learn the needed competency. Exercise 19 offers such a strategy.

EXERCISE 19

Crafting Assignments

Employees and managers will have an easier time designing development assignments if they can identify a particular skill that needs
development and then consider assignments as falling into one of
three categories: (1) Conscious Observation, (2) Selected Participation,
and (3) Key Responsibility.

Skill to be learned? _____

Conscious Observation: Who does this well? Can I find an opportunity to watch this person? What will I look for? What questions
do I have? Afterward, what most surprised me? What can I see myself
doing without much difficulty? With some practice? With a lot of
practice?

Selected Participation: Can I identify a project, activity, or task
where this skill is required? Can I negotiate to take on part of the
task so that I can practice this skill and receive some coaching? What
will I need to do to prepare? Who can help? Who can I talk with
about my experience afterward?

Key Responsibility: Can I identify a project, activity, or task where
the skill is key? Can I negotiate to do this assignment from beginning to end? Who can I enlist as my development coach? What
will I want this person to watch for?

Research done at the Center for Creative Leadership in
Greensboro, North Carolina, has shown further that the best development sources are experiences that indeed do come from assignments. The center's classic research (Lombardo and Eichinger,
1989) describes these five specific types of assignments. Each
teaches distinctly different skills.

- *Small projects and start-ups:* Emphasizes persuasion, learning new content quickly, working under time pressure, and
  dealing with groups of new people. Small Projects and Start-
  Ups are projects that involve a new task, a start-to-finish
  mandate, and end-result accountability. An individual may
  or may not be in charge, but in either case the experiences
  can be powerful.

- *Small-scope jumps and "fix-it" jobs:* Emphasizes team building, individual responsibility, dealing with the boss, development of subordinates, and time pressure. Each challenge
  differs in variety of issues and the progression of one's responsibilities. In this category, an individual must be in
  charge for significant challenges to occur.

- *Small strategic assignments:* Emphasizes intellectual pressure and influencing skills. Studies show that small strategic assignments often shock people out of a parochial point of view by requiring them to go from an operational to a strategic perspective, from the concrete to the abstract, or from a present to a future orientation.

- *Coursework and coaching assignments:* Loaded with intellectual pressure and the challenge of locating something important that is missing, coursework and coaching assignments force individuals to recall how difficult it is to teach or coach. If they are experts in some area, the difficulty often lies in explaining what has become intuitive for them. If they have no expertise, they are likely to face strong intellectual pressure. From either circumstance, a likely benefit is a heightened awareness of what they value and how they think and respond to intellectual pressure.

- *Activities away from work:* Development certainly doesn't occur only on the job. Activities away from work, such as doing volunteer work, and community service, participating in professional organizations, and coaching children's sports are additional assignments that offer important lessons. Any of these, tending to emphasize individual leadership and working with new people, will have elements of learning how to influence and persuade.

These assignment categories are extremely useful to the employee, leader, and practitioner in designing specific skill-building tasks within each of these categories.

Practitioners must also consider two primary questions about learning through experience that must be answered to ensure effectiveness: (1) How will the learning experience be structured to provide the necessary steps toward full learning?, and (2) How will the experience be evaluated so that the learner knows when he or she has achieved competence in that area?

The new model for on-the-job learning is more participant centered than instructor led. Employees are more accountable for designing their own development activities and enlisting a "coach" or "debriefer" to provide assistance in the form of instructional feedback, questions, and suggestions to motivate the employee to develop further or to ascertain the learning that took place. Instead of the instructor being selected for the employee, the employee is in control and looks for people to learn from at different levels.

CASE 27

Debriefing with Colleagues for Enhanced On-the-Job Learning

A manufacturing company decided that the best way to help their managers and employees acquire new skills and then demonstrate them was to publish their competency lists with specific development assignments attached. Although many organizations distribute similar lists, this organization went one step further. It published hints for how each assignment could be debriefed by talking with another individual so that the learnings could be discussed and defined. One example is presented below.

Understanding the Allocation of Resources

Involve yourself in the development of a new product or project that is being considered. Take part in all the meetings where the agenda is the financial considerations related to this project. Before the group or committee makes any final decision, make your own financial evaluation of the project in terms of budget, cost, and revenue projections. Compare your predictions with the group's analysis of the financial issues.

Debrief by talking with a key member of the committee to see if your calculations were similar to theirs. Where were your strengths in analyzing the financial upsides of the project? Where were your weaknesses? What did you learn about your own knowledge of allocating resources? What actions should you be taking to improve your understanding of this important business area?

A Moving Experience

Job rotation, the movement of employees to different tasks at specified intervals, enables them to develop and practice new skills and to determine areas in which they can best use their talents. In addition, this practice allows the organization to add depth and flexibility to its employee base by developing people who are prepared to function in a variety of capacities and by discovering where individual talents fit best in the organization. Job rotation provides a greater variety of work experiences that can broaden the knowledge and understanding that employees require to develop further in their careers.

TABLE 18

JOB ROTATION ALTERNATIVES

Type of Rotation	Objectives
New Employee Exposing new employees to a number of jobs before placing them in a permanent position	■ Provide understanding of operations in different areas ■ Test Skills ■ Determine appropriate placement
Personal Growth Moving employees temporarily to jobs they have not undertaken in the past	■ Learn variety of skills ■ Learn new skills ■ Opportunity for advancement ■ Opportunity for lateral moves
Executive Development Moving managers or managerial candidates to various units of the organization	■ Assess managerial potential ■ Understand total organization ■ Determine next move ■ Reward for level attained
Revolving Door Shifting employees back and forth between jobs at predetermined intervals	■ Broaden skill base ■ Alleviate boredom of doing same job ■ Determine next move ■ Provide depth of talent through cross-training
Continual Reassignment Reassigning employees to different units or geographic locations at set intervals	■ Geographic relocation ■ Facilitate new ideas through diversity ■ Prevent employees from getting stale in one place ■ Use employee talents in diverse settings

The length of a rotational assignment may range from weeks to months. It may be a single event to give an employee a closer understanding of a different function, or it may be a "revolving door," meaning the employee continues to rotate back and forth between two or more jobs. Some common types of job rotation and their objectives are depicted in Table 18.

■ ACTION PROVOKING QUESTIONS

EVALUATING JOB ROTATION PLANS

- What are the objectives of rotation?
- What types of rotation will be used?
- How should eligibility be determined?
- Which jobs can and cannot be included?
- Will specialized training be necessary for participants?
- Will there be limits on the number of persons rotating at any one time?
- What will be the time frames for rotational assignments?
- How will performance appraisal of rotated individuals be determined?
- How will the results of the system be measured?

Depending on its objectives, job rotation may take place within a department or division or between different departments and divisions. The goals that employees identified at an earlier stage of the career development process can help guide the organization in determining how the system should be structured and in identifying which jobs are likely candidates for rotation. Some organizations may only occasionally rotate employees who volunteer for a temporary "swap" in duties, while others may exchange all employees with certain duties at set intervals on a continuing basis. In planning for rotation, the practitioner might consider the Action Provoking Questions above.

Positions in industrial engineering or human resources can provide excellent experience for managers who need to learn more about these areas. Working in these departments brings candidates into contact with nearly every other department in the organization and, as a result, increases their knowledge of the overall organizational structure. Lateral promotions, like rotational assignments, provide an opportunity for individuals to receive guidance from a variety of other managers and to observe many management methods and techniques in action. If these sorts of developmental activities are suggested during the Strategizing Stage, a job rotation program might fill the bill.

Training for Cross Purposes

Common to both job rotation and experienced-based training is the concept of cross-training—increasing skills so that individuals are able to perform a variety of duties. This gives the organization a broader and more flexible base of talent and increased options for placing employees where and when they are needed most.

Cross-training represents a hybrid approach to skill development that combines some of the features of training with some of those of job rotation. The object of cross-training may not be to permanently change an employee's job, but to provide in advance for organizational needs during peak times or vacation periods. For example, one division or department in an organization may have a high seasonal need for additional employees. Through cross-training, the valleys and peaks of seasonal and business project demand can be leveled.

Cross-training has several advantages: (1) Organizational needs are met with permanent employees rather than through hiring temporary help. (2) Employees are exposed to different skills and functions that can help them to make career decisions. (3) A team spirit is usually developed within the workforce that enhances morale and feelings of mutual support. (4) Monotony and routine can be broken up.

Cross-training can also serve as a basis for increasing job enrichment efforts, expanding the awareness of organizational objectives, developing improved relationships between functions or departments, and exploring career alternatives. Most cross-training efforts involve shorter periods of time than job training or job rotation.

Practical Projects

Another aspect of experience-based training is to assign temporary projects that can result in learning and practical experience. These projects may be undertaken individually, such as research assignments; in teams, such as problem-solving and planning assignments; or on committees where employees have an opportunity to gain more responsibility and diversified experience.

These endeavors are often undertaken on a less systematic basis than job training or job rotation, with employee and supervisor or career development practitioner simply recognizing a skill that should be acquired and matching it with a special project that can give the employee a chance to practice that skill. Action plans developed by employees during strategizing can guide the selection of projects. For example, individuals who want to move into financial management may be able to research alternative inventory accounting systems for their division. A secretary desiring to

CASE 28

Temporary Projects: A Chance to Learn New Skills

A manufacturing company's administrative staff participated in a career development effort that utilized the project concept as a way of enriching jobs and preparing participants for possible future career moves.

After participants had worked through a long process of profiling and met individually with a consultant and a human resource practitioner to select a job enrichment goal, the development of the project concept process began. Participants were asked a riddle: "What is it that this company needs that it presently does not have that it would challenge you to do—you would practice new skills, utilize old ones, and grow as a result of it?" Participants answered the riddle by suggesting a range of projects that they thought might benefit both the organization and themselves.

Each project had to meet a series of criteria before it was sanctioned. Criteria combined job enrichment principles characteristic of power defined by Rosabeth Kanter. (Is your project extraordinary? Relevant? Visible? Does it provide an opportunity to make new alliances with peers? Subordinates? Mentors?) Participants assisted one another in the selection. The organization was apprised of the projects so that commitment could be assessed before commencement.

Projects selected by the group were team developed and provided each individual with a chance to practice or learn specific new skills.

advance to administrative assistant may be placed on a project team that reviews the departmental communications and paperflow system. Projects such as these enable employees to learn and practice specific skills and simultaneously provide the organization with valuable information.

SUPPORT-GUIDED DEVELOPMENT

A great many development opportunities during the Implementing Stage come simply from getting employees together with others who can provide instruction, guidance, and support. This may take place within groups of individuals who share some common need or goals or between two individuals who are helping each other. Support groups within organizations can generally be

CASE 29

"Development Quartets": Support from the Group

Following a three-day development program in a financial organization, participants were assigned to "development quartets"—support groups organized to meet on a continuing basis during the six-month period following the workshop. The groups were provided with a variety of activities that could be discussed at meetings and were assigned mentors who met individually and with the entire group to discuss career goals and development plans. The development quartets were organized to represent a cross-section of several major departments within the organization as well as gender and ethnic diversity.

categorized by (1) profession (such as engineers, accountants, or HR managers from various units within the organization); (2) level or rank (middle managers, administrative aides, or department heads); and (3) special interests (such as young managers). These groups may be formally sanctioned by top management, or they may be formed informally by a few interested individuals. Many individuals in organizations formalize support groups and mentor relationships by initiating a structure for their development and arranging times and places for meetings.

Informal support groups can also effectively promote professional development, with individuals meeting over lunch or after work to discuss a variety of issues of common interest. In addition, employees may join support groups outside the organization in order to exchange ideas and promote learning along with others who are in the same profession or have like interests.

Typical activities of these internal groups include (1) providing a sense of togetherness and comradeship that is supportive of group members' career mobility, (2) sharing information about business operations and norms in various units, (3) helping individuals learn and grow, (4) identifying issues that need to be brought to the attention of top management, (5) conducting special projects concerning issues of interest to group members, and (6) encouraging favorable treatment of members by the organization.

Occasional meetings that cross departmental lines can provide learning opportunities as well as support. Most organizations have regular meetings of department heads and division heads, and some have periodic meetings of budget analysts, HR specialists, and others. The practitioner may want to institute special days during which individuals from various departments meet to discuss and demonstrate the operations of their groups. This can be set up as a display hall environment, with booths and tables where departmental operations are discussed and literature is made available. Employees can be invited to circulate through the area and meet people from different departments and functions in order to learn more about the organization and the opportunities it offers.

Mentor as Teacher

One of the most effective supports for growth and development is the mentor-protégé relationship. Traditionally, this was a one-on-one relationship, but a more structured group approach is especially applicable to learning organizations.

An individual who finds another person (generally with longer tenure in the organization) who can teach, coach, and advise gains access to information and assistance that can contribute to acquiring the skills necessary to reach a particular goal. During the Implementing Stage, the mentor (1) grooms an individual for new responsibilities or advancement; (2) coaches and counsels an individual in behavior and skills that can facilitate career progress; and (3) shares information and expertise that has been specially acquired.

The environment created by this relationship is unique in the way it fosters learning and enthusiasm in the employee. Mentors must be willing, however, to let the protégés learn on their own, which includes permitting them the freedom to make mistakes. Protégés are allowed leeway to question their mentors' opinions so that they can learn and understand. The protégés must be able to accept criticism without becoming defensive, while also asserting individual feelings and views. The structure of the mentor relationship makes this possible. Since mentors are not forced to protect their jobs and the protégés are not evaluated as protégés, the environment is conducive to learning. The mentors must be willing to devote time to aiding, supporting, and instructing a protégé. The protégés must also be willing to devote time, often outside of work hours, to the relationship.

Typically the mentor-protégé arrangement is an informal one, adopted by two individuals who simply feel comfortable with each

EXERCISE 20

Know What You Want

Protégés who know what they want and see the benefit in taking action to achieve it can be more proactive with their mentors.

Protégés could fill in each of the WANTS listed below that relate directly to their long-term goals and short-term objectives. After each WANT, they should describe how it will benefit them in reaching their goals.

Example: *"I want to get straight feedback on my depth of new product knowledge because I need to know if I should sign up for additional training."*

I WANT to get straight feedback on:

_____

Because . . . _____

I WANT to learn a specific skill like:

_____

Because . . . _____

I WANT to hear about opportunities such as:

_____

Because . . . _____

I WANT to get information about:

_____

Because . . . _____

I WANT to get help with an idea like:

_____

Because . . . _____

I WANT to demonstrate a strength like:

_____

Because . . . _____

EXERCISE 20

Know What You Want (continued)

I WANT to get a specific job like:

_____

   Because . . . _____

I WANT to gain visibility with:

_____

   Because . . . _____

I WANT to find new contacts that can:

_____

   Because . . . _____

other. However, many organizations have formalized the system, generally by asking for volunteers to form a pool of mentors and matching them with individuals who are relatively new to the organization. Their informal meetings are supplemented by structured occasions to bring all mentors and protégés together for discussion and learning sessions. In Exercise 20, protégés can list what they want from their mentors and how their interaction will benefit them in reaching their goals.

Other organizations develop formal mentor programs for select groups of employees who may be on the organizational fast track. Some of these organizations are experimenting with a new approach to mentoring that does away with the old one on one approach and recommends learning groups.

When mentoring is approached from a group perspective, the mentor becomes a *learning leader*. This learning leader works with a group of new or junior employees, but also remains tightly networked with the employees' supervisors and managers. The group will consist of about six employees who can thus learn from their peers as well as the mentor. The learning leader must demonstrate

CASE 30

A Formal Mentor Model

A large bank devised an Advanced Opportunities Program. Its purpose was to prepare a group of individuals to assume certain targeted senior management positions; to aid from throughout the system a mentor was assigned to each one. The mentors included individuals who had the following characteristics: (1) senior members of management, (2) interested in and capable of developing others, (3) willing and able to commit the time required to act as a mentor, (4) knowledgeable about the necessary technical skills and the developmental requirements for the targeted area, (5) able to convey that knowledge of the technical area to others in a coaching situation, and (6) willing and able to provide coaching and to share insights about the political fitness and organizational norms appropriate to the targeted area.

It was the mentor's responsibility to provide information and make suggestions to his or her protégé concerning the skills, knowledge, experience, training, and other developmental requirements an individual would need in order to qualify for the senior management level. Whenever possible, the mentor was expected to suggest sources for acquiring this expertise.

most of the attributes of the typical mentor, but in addition it is especially important that the leader maintain sensitivity to diversity. The traditional mentor-protégé relationship has fostered homogeneity as both mentors and protégés tend to seek out people similar to themselves. The learning leader–group approach offers an invaluable opportunity to support employees from diverse backgrounds.

Support from Afar

The proliferation of professional groups has resulted in an organization for almost every line of work. These groups and societies provide an excellent opportunity for learning and growth. Many individuals might not be aware that they are eligible for the specialized services of a number of associations. For example, an accountant in a government agency may find opportunities available from an organization of professional accountants or from an organization of government employees. Women, or members of racial or ethnic minorities may discover opportunities in a group representing professional women or minorities. Through their meetings and training programs these groups can provide a good source of personal contacts and professional learning. Since these organizations contribute substantially to the development of their members, many employers pay for membership dues and conference travel expenses and grant time off for attending meetings and conferences.

Other groups outside the organization address special interests and development needs. Public-speaking groups, for example, are an excellent vehicle for skill development. They have had particular success in helping members learn and practice the delivery of speeches and presentations. Similar groups range from those that help members develop writing skills to those that assist members in starting their own small businesses.

Clearly the acquisition of skills does not have to be restricted to the confines of the organization. Ambitious employees will use all the sources available to them both outside and inside the organization to execute career goals. The leader's job is to help employees discover these opportunities and become involved in them. And as organizations find themselves operating in more severely restricted environments, with cutbacks and definite limitations on expansion, they will continually need to look to the creative sources outside the organization's boundaries for the development for their employees. Employees, too, are expected to be increasingly better educated, up-to-date, and career self-reliant.

Demonstrating Competencies

HOW DO WE KNOW WHAT THEY'VE LEARNED?

So far in this discussion of the Implementing Stage the attention has been mostly focused on support and guidance in terms of development activities. What sort of a responsibility do the participants in a career development effort have in making certain that the Implementing Stage effectively achieves the plans they developed to accomplish their career goals?

The proof of the pudding is said to be in the eating. The proof of developmental efforts is in demonstrating the newly acquired skills, techniques, and behavior gained from the implementation of career development plans.

The Four Stages of Learning

Before acquiring a particular skill, employees are at the first stage of the learning process, the level known as Unconscious Incompetence—they don't know (even what it is they need), but they don't know that they don't know.

As employees begin to learn about themselves and what they want to accomplish, they begin to see new opportunities for growth and development. Slowly they begin to realize how much they do not know in a certain area, and as a result, they are able to name specific areas where they need further skill development. Thus they reach the second level of the learning process, Conscious Incompetence—they don't know, but now know that they don't know.

After goals have been established, plans have been developed, and resources for learning have been discovered and pursued, participants can begin to learn specific new skills and to develop new behavior. Step-by-step they achieve the third level of learning, Conscious Competence—they now know, but they know only well enough to be able to perform with a great deal of concentration and effort.

This is the most uncomfortable stage of learning. The skill being learned, the behavior being attempted, or the technique being practiced can only be done by applying determination and effort. Often the natural inclination at this point is to quit, to walk away because doing it is too hard. The urge to go back to the comfort of the Unconscious Incompetence is great. At this stage employees will need all of the support, encouragement, and help that practitioners, managers, supervisors, peers, and the organization can muster. If they receive that support, if their efforts are noted and rewarded, employees will reach the fourth level of learning, Unconscious Competence—where they know, and know so well that the newly acquired skills and behavior become automatic—and they are ready to progress onward with those skills to some new career opportunity.

The purpose of the Implementing Stage is to help employees achieve the third level of learning, Conscious Competence, and to know that the fourth level, Unconscious Competence is possible, but requires a great deal of practice. Figure 7 lists the four stages of learning.

FIGURE 7

The Four Stages of Learning

IV	Unconscious Competence
III	Conscious Competence
II	Conscious Incompetence
I	Unconscious Incompetence

Come Blow Your Horn

Most people have a tendency to be modest about their achievements. So employees will, for instance, enroll in a developmental program or project that could greatly enhance their careers, but through modesty or reluctance to toot their own horns, they fail to let managers or anyone else within the organization know about it. Practitioners must ensure that employees keep the organization informed about what they are doing, how they are doing, and what help they need.

Demonstrating skills gained through career development efforts is more than just letting others see what has been learned. At the level of Conscious Competence, employees will be trying to demonstrate these new skills, but because these skills are not fully internalized (to the point of Unconscious Competence), mistakes will be made. If these mistakes are noted and the reasons for them are not appreciated, employees are very likely to give up or at least be reluctant to attempt the demonstration of other learning. Progress toward goals must be known so that support and reward can be given.

Practitioners and leaders, therefore, have a very special responsibility to (1) encourage employees to make their efforts known, (2) document those efforts, and (3) keep others involved informed as to where they stand.

The responsibility for the demonstration of competencies is, of course, that of the employee. Only employees can show what they have learned, and only they can build upon those learnings to advance their career development efforts.

Practitioners and managers have the responsibility to provide support and feedback—support that encourages progress and feedback that keeps the participant aware of achievements and learning.

> **CASE 31**
>
> *Showcasing New Learnings:*
> *Exposing Individuals' New Talents and Skills*
>
> A high-tech organization provided an intensive development opportunity to a target group of individuals who needed to learn a new skill set. The individuals worked in teams to define a project that met a business need and also utilized one or more of this particular skill set. Projects lasted six to nine months, were seen as developmental, and were done in conjunction with the current job. At the conclusion of the project, each team was invited to present their results to the executive committee and a team of senior line managers. The presentation provided an opportunity for these individuals to showcase their skills and also served to expose the group to senior organization members who might not have known their talents.

WHERE CAN SUPPORT BE FOUND?

One of the most time-consuming and complex tasks encountered during the Implementing Stage is locating the educational, training, and developmental resources required to reach goals set during the Targeting Stage. To accomplish this, practitioners might emphasize not only the importance of employee participation in the search for information about resources, but also the necessity of communicating that information to the organization.

Employee Responsibilities

This point in the process requires a great deal of self-direction, motivation, and tenacity as the employee searches for and pursues resources that will be necessary to implement the career development plan. The primary responsibilities of employees are to (1) identify specific ways in which they can acquire resources to facilitate their development, and (2) use those resources to develop the skills and relationships necessary to move toward career goals.

The first of these roles is largely an information function. As described earlier, employees need to continually search for information about training and development opportunities, experiences, and support that may assist their progress. They may need to talk to colleagues in other departments, supervisors, and friends

CASE 32

Development Assignments with
the Support of a Learning Team

A chemical company, committed to the development of its bench strength, offered a year-long program to a select group of technical professionals. All were provided with a 360-degree feedback assessment of their technical and managerial strengths and weaknesses. Each individual had to devise a development assignment that would serve to strengthen a capability. The assignments were reviewed by their learning teams and also by their own managers. The review helped the professionals fine-tune these goals and, to a great extent, devise even tougher assignments. Assignments were discussed at the conclusion of the year for the learning points that they taught, and for the new insights that participants gained that would help them in their future development.

to gain evaluative information and advice about what specific training is beneficial. They may need to investigate opportunities offered by local educational institutions or through professional associations. In some cases, they may need to talk with supervisors about special projects or job revisions that could be undertaken to provide developmental work. And, most important, employees themselves may need to initiate ideas for on-the-job learning.

Using those resources may mean taking courses, attending training, completing special projects, trying new skills on the job, or forging new relationships with others. All require an expenditure of time and sometimes money, as well as a willingness to stick with it when the initial excitement of doing something new wears off.

At the same time, employees should continually appraise their experiences and look for ways to capitalize on them for career growth. They should keep managers and career development practitioners informed about their activities and their future plans. And they should try not to operate in a vacuum but rather seek support and guidance from others in pursuing career development resources. Anything that the practitioner can do to engender this spirit in employees will contribute substantially to the program's success.

Practitioner Responsibilities

The career development practitioner needs to see that the resources employees want to use are made available by the organization and that employees are informed about these resources. To do this, the practitioner needs to track and monitor information gained from the other stages of career development. In addition, the practitioner serves as a liaison between top management, employees, and the direct managers of career development participants in order to inform each of these groups and guide them in contributing to the program.

It is at this point that practitioners might consider revising old internal programs, terminating those programs that appear to have outlived their usefulness, and instituting new ones that may be required. It may be, for instance, that people within the organization have been discussing the institution of a job rotation program, a broader application of tuition aid, or an after-hours technical training effort. Practitioners armed with the requirements defined by employee career development goals are in an ideal position to help organizations recognize their needs, to help direct the organizational response, and to serve as a prime element in making changes.

The practitioner must also identify which resources can best be provided outside the organization to meet a variety of training needs. This may include gathering information about these methods as well as keeping up-to-date on the programs offered by local colleges and universities, training organizations, professional associations, and adult education institutions. The practitioner will need to ensure that time and money are available for employee career development pursuits. The organization's top management should be encouraged to adequately budget for learning needs and to set policies that allow employees time to pursue their developmental plans. The Action Provoking Questions on page 224 provide a guide for practitioners who want to assess the degree to which their organization provides these activities.

Ensuring that employees are informed about developmental resources available within and outside the organization is another responsibility. This may be done through written communications, face-to-face information sessions, computer-based information systems, and so forth.

Practitioners must not do it *all*. Managers and employees need to take responsibility for their own continuing education, and leaders need to take responsibility for the development of their employees.

■ ACTION PROVOKING QUESTIONS

EVALUATING IN-HOUSE DEVELOPMENTAL RESOURCES

- What additional resources should we consider developing?
- Do all employees have equal access to the organizational resources?
- Are employees at all levels adequately informed about resources that are available?
- Do we have a system for tracking how organizational resources are used?
- Have I done all I can to encourage employees to actively seek resources?

One organization encouraged self-management on the part of employees by initiating a self-monitoring chit system for spending training and development dollars. Under this system each employee was given a limited number of chits, representing dollars, for time spent in learning experiences. Employees themselves decided how and when to spend these chits on developmental experiences. This system, combined with thoughtful career goal setting, encouraged employees to make responsible decisions about how to spend their development resources.

Practitioners may need to go to bat for increased funds for a tuition assistance program, recommend a more equitable arrangement for funding membership dues for professional associations, install computerized tools, or encourage a more liberal policy on interdepartmental job rotation. To pave the way for these suggestions, practitioners should continually inform top management of program activities and results. This may be accomplished through periodic briefings and memos that report on what is being done and demonstrate the benefits accruing to the organization.

Manager and Leader Responsibilities

Few managers or leaders today can afford not to be involved in their employees' development. Special orientation and training sessions are often conducted to help develop coaching skills, determine ways to develop learning experiences, and understand how to best provide an arena for the testing of new employee skills and abilities.

For a variety of reasons, most organizations find it greatly in their interest to support managerial involvement in the development process at this stage: (1) Closer ties are established between manager and employee. (2) Individuals closest to the actual work situation devise ways to increase its learning potential and to give rewards and recognition. (3) Employees can turn to the most available resource for advice and information. (4) Managers are more likely to fulfill ongoing responsibilities with employee career development in mind. (5) Less time is required of human re-source staff or other career development practitioner resources.

When managers do take an active part in the Implementing Stage, coaching developmental opportunities is their primary responsibility. And this is often the function for which they are least prepared unless they are given special orientation and training. Managers need to acquire both substantive knowledge that can be passed on to employees and the process skills that will help them conduct these coaching sessions.

The areas of substantive knowledge are (1) knowledge of basic human resource requirements and plans in the organization; (2) understanding of the resources available—internally and externally—that can facilitate employee development; (3) familiarity with roles of others in the organization who may be able to provide further information and advice to employees; and (4) understanding of ways in which developmental experiences might be structured in the immediate work setting.

Managers who are prepared with appropriate information and skills should be able to conduct discussions that give employees advice and suggestions as well as general support and encouragement to select means of building skills. Discussions at this point may review previous stages of career development or may be limited to Implementing Stage activities. Managers should review employees' career strategy or action plan and any other pertinent information. The discussion is generally open-ended, using examples that allow the employee to discuss a wide range of development concerns. As a resource planner at the Implementing Stage, the manager is also called upon to exercise a high degree of creativity and to work closely with subordinates to develop new opportunities that do not conflict with accomplishing the necessary ongoing work.

Three key questions should be continually asked by the manager who acts as resource planner:

- What can I do to help employees learn and grow?
- What can I do to reward their efforts to learn and grow?
- How can I help them to recognize their learnings?

Career discussions at the Implementing Stage may include conveying to employees that the skills they gain may not immediately lead to actual job changes. They are, nevertheless, valuable to both the organization and the employee in the short term and, with proper assistance, will brighten the long-term prospects for all concerned.

The Implementing Stage is an important one in which the organization, management, the practitioner, and the individual all play strong roles. The results of successfully completing this stage are worthwhile—employees acquire new skills and become more proficient in their present jobs while preparing themselves to move on to one or more targeted career goals. The organization gains employees who manage their own growth and development and who are, due to the energizing quality of this stage, more productive. The next chapter investigates the importance of sustaining the entire career development experience through an array of maintenance vehicles and a thorough evaluation process.

|7|

Remaining Relevant

THE SUSTAINING STAGE

"Stayin' alive."
—THE BEE GEES

I n our era of rapid and dramatic change, it is critical to find ways to sustain the energy and momentum of the career development effort. Far too many career development initiatives fade just as quickly as they've been implemented. Bottom-line questions, too, are being directed at career development programs with increasing urgency. Ideas that sound smart may not translate into "good dollars and sense." In fact, a lot of promising programs are generated only to fizzle out or be abandoned not long after their creation. Career development programs need to be adapted to changing conditions by designing a variety of sustaining systems that keep the program alive.

It is also crucial to recognize that these systems will not work if they're tacked onto the end of a career development program; they have to be designed in and considered at the preparation stage and attended to at each of the succeeding stages. Many of us know this intuitively: We've probably felt, if not actually documented, those moments when organizational and individual commitment to a particular career development effort begins to wane. There are several ways to help avert such an outcome. One is to ask three "guiding questions" at each stage of the effort:

- How do the career development needs we've identified link with our overall business direction?
- How can we create interventions that are flexible and adaptable enough to meet changing needs and audiences?

■ How can our career development efforts be made to outlive individual stakeholders and particular actions so they become part of the fiber of the organization?

The point is to stay loyal, throughout the entire life of a career development effort, to the notion that development, like all change efforts, is an ongoing and long-term process. This chapter will address the importance of sustaining the career development effort once it has begun, by addressing two distinct sets of ideas: (1) What kind of *maintenance mechanisms* can be designed to keep the effort evergreen?, and (2) How can *evaluation systems* be designed to bring continuous improvement to the development effort?

Maintenance Mechanisms

Depending on an organization's size, its culture, and the scope of its career development efforts, practitioners should be aware of a wide array of mechanisms for maintaining their development efforts. In an earlier study with Zandy Leibowitz (Kaye and Leibowitz, 1994), five mechanisms were determined: (1) follow-on functions, (2) human resource linkages, (3) communication vehicles, (4) accountability approaches, and (5) reward structures. Within each of these general categories, of course, numerous variations are possible.

FOLLOW-ON FUNCTIONS

Most training efforts can be enhanced and energy maintained by structuring ongoing events that begin when the training has ended. Practitioners can check themselves on their attentiveness to follow-on functions in the Action Provoking Questions on page 229.

Career action teams can be a very successful mechanism for maintaining energy. These employee-based support groups offer a chance for employees to meet periodically to help one another with career development activities. Career action teams can work as effectively for managers as for employees. In fact, many managers enjoy the opportunities for sharing ideas and talents that these teams can and do provide. When these teams are designed to maintain energy, they should be introduced as part of the training effort itself. In other words, employees would recognize that attendance at the workshop means one or two days *plus* the agreement to meet with a career action team for three to four sessions afterward. Practitioners can rely on the fact that if these groups don't

---

■ ACTION PROVOKING QUESTIONS

FOLLOW-ON FUNCTIONS

- Does the career development effort offer opportunities for on-going support meetings between program participants?
- Do managers see their own staff meetings as a forum for continued dialogue about development issues?
- Does the organization support continued work on the part of managers and employees through the use of special coaching sessions, and/or resource centers containing in-depth information?
- Has the organization made an effort to make its specialized talent available for networking purposes?

"click" after three to four sessions, they probably never will. Those that do, however, will probably continue for quite some time.

Team/staff meetings with an emphasis on career development or information sharing (i.e., on future changes in the business as a whole), job enrichment, trading or sharing workteam responsibilities, and so forth, are another excellent vehicle. Sometimes, the practitioner will need to devise "scripts" for the managers who lead such meetings to help them frame the issues. These scripts usually include exercises that managers could do with their staff, discussions they could lead, and questionnaires they might distribute, as well as an overview of what might be expected in the employee program.

Coaching clinics are another means of building skills and maintaining momentum. They work well when designed as a follow-up to individual career development discussions or "one-shot" training sessions. Often these clinics are problem oriented, addressing thorny issues such as plateauing, developing minority employees, and so on.

Career resource centers are locations that house career development support material such as job information, organizational information, publications, videos, software tools, training materials, and an array of assessment tools. These centers provide a convenient base for activities that complement seminars or group meetings. Often skills workshops, speakers, discussion groups, and informal brown-bag sessions are held in the center as well.

For the most part, these centers are not meant to be made of bricks and mortar, but simply are specially designated locations—

a room, common area, bookshelf, or section in the learning center or training facility. Employees of all levels are invited to use these centers; they usually want to know more about the career development process, augment what they received during other parts of the effort, or gain detailed information about the organization, its divisions, or its future plans.

Information guides can also be invaluable. These individuals might be technical specialists, functional specialists, or simply managers who like talking with people about specific career interests. Regardless of their organizational title, they can be established as a resource with commitment, energy, good humor, and perspective on the process of shaping and cultivating a career. Selecting these specialists can make the difference between a straightforward career intervention and a genuinely exciting set of career initiatives undertaken successfully across divisions or even throughout an entire organization.

HUMAN RESOURCE LINKAGES

Another vital way of sustaining momentum and maintaining the integrity of the effort is to very deliberately link development with other HR initiatives. We might well argue that from a customer point of view that integration is long overdue. People are growing weary of the HR "flavor of the month"; they want some coherence. The job of the practitioner is to point out how everything connects with everything else: that is, to show how various HR initiatives support one another. Practitioners can check themselves on their attentiveness to human resources linkages in the Action Provoking Questions on page 231.

Performance appraisal is one HR link that many practitioners talk about in the same breath as career development. Because they're clearly "first cousins" in some ways, many organizations try to do them at the same time. But in order for the benefits of integrating these two programs to be felt over the long term, managers must first be alerted to the difference between developing employees to carry out current responsibilities and developing them to meet future challenges and opportunities—a subtle but crucial distinction. Only after it has been pointed out in clear terms can an organization hope to link career development meaningfully to appraisal of performance. The important point is that both need to be defined in terms of the inevitability of change and the need for new skills, attitudes, and flexibility to encounter that change effectively.

■ ACTION PROVOKING QUESTIONS

HUMAN RESOURCE LINKAGES

- Does the performance appraisal require a development plan? Does our performance appraisal hold managers accountable for their role in developing people?
- Have we made the link between career development and quality initiatives obvious to all employees?
- Are we actively using our competency lists within our career development effort?
- Do our training and development programs support the needs identified in employee development plans?
- Does our current orientation program introduce our development philosophy effectively?

Quality initiatives also come to mind readily when we think about various career development linkages. Both initiatives focus on taking responsibility, setting goals, using information aggressively, and communicating well. Yet these two initiatives are too often launched, monitored, and assessed by completely different parts of the organization. One way to begin merging them is to use the language of quality in career development efforts—in particular, the notion of continuous improvement, which is the cornerstone of quality.

Competencies, too, are an excellent link with the development effort. Competencies can become the "currency" of career development—tangible, desired groups of skills that individuals can work to acquire. Competencies can also frame and structure profiling discussions. Rather than groping for language to talk about strengths and improvements, managers can draw on their own organizational competency studies that have already been done (often with considerable effort and expense) to define the key skills and knowledge people need now and in the future.

Training and development choices also need to be driven by identified development gaps—and employees need to receive information and a process for identifying those gaps. Competency instruments are used by many organizations to identify skill and knowledge deficiencies.

These reports are coupled with lists (often computerized) of training courses that support these identified needs. Such lists are geared to the organization's training menu, or they describe training opportunities nationwide. Organizations that demand a specified number of training hours each year can utilize this particular mechanism to enforce this type of maintenance system. Practitioners today recognize the importance of coupling training and development classes with on-the-job learning assignments; both address development gaps.

Orientation programs are becoming a "hot-button" issue as organizations realize that the reservoir of new employees is no longer as deep as it once was. For this reason, the orientation of new workers is an ideal initiative to link with career development. The questions that confront employees at the point of organization entry are essentially career development questions. How does my job fit into the bigger picture? How can I learn more about the rest of the group and about the business as a whole? The ways in which organizations handle these questions depend considerably on whether career development initiatives are effectively "mated" with the organization's orientation program. Savvy organizations know that if a new employee is going to leave, he or she is likely to do so within the first three years of employment. The idea is to get to people with information and resources that will help them make positive career choices sooner and thereby enhance their contributions to their workteams.

Clearly, these are just a few of the HR structures for the practitioner to consider. Linking career development and other HR structures is a challenging task, one that demands attention from leaders and practitioners alike. It can be a very powerful way to maintain the momentum of a career development effort because it addresses structures and policies in an organization, not just behavior change.

COMMUNICATION VEHICLES

Many career interventions have died for lack of a solid communication strategy. Practitioners can check themselves on their attentiveness to communication vehicles in the Action Provoking Questions on page 233.

Commitment meetings are an excellent communication technique that can force large-scale information sharing and planning. After data collection, for example, an open forum can be held. The walls of a large conference room can be literally covered with data (gathered from surveys and focus groups) about various career-

---

■ ACTION PROVOKING QUESTIONS

COMMUNICATION VEHICLES

- Are we continuing to build commitment to our development effort with all our constituencies?
- Are we publicizing the effort continually? Do we have a marketing effort in place for all aspects of career development, not just the training program?
- Is our career development advisory group in continued contact with senior management?
- Are we making full use of all organization communication vehicles to build our communication for career development?

---

related resources, their users and usage rates, their successes and needs for improvement. Employees can be asked to "edit the walls," noting aspects of various initiatives that they want to see emphasized. If sufficient numbers of people are involved, this highly interactive buy-in process can help those who participate to feel that they helped invent the system.

Career renewal meetings are another communication technique. Here, employees and managers are asked to convene periodically to review and discuss how a particular career development process is going for them. Regardless of the specific mechanisms chosen, however, the need for open communication remains a constant— and has to be addressed at all organizational levels.

Planning teams are often time-consuming, but they always pay off. There's simply no substitute for a team of line people to inform upper management of what to do and how best to begin doing it. HR professionals just can't create certain kinds of career development systems by themselves. The longer a planning team functions, and the more diverse its participants, the greater its contribution to the development culture.

Designated alliances are another surefire means of maintaining a communication strategy. Here, alliances are determined between people at the top and members of planning teams. Senior leaders can give tips, advice, and general guidance. These alliances rely heavily, of course, on the ability of the people involved to communicate openly and directly. The greater the reach and substance of interpersonal as well as divisional communication, the more

---

CASE 33

*Managerial Accountability: Choosing
What Works for Them*

A high-tech company gave all managers a choice of how they wanted to be held accountable. Managers were asked to select from an array of commitment statements such as: "I will meet with each of my employees for forty-five minutes twice a year." "I will create an open-door policy for all my people who want to discuss career issues one Friday a month." "I will hold staff meetings every other month specifically directed at career issues." Managers made their commitments known to the practitioner and also to their own direct reports. The system encouraged managers to be creative, to do "something," but to promise only what was comfortable for them.

CASE 34

*Joint Accountability: Employee
and Manager in Partnership*

A n oil company dealt with the accountability issue by requiring that all employees submit three enrichment goals to a Personal Development Committee made up of their own supervisor and the supervisor's peers. The employee was held accountable because the goals had to be in writing and submitted at a certain point in the performance management cycle; managers were held accountable because they were expected to come to the Personal Development Committee meeting having completed development sessions with all their employees and prepared to discuss their employees' enrichment goals.

---

likely the organization is to maintain well-linked, successful career development efforts.

Marketing plans are integral to the communication strategy. The marketing of a new program shouldn't cease as soon as training

∎ ACTION PROVOKING QUESTIONS

ACCOUNTABILITY APPROACHES

- Have we been assertive in our approach to holding managers and employees accountable for their development?
- Have we involved managers and employees enough in the design of the accountability mechanisms?
- Do our development accountability systems reinforce other HR initiatives?
- Are we publicizing the success (or failure) of our accountability mechanisms?

has been announced. Instead, it should be continuous, and it should "piggyback" on other in-house marketing efforts. In essence, employees and managers alike should be receiving multiple messages, from many and mutually reinforcing sources, about the necessity and benefits of taking responsibility for career development—and about how the organization can support individuals in this undertaking.

ACCOUNTABILITY APPROACHES

There is a saying in our field that suggests that people will do what is "inspected" not necessarily what is "expected." This seems to be quite true today, given the pressure on individuals at all levels to do more with less. Still, manager and individual accountability is vital, and an important maintenance mechanism. Practitioners can check themselves on their attentiveness to accountability approaches in the Action Provoking Questions above.

Manager accountability for developing the careers of their subordinates is all too often neglected by leader and practitioners. Under pressure for results, managers become so concerned about operations that they often overlook opportunities to identify and develop talent. Their time, energy, and attention is devoted to increasing production, improving sales, and reducing costs. As a result, opportunities that lead to supporting the growth of employees is often neglected.

It is vital to the sustaining stage that managers obtain feedback on how they're doing as developers. In this regard, a variety of upward appraisal systems that allow employees to give their managers feedback on their development behaviors are being implemented in organizations. Another powerful assessment vehicle is the "skip-level" meeting, in which the employee talks to his or her manager's boss about how well the manager is performing as a developer.

Many organizations have also discovered that going public with exceptional development practices creates a strong incentive for managers to "walk their talk" as coaches and advisors. The key is to emphasize both technical competence and development competence as central to management effectiveness. The objective isn't to intimidate managers into developmental behaviors; rather, the aim is to create and support an atmosphere of continuous improvement within which managers will feel encouraged to expand their repertoire of developmental skills and use those skills on a daily basis, just as they use their technical skills.

Employee accountability has become more and more important as leaders and practitioners drive home the self-responsibility message. At one time, accountability systems were all devised with the manager in mind. While many organizations still do this, some are experimenting with holding individuals accountable in similar ways. Several organizations have placed words like "development-minded" on their appraisal systems. These organizations are interested in the degree to which an individual has taken charge of his or her own career and moved toward a series of development goals. Others are providing self-appraisals to individuals to ascertain their own proactivity around development.

One organization includes a list of twenty-one development practices with its performance appraisal criteria. The degree to which employees take action on these practices is rated as seriously as the performance skills and traits. Development practices include such capabilities as: *enlists others as coaches, knows weaknesses that must be addressed, recognizes strengths,* and *makes appropriate changes in response to feedback.* Employees must be able to describe their actions in several of the twenty-one practice areas.

REWARD STRUCTURES

Practitioners attempting to find ways to sustain career development programs will be faced with a host of problems when the subject of rewards comes up. Providing rewards and recognition that are meaningful to the individual is a task that requires a great variety of responses.

■ ACTION PROVOKING QUESTIONS

REWARD STRUCTURES

- Are we rewarding employees for other than upward mobility?
- Are we rewarding managers for their support of the development of their direct reports?
- Is our reward system for development public?
- Have we been creative about non-monetary rewards for development?

These responses may include rewards for employees who increase their learning and performance, rewards for development-minded managers who contribute to the growth of employees, and the establishment of monetary and nonmonetary systems for determining and administering new forms of compensation and promotion opportunity. These options must be within the realm of practicality for the organization, and they must be supported by a system that is perceived as equitable.

Perhaps no other organizational tool is as powerful in changing collective values as a firm's reward system. This area deserves serious consideration because of its influence in aligning career patterns and aspirations with changing corporate needs. Fortunately, the repertoire of compensation and reward choices has expanded significantly in recent years, as organizations have attempted to respond to varying employee needs and to search out less costly options than pay raises alone. Unfortunately, however, the options are still geared toward incentives and rewards for upward movement, with little support for employees who might prefer alternate career routes.

How to best compensate these alternate career moves and signal their value to the organization is a complex issue that creates yet another barrier to accomplishing a change toward a full range of career options. But, with sensitivity and creativity on the part of leaders and practitioners, the questions can be addressed. The author worked with Kathryn McKee (McKee and Kaye, 1989), compensation specialist, to address these issues. Practitioners can check themselves on their attentiveness to reward structures in the Action Provoking Questions above.

Lateral moves often provide intensive rewards, such as opportunities for new learning and the challenge of a new work environment. By encouraging such movement through a lump-sum payment or "transfer" bonus, organizations can continue to challenge employees. Skill-based pay systems can be particularly valuable in supporting these moves, as employees generally begin to add skills—through training and new experiences—shortly after the move. A compensation program that is designed to reward the acquisition and continued use of new skills can be a powerful incentive for employees to move across or "over" in the organization.

Enrichment on the current job—staying but not stagnating—is another career development option that is often overlooked by organizations and employees. Utilizing a skill-based pay system wholly or partially allows organizations to reward employees for further acquisition of additional skills. Such a system adapts best to situations where job opportunities are flexible enough to utilize a variety of skills, rather than to fairly routine situations that do not accommodate personal growth and learning. In addition, skill-based systems are most likely to succeed in organizations that are willing to support career development programs and commit resources to training. When enrichment involves serving on special committees, undertaking one-item research, joining a project team, or assuming new tasks, a one-time cash bonus compensation can be considered. Short-term, noncash rewards also can be used, such as providing for attendance at out-of-town conferences, greater autonomy in performing the work, and public recognition.

Exploratory moves often provide an essential first step by helping individuals determine interests and find paths to follow. Rewards can also be structured for exploration in areas that support learning—such as attendance at conferences, enrollment in seminars, or tuition reimbursement. One-time bonuses and public recognition also are highly appropriate for employees who are willing to explore a number of options in order to discover their own niche in the firm. Organizational compensation systems can accommodate exploring by holding the employee's salary constant during the period of exploration.

Realignment moves have been viewed negatively in the past, with the only reward being the elimination of a job that may not have suited the employee at all. Generally, downward moves have meant "demotion"—in pay, status, authority, and esteem. Compensation in this area today should at least consider ways to alleviate punitive and demeaning possibilities. Positive practices might include no cut in pay for a period of time, a gradual lowering of the salary, retention of perquisites, continuing education, or recognition as a special contributor.

These ideas are meant to ease the way in an effort to stop the traditional use of promotions as the only mark of career development. Follow-through will be different in each organization. Change can begin to happen only when total commitment—and patience—exist at the highest levels. Organization leaders must be the first to signal support for new compensation patterns, and other top managers must join in the commitment to alternative types of plans that consider individual needs and recognize that new compensation strategies are indeed essential to ensure the highest potential utilization of human resources.

Evaluation Efforts

Evaluation is a vital maintenance mechanism and deserves special attention at the Sustaining Stage. Developing systems that effectively evaluate career development efforts is often a headache. Although elaborate methods of human resource accounting are constantly being developed, evaluation methods are still often inadequate and it is often difficult to judge the quality of organizational career planning practices. Despite much research in this area, it is difficult to quantify the specific return on investment that organizations receive for their human resource development efforts, especially in the area of career development.

A recent survey of 1,000 U.S. corporations (Gutteridge, Leibowitz, and Shore, 1993) showed that, overall, career development practices get a very low rating by human resources executives. The highest-rated practices—tuition reimbursement, in-house development programs, and job posting systems—were rated as effective less than three-quarters of the time. Workshops were rated as effective only half the time, and computer-based approaches were considered effective less than half the time. Counseling and career discussions by leaders were rated as effective less than a quarter of the time, and job rotation or job enrichment programs were considered effective less than half the time.

The results of this survey probably reflect less upon the essential effectiveness of career development programs than on the difficulties encountered in designing and carrying out effective evaluation mechanisms. The survey demonstrates the need for establishing more reliable methods for determining the effectiveness and benefits of career development programs.

Interestingly enough, many organizations underestimate the importance of evaluation and are content with a cursory evaluation from participants following the workshop portions of the career development program. Practitioners may be swayed by management to avoid this step (after all, it's costly, time-consuming, and may not provide the desired results) but should argue for its inclusion. Several ideas for evaluation are suggested in the preparation chapter since, ideally, evaluation technologies should be established at the inception of the program and continue throughout all six stages.

DETERMINING FACTORS

The evaluation section of this chapter is designed to remind the practitioner of some crucial questions (Who? What? When? and Where?), to elaborate on some simple "how's," and to press for, at minimum, a tracking or documentation of the various program components.

Who?

All too quickly, leaders and practitioners choose the program's target group to be the primary source of evaluation. Often the target group is not the best audience with whom to test the waters. Program participants may be overly optimistic because a trainer has been particularly dynamic or an activity personally meaningful, or they may have a negative predisposition because they have been coerced into attendance. These and other factors may influence their views and bias may result. Participants should be polled, but they need not be the only group to evaluate the effectiveness of the program.

Every programmatic intervention in an organization affects numerous important audiences. If these audiences are identified early, appropriate evaluation techniques can be designed to gain their feedback as well. It is important to consider the different vantage points of each group in order to understand just how the career development effort affects them. Some of the audiences to consider in determining an evaluation design include:

■ Participants in the program—all those who have been targeted to attend the program

- Managers or team leaders of program participants—those leaders whose subordinates have attended the program
- Top management—those at decision-making levels in the organization who approved the program and allocated funds
- HR staff—other human resource development specialists such as recruiters, and wage and compensation professionals, who may be affected by the program

What?

By polling the various audiences, the practitioner will learn what each audience will consider as evidence that the program has been successful. Once these "success indicators" have been collected, the list can be shaped further by considering whether or not a particular indicator is "measurable" either in a qualitative or in a more quantitative form.

Most practitioners have their own ideas of what should be evaluated beforehand, but it is best to move cautiously until all potential audiences and areas of evaluation have been studied. Some areas of evaluation for the various audiences have already been suggested in the preparation chapter. Practitioners, working with the organization's leaders, can develop their own list by questioning a random group of representatives of a particular audience about the indicators of success that are important to them. Leaders and practitioners can then decide what can feasibly be measured and what is useful to the organization.

When?

Some evaluation activities can take place concurrently with the actual implementation of the program. Individual career development workshops can be evaluated at their completion, and again later on. Records can be kept on job posting systems as they are used and on the impact of their use on internal job changes over a certain period of time. Career development programs can also be evaluated in terms of short-term changes, three to twelve months following completion of the effort, or long-term changes, anywhere from one to five years after the initial implementation of the effort.

Determining when to gather data also depends on the kind of data one is going to collect. Initial reactions to the intervention, for example, are probably best collected immediately after the program has closed. On the other hand, data concerning learning and behavior change, as well as organizational and job change, is best collected after a certain time period has elapsed. Data on reduced turnover, improved performance, and so on, is also best collected after a suitable period of time has elapsed.

Administering a pretest and a posttest with the same group would be ideal. Gaining information about a group prior to an intervention and then collecting data afterward and measuring the change provides excellent data for evaluation. Preprogram data can be collected from any or all of the audiences or from a general sensing of the system.

Some organizations administer a climate study, a study that measures a wide variety of variables, several months prior to a program. The same study is then administered following the intervention. Companies using a climate study for career development then pay particular attention to the questions that address career development principles.

Evaluation should occur after the intervention and several times thereafter, covering a predetermined period of time. Practitioners are advised to recognize that the more they can evaluate at different points in time, the more chances they have to gain valuable data.

Where?

Although the evaluation is conducted where the program has occurred, the practitioner should not forget that other parts of the organization will also be affected. A change in one part of the system will produce changes in other parts.

If it is possible to use a control group, a group that has not experienced the intervention, and compare it with the group that has, the evaluation results are all the more credible and valuable to the organization. In the preparation chapter, leaders and practitioners are warned to think carefully about where the effort should be launched, to start small, and to choose target groups carefully. Heeding these warnings will pay off in more effective evaluation at the Sustaining Stage.

How?

There are a variety of methods for selecting data that can be used to evaluate the results of career development efforts. Using any one of them does not necessarily preclude the use of others. The method or combination of methods that leaders and practitioners select will be contingent on the organization's specific informational needs and the results of the "who, what, when, and where" diagnosis.

EVALUATION APPROACHES

Regardless of the type of development program, organizational consultant Donald Kirkpatrick (1985) maintains that information must be gathered on four levels: participants' reaction, learning, behavior, and program results. This section will address issues such as participants' evaluation of the program, participants' training, new skills acquired, and change in attitudes. Furthermore, are the new skills being applied on the job? Has behavior changed? Finally, what are the bottom-line results?

Three approaches to gathering the data will be described briefly here: the use of records, observation techniques, and self-report measures. The intent is not to describe every facet of these methodologies but to provide a summary of how each might be used in evaluating a career development effort.

Use of Records

Records are accounts of events that regularly occur in the system. When extensive records are kept as a matter of course, it may be easy for the practitioner to extract a substantial part of the data needed to determine specific activities that occurred, materials that were used, how and with whom activities took place, and changes that occurred over time. These records may include minutes of the planning and progress meetings; summaries of training sessions or other developmental efforts; attendance records of development or administrative sessions; progress reports of subgroups and committees; individual project or development plan progress reports; and results of attitude surveys, including the changes in employee ratings of career development programs over time.

Today, with so many records on computer systems, it is easy to tap into even more data to evaluate career development activities. Record data is considered credible evaluation information because it provides evidence of program events accumulated as they occurred rather than reconstructed later. Furthermore, they are not affected by the experimenter's bias because they are independent of the career development practitioner. The major drawback of using existing records is that abstracting information from them and reorganizing that information into a usable form can be time-consuming. Also, ethical or legal constraints are often involved in examining certain records. Some examples of existing records that might be used in evaluation efforts include documentation of instances in which employees (1) sought supervisory help or help from the HR staff, (2) visited the career planning center, (3) updated their skills inventories, (4) used the job posting system, (5) requested tuition reimbursement for further skill training, or (6) sent unsolicited memos regarding their career progress or feelings about a particular part of the program. Another record would be the employee's annual performance appraisal.

One might review the record and performance rating prior to the career development effort and again afterward to see if there have been any changes in the employees' performance in any number of evaluation dimensions as viewed by their managers. One could also record changes in employee-initiated grievances— these grievances *could* indicate a change in morale or a change in attitudes toward career paths and development possibilities. Asking to see records that are kept by the organization as a matter of course will usually not be seen as burdensome by those departments asked to share them. Often the extra burden of specially recording events is the major drawback to fully using this particular evaluation device. Table 19 outlines the major evaluation steps based on the use of records.

Observation Techniques

Using observation as an evaluation method requires that one or more individuals devote their attention to the behavior of current or former program participants for a prescribed time period. In some cases, the observer may be given detailed guidelines about who or what to observe, when and how long to observe, and the method for recording that information. A tally sheet might be devised for such purposes. (If supervisors serve as observers they will need special training and guidance as the "halo effect" or the "horns effect" (a rating higher or lower than is fair due to predetermined biases) can impair their observations.

One way to enhance the credibility of observations is by demonstrating that the data from the observations is consistent, within acceptable limits, among different observers over time. An advantage of this method is that observations can be highly credible when seen as a report of what actually took place.

TABLE 19

EVALUATION STEPS BASED ON THE USE OF RECORDS

1. Develop a list of critical features.
2. Determine what records are already being kept that are available (for example, performance appraisals—changes in performance appraisals might indicate behavior changes).
3. Match the critical features list with available records. For each type of record, try to find a critical program feature about which the record might give information. Think about whether a record will yield evidence of duration or frequency of an activity.
4. Prepare a sampling plan for collecting records and a plan for transferring data from the records examined.
5. Consider a means for obtaining access to records that does not inconvenience other people.

Furthermore, observers can provide a point of view different from that of staff members who are more closely connected with the program. (This is especially true if observers are seen as disinterested viewers.) One disadvantage of the observation technique is that awareness of the observers' presence may alter what takes place. Also, much time is needed to develop observation instruments, to locate and train credible observers, and to organize schedules.

Events that might be observed during or after a career development effort are behavior changes toward colleagues and leaders, the way employees apply to their present jobs the information they have gained, changes in the way leaders guide their employees, increased assertiveness, or requests for more responsibility. Table 20 lists the critical steps in evaluation based on observations.

Self-Report Measures

Self-report measures are collected through interviews, questionnaires, logs, or journals. If collecting information from everyone who experienced the program is too time-consuming, self-report descriptions can be culled from a random sample of participants. Since different groups of participants in a program might have divergent perceptions, it is important to gather self-report information from all levels of employees within the organization who

---

TABLE 20

EVALUATION BASED ON OBSERVATIONS

1. List the critical program features.
2. Prepare descriptions of positive actions, such as assuming more personal responsibilities or seeking on-the-job training that participants might demonstrate after the program.
3. Prepare descriptions of negative actions (alternative but undesirable program side effects, such as demanding promotion today or complaining about the transfer policy). Describe the most likely ways in which things can go wrong so that observers will know what to document.
4. Choose an observation method and decide how long each observation time sample should last in order to yield acceptable data.
5. Prepare a sampling plan for conducting observations.
6. Prepare observer tally sheets.
7. Select and train observers.
8. Try out the instrument.
9. Inform the program staff about the forthcoming observation.
10. Conduct observations, then score and prepare data for interpretation and presentation.

---

have been involved in the program—nonexempt and exempt employees, first-line supervisors, middle managers, and members of senior management. Self-reports may also be solicited from members of the HR staff who supported the program and from clients or organizational peer groups who may have experienced spin-offs of program results.

Data generated using self-report measures is best used to substantiate or enhance other more quantifiable findings. Using this evaluation method by itself, however, may leave the practitioner open to questions of data validity. Those who are closest to a program will be inclined to see such information as highly credible, while those more distant from the program (higher levels of management) are less likely to trust the self-reported information published by the practitioner's staff. They have a point. Sometimes those providing self-report information have a vested interest in making the program look good or bad, and they may not even be aware of it. If, as often happens, certain subconscious mechanisms reduce cognitive dissonance, individuals may overlook (or rationalize) program shortcomings or disregard potential problem

---

CASE 35

A New Twist to Evaluating Training Classes

A telecommunications company decided to add an interesting evaluation component to its training classes. All participants in training were asked a series of questions that forced them to comment on their degree of "openness" to the particular topics being taught. By utilizing this series of questions in a variety of ways, with all their classes, the organization was able to make participants in their curriculum more aware of their own learning habits, and to gain a perspective on some of the barriers to classroom learning.

---

areas. A great many programs are judged to be successful if participants have had a good time or have experienced a high-energy, motivating presentation even though they have learned little that is of lasting value. The real test of a successful workshop or seminar lies in the amount of learning retained and the length of time that the information is retained by participants. Experiences that are enjoyable while imparting constructive knowledge will always rate high with participants, but first reactions often measure only the level of pleasure the program provided.

The *questionnaire* method of self-reporting has several advantages. It can (1) provide answers to a variety of questions in a relatively short period of time (especially if questionnaires are precoded), (2) be given to many employees throughout the company simultaneously without having to train interviewers, and (3) present uniformly organized information by asking all respondents for the same information. Questionnaires allow the respondent time to think before answering, thereby providing a chance for reflection and personal insight.

Questionnaires have disadvantages in that they do not provide the flexibility that interviews do. Some people are better able to express themselves in writing than others. And unless the wording of questions is carefully thought out and pilot-tested for clarity, it is not unlikely that respondents may have imposed their own unique interpretations on the questions, thereby providing little

---

CASE 36

Using a Follow-Up Survey to Track Results

A large bank followed up on its two-day on-site workshop with a sixty-day follow-up evaluation. Participants in the program were both managers and associates. Objectives included getting the associates to (1) take charge of their own development, (2) acquire the tools to do so, (3) understand the skills and behaviors needed for success, (4) set specific development goals, (5) draft a development plan for discussion with their manager, and (6) appreciate the role of diversity in the development process.

A two-page follow-up survey was sent to all participants and their managers. The survey was designed to measure the program's effectiveness and its impact on associate development practices. According to the survey findings, results of the program included:

- 96 percent of managers reported a strong or very strong impact on associates' level of ownership in their own development.
- 84 percent of associates had development discussion meetings with their managers; of these at least 20 percent had never had a development discussion before and 75 percent rated the value of this discussion as higher than before.
- Over 87 percent of associates had completed a development plan as a result of the program, and most participants and managers had great confidence in these goals.
- Over 93 percent of participants gained a greater understanding of the impact of diversity in the workplace.

Furthermore, associates reported a significant increase in the level of support for professional development from their managers.

---

usable data for analysis. The unpredictable rate of return poses another serious problem of using questionnaires. One must plan several appeals for the return of questionnaires if this method is to be effective.

Interviews, on the other hand, are good for those who communicate best verbally. Interviews permit flexibility and allow the interviewer time to pursue unanticipated lines of inquiry. The interviewer can often gain a great deal of information. Disadvantages are, however, that interviewing is time-consuming and that sometimes the interviewers can by their nonverbal or verbal behavior unduly influence the response of the interviewees.

It is important to remember when conducting interviews to always ask open-ended questions. Questions that can be answered yes or no and those that imply a specific answer will not generate a great deal of information. It may occasionally be necessary to probe participants in order to gain additional information. The interviewer may need to encourage the interviewee to give additional information relating to the previous question. Probes might be statements such as "Tell me more about that" or "Expand on that, please" or "What are some of the likely long-range consequences of that action?"

The major drawback to using interview data in evaluating a program lies in the difficulty experienced when trying to quantify and summarize it. Although feelings, opinion, and experiences can be extracted, they seldom fall into any but the most generalized categories for quantification. It is possible, however, to ask quantitative questions and use the open-ended approach to provide back-up data.

Logs, journals, and diaries are less formal descriptions of activities, experiences, and feelings written by a participant either during or after a specific career development activity. Asking people to keep self-reports with accounts of their experience can be an effective data-gathering device, provided there is agreement from participants and an understanding between participants and their managers that this will not in any way affect job standing. When analyzed at the end of the program, these accounts can aid the practitioner in understanding the positive and negative experiences of participants with various components of the program. In addition, the logs might reveal patterns of attitude change. Logs and journals can also be kept by leaders to record changes in the work habits of subordinates who have been involved in career development activities. Diaries, on the other hand, are more private self-report instruments. They are kept by participants themselves, and while they cannot be collected and read by program evaluators without prior agreement, participants can be encouraged to review them prior to providing interview or questionnaire responses or to use them as a source from which to provide evaluators with representative quotes or extracts.

The advantage of these informal procedures is that they provide information about a person's experiences and feelings. The disad-

CASE 37

Using Journals to Track Results

A telecommunications company used the journal approach to gather data from both leaders and employees participating in a career development effort. Journal questions included:

- What was your reaction to the learning experience? What are your thoughts at this time? What were the best new ideas you got from the learning experience? What are your concerns about career development?
- What are your hopes and concerns about your leader's reaction to his or her learning?
- How did you prepare for the trial career development discussion with your leader? What were you most apprehensive about? What did you feel most confident about?
- Comment on each of your development team meetings.
- What is the best outcome that this program and the whole career development effort at this company could produce? What are your realistic positive expectations? What is your worst fear?
- Has your perspective on career development changed from your first journal entry to the last? How?

Program participants, both leaders and employees, were asked to choose three complete responses out of their journal to submit to the program designer. These were submitted anonymously and were used by the design team to evaluate the outcomes of the development effort.

vantage lies in the problems of extracting, categorizing, and interpreting the information and in the ethical issues raised when using such information. To score and interpret information in this process also requires time and expertise. Accordingly, deciding to use logs and journals and establishing plans for collecting and using the information they contain must occur at the beginning of the program if this method is to be used.

Clearly, an advantage of this approach is that minimal demands are made on the career development staff to record data. Furthermore, by submitting these written reports, participants feel as if their experiences are noted and considered important, and

TABLE 21

EVALUATION BASED ON SELF-REPORT MEASURES

1. List the program's critical features and the questions you want answered.
2. Decide if you already have the information in existing records.
3. Decide whether to distribute questionnaires, to interview, or to do both.
4. Write questions, based on the critical program features, that will prompt people to tell you what they said and did differently as a result of participation in the program.
5. Assemble the questionnaire or interview instrument.
6. Determine how many times to distribute questionnaires or conduct interviews, when to do it, and to which people/groups.
7. Try out the instrument on a small subsample. (Revise if needed.)
8. Alert people that you will be requesting periodic information.
9. Administer the instrument according to a predetermined sampling plan.
10. Record data from questionnaires and interview instruments.
11. Prepare a data analysis summary.

they are more inclined to observe incremental changes in themselves and their behavior over time than they would be without this historical comparative data. Table 21 lists the key elements of evaluating based on self-report measures.

RETURN ON INVESTMENT—THE BOTTOM LINE

One of the most important, yet also most difficult, calculations about the effectiveness of a career development effort is the total cost savings for the organization. How can the organization put a price tag on the dollars that have been saved, and how does that compare with dollars that have been spent implementing the program?

Measuring the human return on investment of any program— be it a long-term career development effort or a one-time training endeavor—has been the subject of much debate and experimentation in business and industry. It requires that human resource costs be viewed as investments similar to capital investments and that the return on the dollars invested somehow be translated into quantifiable terms that can be compared with the investment expenditures.

One method for making such calculations is to compare earnings—the ultimate goal of most companies—with payroll expenses. Return on investment in human resources can be measured by dividing the total payroll costs (including fringes and training) into pretax earnings. A department that increases earnings faster than it increases payroll costs can be viewed as increasing its human return on investment. This may be due to higher employee productivity, increased employee skills, holding the line on salaries, or workforce reductions.

When such measurements are taken before and after a program aimed at human resource development, they may indicate some tangible results of that program. However, several problems are inherent in this method of measurement. First, there are likely to be numerous confounding variables operating during the measurement period that make it difficult to determine whether or not the program concerned is responsible for the noted results. At any given time other factors may be occurring—such as the introduction of new technology or new operating procedures—that could also be responsible for changes in earnings and payroll. And second, not all units of the organization are directly concerned with earnings. Thus, staff offices such as human resources or accounting would need different methods for measuring return on investment in human resources.

Another method of calculating the return on investment within the participating target group involves measuring changes in those cost areas that are most likely to be influenced by the career development program and other intervening variables. Three major areas that may be adapted to such measurement are reduced turnover, improved performance, and fewer grievances. Examples of cost savings calculations in these areas follow.

Reduced Turnover

The employee turnover rates within the participating group could be determined before and after the career development intervention. The change, expressed as a percentage of the prior rate, is one measure of the program's contribution to reduced turnover. As an example, suppose the turnover was initially 10 percent per year, and the postprogram rate drops to 8 percent; the turnover reduction is 2 percent per year, corresponding to an improvement of 20 percent. Of course, one obvious disclaimer is that the career development program is not performed in a vacuum; many outside factors will almost certainly influence the turnover rate, such as changes in the economy, management decisions, and variations in the demand for certain professional services.

Then one computes all of the costs associated with turnovers within the target group. These include severance pay for the departing employees; lost productivity during the periods their positions are vacant; and the recruitment, selection, and training of their replacements. These costs should be expressed on a per-turnover basis.

The resulting annual cost saving is simply the number of program participants, times the reduction in turnover rate, times the turnover cost. For example, the reduced turnover financial gain might be 300 participants times 2 percent less annual turnover times $20,000 replacement costs, which equals $120,000 per year.

Improved Performance

It should be stated immediately that increased productivity is difficult to quantify. There are, however, cases such as where there is increased sales volume or some other measurable quantity of work output, or alternatively, the need for a smaller number of employees to accomplish a specific task due to increased efficiency, job enrichment, or newly acquired skills on the part of current employees.

An example of a case involving increased sales volume might be the case of a retail store where sales in a particular department increase by 5 percent, from $200,000 per month to $210,000 for a productivity gain of $10,000 per month, after the completion of a career development effort.

An example of a case involving increased work output might be the case of an organization where administrative assistants, having identified career goals in common with company needs, complete some basic accounting courses, saving the company $35,000 per year for a bookkeeper.

Fewer Grievances

Improved compliance on the part of management with diversity goals may ultimately reduce the number of grievance actions with resultant savings in legal costs and back-pay settlements.

For example, if the incidence of employee grievances drops by 25 percent within a minority target group, the company might reduce its affirmative action legal expenses by several hundred thousand dollars per year, with corresponding savings in settlement costs.

There are also many important aspects to a career development effort for which the return on investment (ROI) must necessarily be assessed in nonmonetary currencies. These can include:

- Improved morale and commitment to the organization resulting from the feeling that the company cares about its employees
- Appreciation of existing skills and their applicability to other job functions within the organization
- Increased self-esteem and self-confidence
- Identification of individual career goals and the means to achieve them
- Heightened sense of community and the establishment of organizational support groups
- Increased understanding of internal human resource development processes, such as performance appraisals

It is also important to realize that the career development effort's payoff does not come only after the individual has moved through all six stages; there is substantial qualitative and quantitative return on investment for the individual and for the organization at the conclusion of each stage. During the preparation stage, leaders and practitioners may have developed their own lists of ROI factors for each stage (a good selling tool for top management), and they may now want to refer to it again to guide or check their program results. Table 22 shows the potential return on investment at each stage of the effort.

AT LEAST DOCUMENT

If serious evaluation is not possible, leaders and practitioners should at the very least document and report on the process. Documenting a career development effort details the way in which the various stages were implemented and makes results available to all those who need to use them further.

Few documentation efforts pay enough attention to the program processes that helped achieve certain outcomes. Although some reports might contain short descriptions of the program's major features—such as the workshops developed, the leader-employee interactions, the structural supports, and the special skill training programs—most reports leave readers with only a vague notion of how often and for what duration particular activities occurred or of how components combined to affect the daily life

TABLE 22

POTENTIAL RETURN ON INVESTMENT AT EACH STAGE

Stage	Return on Investment
Preparing	■ Increased organizational insight: Organization has assessment of how individuals view their careers and where the greatest problems lie. ■ Special selection of target groups: Group needs are identified. ■ Formalized planning: Organization has a formal plan for developing its human resources. ■ Employee commitment to program and organization: Individuals are apprised of programs and have opportunity to affect what happens to them. ■ Increased management commitment to organization goals: Managers are prepared and apprised of their role in the process.
Profiling	■ Increased self-understanding: Employees gain understanding of their own personal, technical, and conceptual skills, their values and preferred work contexts. ■ Accurate self-appraisal: Employees seek opportunities to test the realities of their self-assessments in their professional and personal net work. ■ Improved communication on performance appraisals: Employees will be able to determine their professional strengths and weaknesses and the areas that they wish to develop.
Targeting	■ Employee understanding of organizational goals and directions: Future trends and their impact on career discussions and alternatives are clear to employees. ■ Flexibility in career goals: Employees have set a variety of career goals. ■ Matching of organizational goals and employee goals: Goals are viable and used by the organization in its human resource planning. ■ Increased employee understanding of organizational job requirements: Employees will have clear understanding of performance criteria and performance expectations.

TABLE 22 (CONTINUED)

POTENTIAL RETURN ON INVESTMENT AT EACH STAGE

Stage	Return on Investment
Strategizing	■ Increased management-employee interaction: Development plans are devised and commitment is strengthened by dialogues between manager and employee. ■ Training and development options studied: Individuals are aware of strengths and deficiencies and of resources offered by the organization to improve certain skill areas. ■ Training and development needs identified: Practitioners are aware of the training and development that will be needed by employees and can formalize plans to offer such programs. ■ Goals and timetables developed: Affirmative action candidates develop action plans for mobility in the organization. These are in line with affirmative action goals. ■ Increased employee understanding of organizational direction: Individuals will be abreast of organizational directions and will be able to plan their careers accordingly. Employees will meet career goals.
Implementing	■ Improved selection of training and development activities: Employees are selective about the developmental options they enter. ■ Documentation efforts strengthened: Skills and competencies are strengthened by the organization as they are acquired by individuals. ■ Cost-effectiveness in training and development: Training programs that are frills (not related to any specific career goals) are eliminated.
Sustaining	■ Evaluation systems developed: Support is provided for improvements. ■ Career development efforts documented: Practitioners can enhance and continue the career development effort. ■ Reward systems strengthened: Compensation systems support other directions besides upward mobility. ■ Greater organizational flexibility: Organization will be able to keep abreast of and be responsive to changing workforce trends and patterns. ■ Improved work climate. Organization will have a healthy growth climate and stable workforce.

CASE 38

Documenting the Career Development Effort

A high-potential career development effort in a large chemical company documented the first program with an evaluation report. The report was organized to demonstrate the process used to evaluate the relative effectiveness of each of the major elements in the program. The evaluation objectives used to gather data included:

- Determining the overall effectiveness of the program from the perspective of all who participated (employees, leaders, and learning leaders)
- Obtaining information and recommendations to assist in future iterations of the program
- Determining the usefulness of each unique element of the program and its value added to the program
- Assessing the degree to which the program accelerated growth

The report furthermore contained information on each program element, such as:

- A brief summary of the particular element
- An overall analysis of the data
- Quotable quotes taken directly from interviews
- Recommendations from the interviewers as they related to each element

Focus group interviews were the main method used for collecting data from participants. Questions focused the group on (1) their overall reaction to the program as a whole, e.g., their memorable moments; (2) their reactions to each individual element, e.g., the highs and lows of each; (3) their recommendations for future programs; and (4) their insights and what they learned.

of employees in the organization. Few reports clearly picture what the program is actually like, and of those that do, most do not give enough attention to verifying the picture that is presented. Some form of final report is essential—it forces the practitioner to pay attention to all critical features, provides a way for others to continue the program once the first effort is completed, and helps the reader to understand the differences between a good and poor career development effort.

A report of program implementation should contain (1) a description in as much detail as possible of the interventions (such as workshops and counseling) and the structural elements (such as performance appraisal and job posting systems) that characterize the career development effort, and (2) a description of back-up data that comes from a variety of sources and ensures thoroughness and accuracy.

A Worthy Fuss

It is important to record a description of the career development effort for internal and possible external documentation purposes. This kind of documentation can be useful to an organization in a variety of ways. However, the job is not easy. Sometimes the expected outcomes of career development efforts are intangible and difficult to measure. Sometimes the outcomes are removed—they often occur after the program has concluded and the participants have moved on. (Career success stories, continued job mobility, and continued coaching of one's own employees are good examples.) In such instances, judging a program completely on the basis of immediate outcomes would be unfair. Even when career development activities result in intangible or removed outcomes, it is crucial to precisely specify the processes that were used.

A documented report may be the only description of the program that will remain after a particular career development effort has concluded. Reports should for that reason provide an accurate account of the program and include sufficient detail so that they can serve as a planning guide for those who might want to expand the career development effort to another division of the company. Furthermore, other professionals need to know the characteristics of the program—the materials, activities, interventions, and interchanges that brought about the program's outcomes. A documented report about a particular effort can strongly suggest to organization decision makers that using similar processes for other programs or aiming toward other similar goals is a positive move.

Clearly, knowing how a report will be used will help the practitioner to determine how much effort to invest in it as well as what information about actions and changes will be most useful to top management or planners. If accountability is the major reason for the documentation effort, the practitioner should be ready to provide back-up data to show whether, and to what extent, particular events vital to the process occurred and were successful. The more skeptical the audience, the greater the necessity for providing formal back-up data to verify the accuracy of the program description. Sometimes reports must be backed up with measurement, such as coded observations by trained observers, examination of program output, structured interviews, or questionnaires. Carefully planned and executed measurement will allow the practitioners to be reasonably certain that the information they report describes accurately the situation at hand, especially if the practitioner expects to confront a serious skeptic.

A documentation report on the implementation of a career development program should include as a minimum the following five sections:

1. *Summary Statement.* A summary should give readers a quick synopsis of what is contained in the report—why the program was conducted, the type of evaluation mechanisms used, and the major findings and recommendations of the evaluation.

2. *Program Description.* A description of the program context should focus on the settings (off-site, on-site), the employees involved, and special resources that were prepared and used. This section would also describe how the program was initiated, what it was supposed to do, and how resources were used. The origins of the program and historical background, the factors that went into preparing the program, and the selected target groups are all described in this section.

3. *Critical Features.* This section should describe the program's most critical features as prescribed by the original program design at the Preparing Stage. Here the practitioner could describe what the program was supposed to include, how much variation it allowed, its theory on philosophical stance, the rationale underlying the program, the provisions that were made for reviewing the program, and the results of planning meetings that helped to remedy programmatic problems as they occurred.

4. *Evaluation Measures.* This section should specify the focus of the evaluation, the range of measurement instruments for data collection, the checks that were made on validity and reliability, and the limitations or deficiencies that might be inherent in the sampling process.

5. *Program Results.* This section should describe the extent to which the program as implemented fits the design that was

originally planned at the Preparing Stage. It should describe what was found through analysis, noting variations of the program across divisions or time. The report should conclude with an interpretation of the results and suggestions for further program evaluation or program development.

Tell, Tell, Tell

Career development practitioners and leaders have responsibility not only for documenting the results of their efforts but also for distributing the report to various organizational audiences. Publicity is necessary for future efforts. There is no such thing as an evaluation that is free of political considerations. Presenting evaluation information provides an opportunity to gain continued support for the career development effort. The desires of various audiences should be seriously examined, both at the beginning of the evaluation and throughout the evaluation process. Already identified are the participant, the participant's leader, the organization's top management, and the career development practitioner. Additional audiences might include a customer or client, a group or division that did not yet participate in the program, or other members of the human resource development staff anxious to see the results. Neglecting to correctly identify one or more of these groups is a common mistake, and an ignored audience may cause problems and be nonsupportive of future program efforts. Identifying the audiences who are to receive the evaluation report is critical if the practitioners hope that their findings will lead to approved continuation of the career development efforts.

It is also important to find out what information each group needs and why it needs it. This is a vital component in producing a good evaluation design and in reporting evaluation results. Different groups want different information—often even when they ask the same question. Some groups will be certain and candid about what they need because they want the evaluation of the career development program to support a particular point of view they hold. Other audiences will not know what they want until they *don't* see it. If the career development practitioner wants the audience to listen carefully to the findings, attention must be given to each group and their specific idiosyncrasies.

Clearly, if the practitioner does not have evaluation experience and skills, this may not be the methodology selected at the

Sustaining Stage. Yet, attention to evaluation is becoming so extraordinarily important that practitioners can no longer afford to ignore it. The choices are wide and varied, an approach commensurate with the ability of the practitioner and budget of the organization must be considered at the outset.

NOW WHAT?

A completed and institutionalized Sustaining Stage does not mean that the practitioners' efforts are completed and that they can sit back on their laurels. Completion of one cycle merely means that the time has come to begin again. It may be that the time has come to expand the program. It may be time to try a different approach, one that is aimed at a different target group, or one more adapted to the organization.

Every organization is different. Managers will differ in their acceptance of and approach to career development, individual employees will want different outcomes and have different goals. Mistakes will be made, different barriers will be encountered, different aids and supports will be found each time a career development program is instituted. The first time around a practitioner may find it necessary to take each step carefully and weigh each move finitely. The next time around the process will be easier. Eventually, if all goes well, what develops may be totally different from what is suggested in these pages.

This book is not the be-all and end-all of career development; it is a guide, a starting point for those interested in this particular journey. When the journey begins, the pioneer needs help. This book is intended to provide that help. Once the way is known, it should bear the name of its discoverer; it should bear the imprint of the practitioner who blazed the next trail.

But what about the practitioner? Do practitioners ever take time to consider their own careers?

|8|

Participating Practitioners

*"We do not need competency skills for this life.
We need incompetency skills, the skills
of being effective beginners."*
−PETER VAILL

Career development practitioners are no different from other professionals. Just as doctors have excellent backgrounds and opportunities with which to guard their own health, lawyers have the resources to keep their own legal affairs in order, and accountants have the ability to balance their own books, career development practitioners have, by the very nature of their work, exceptional opportunities to define and enhance their own careers.

Practitioners know from experience how difficult it can be for busy employees and managers to address career issues in a thoughtful and carefully planned manner; in fact, the same constraints apply to their own lives and careers. Too many practitioners seem to assume that since they have responsibilities for the career planning of others, they can pursue their own development by osmosis. The attitude seems to be: "I spend days and weeks dealing with self-assessment and the issues involved in setting goals, so I'm naturally aware of my own needs and options." But is that really the case? Many practitioners have not even taken the surveys and exercises that they request be completed by program participants.

Practitioners' knowledge of the organization and the greater world of work, as well as their grasp of career planning tools, gives them a substantial advantage in making the career development process personally beneficial. The practitioner should have a more complete understanding of the organization and its resources, thereby making it easier to collect and analyze the information necessary to examine all options. This knowledge base provides a powerful career development tool for those professionals who are willing to practice for themselves what they typically have preached to others.

Something Gained

One very interesting and rich starting point for practitioners is to consider exactly what they have gained from their work in the career development arena—including professional skills, organizational knowledge, relationships with others, and of course, personal lessons learned along the way. Examining these factors can often stimulate a greater sense of extended alternatives than may have been previously recognized.

The skills that practitioners bring to bear in initiating and implementing career development programs can be transferred to a wide range of career options. For example, during the Preparing Stage, practitioners and leaders will develop or enhance their skills in planning, budgeting, and scheduling, as well as in negotiating with and gaining commitment from others. Many practitioners are also involved in conducting meetings and workshops at the succeeding stages and thus increase their skills in public presentation, training, and group leadership. The technical elements of the design and delivery of training sessions, program analysis, and financial management also add to the practitioner's skill repertoire.

It is important for practitioners to also recognize the interpersonal skills they have acquired through contact with program participants and with top managers who need to be informed of the progress of career development efforts. These may range from individual coaching to communication and conflict resolution skills—the abilities required to effectively work with, report to, and assist others, as well as skills in one-on-one negotiation, teamwork, and participative decision making.

KNOWLEDGE AND INFORMATION

Career development practitioners are in an ideal position to gather extensive information about their organization as well as about other organizations in their industry. They can then use this information to increase their own knowledge about options for personal career futures, as well as becoming better information providers to others.

For example, by collecting and cataloguing information about the organization, its future, and its human resource needs, practitioners gain a sense of probable future directions. They have also gained a valuable understanding of exactly how the six-stage process of career development works and why it is important to move through the step-by-step procedures in careful and logical sequence. By assisting others in the process, they begin to recognize how the stages can be used to facilitate their own development. And it is likely that when practitioners are working with others, they are also using the process to define personal goals and to mentally determine strategies for themselves. If practitioners have kept active in their own professional organizations, they will find that this knowledge and information is not only helpful but often absolutely critical to their own careers. Learning how others with similar backgrounds are using and applying their skills in other environments provides a wealth of creative ideas that can always be self-applied. Also, in a context where many HR specialties are being outsourced, the practitioner must continually be aware of what organizations would consider their skills and expertise as core to their mission. Keeping abreast and staying connected with professional groups is one way to keep vital information channels open.

RELATIONS WITH OTHERS

Throughout the implementation of the career development program, practitioners come into contact with individuals at all levels in the organization. Most practitioners also increase their contacts with individuals outside the organization, such as potential providers of resources from educational settings, other career development practitioners, and training and HR professionals from other organizations.

Practitioners should recognize the support and assistance they can receive from these persons for their own career development. These new contacts may be mentors who can offer advice based on their own experience, top level managers in a position to make decisions that assist practitioners' achievement of goals, or colleagues who can offer encouragement. Practitioners, because of the wide range of relationships developed through their work, are in an excellent position to form a network of resource persons who can greatly enhance movement toward career goals.

Another benefit is the visibility practitioners gain throughout the organization. The expertise that they have the opportunity to demonstrate becomes widely known, and successful practitioners are often recognized as people who can plan, organize, implement, and evaluate. Practitioners, of course, like everyone else, need to be able to talk convincingly about all these transferable skills. The skills required to design a systemic organization intervention are numerous, but if the practitioner is interested in a move to a line area (where many of these management skills are often required) or another staff area, or perhaps even another kind of organization completely, he or she will need to be exceedingly articulate and specific about the myriad of talents that were utilized in the launch and implementation of this effort. This implies a call to action on the part of practitioners in the form of an increased willingness to move through the career development process with the same concerted effort requested of program participants.

Beyond Professional Development

Practitioners may also need to lead the way to broadening the traditional definition of development from just professional growth as described in these chapters to a more holistic model that integrates a number of work and life arenas. This would more accurately reflect the reality of the complex network of life concerns that employees bring to the job. The chapters in this book have been concerned primarily with two of the four arenas of life: *employment,* finding satisfaction in the current job, and *development,* seeing satisfying options in the future. Two other arenas, due to the book's focus, have been omitted, but need to be addressed, albeit lightly, here. These are the equally important arenas of *commitment,* finding and developing satisfying relationships, and *nourishment,* taking care of mind, body, and spirit. The remainder of this chapter will be devoted to helping the practitioner look at each of these arenas, in order to understand and act on the need for balancing these elements. For if any of these areas is underdeveloped, individuals and, in turn, their organizations are likely to suffer (Jacobson and Kaye, 1993).

EMPLOYMENT: SATISFIED WITH THE PRESENT
We spend most of our waking hours doing our jobs, thinking about work, and getting to and from our workplaces. When we feel

good about our work, we tend to feel good about our lives. When we find our work unsatisfying and unrewarding, the opposite is true. Jay Rohrlich (1980) suggests that work defines who we are. Work is key to belonging in contemporary society. It's the label that others use to identify us and which we use to present ourselves to the world. According to Rohrlich, work gives us order. Work gives us a reason to get up in the morning and a place to go. We find comfort in our jobs and in seeing familiar faces at work. Even when we're about to come apart at the seams, we often (amazingly) manage to present a professional image at work. At those times, we recognize that work is what holds us together.

Work provides challenges. Most of us like the feeling that comes from having solved a tough problem that our work presents. Work offers tangible rewards. Salaries help individuals define the importance of their work and help determine their willingness to work. For many, pay influences one's level of motivation, satisfaction, and self-worth. Work thereby contributes to our psychological well-being. Most work involves meeting goals, and it is through the accomplishment of our objectives that we gain a sense of achievement. For many, work provides a guideline by which we measure success and failure. Practitioners should continually ask:

- Is my current work still interesting to me?
- Around what part of my current work do I feel the most excitement?
- Do I feel recognized, nurtured, challenged in my current work?

DEVELOPMENT: SEEING SATISFACTION IN THE FUTURE

Our vision of the future—whether conscious and calculated or subconscious and subtle—affects our self-identities, our feelings about ourselves and others, and our performances on and off the job. As we have seen throughout this book, the term *development* no longer connotes just higher salaries or higher job levels. It has come to mean doing something in the workplace that is personally meaningful. And if, in fact, development may not imply movement, then we still need to be able to define it as something we can get right where we are. Practitioners who are active learners, who embrace an attitude of continual or lifelong learning, will find this area a natural and easy one to maintain. These individuals will see exciting new skills to hone and knowledge areas to incorporate, all with an inherent element of risk built in. This will keep their devel-

opment adrenaline going—even in times of organization maintenance or downsizing. Practitioners should continually ask:

- What's next out there?
- How can I negotiate to do that more within my own
  current responsibilities?
- What will put me ahead of the game?
- What will ready me further for the future?

While these first two arenas are more natural for many, they do
not provide the vital balance that we all need so much in our lives.
The current organization climate requires us to do so much more
with so much less that it is easy to succumb to the pressures of late
hours, weekend catch-up, and early morning meetings. If this goes
on for too long, or gets too one-sided, we rob ourselves of time in
the other two critical arenas: commitment and nourishment.

COMMITMENT: FINDING SATISFACTION IN RELATIONSHIPS

Our connections with other people affect all aspects of our
lives, including work. Our personal relationships help determine
our feelings about ourselves, our work, and our futures. When our
relationships are good, they provide a network of valuable support
that can enhance our abilities to accomplish goals. When they're
bad, our relationships leave us feeling isolated. We may start to
doubt ourselves and everything we do.

The most rewarding relationships result from two-way commitments with people who are significant to us. From these relationships, we get a sense of security and connection. We may want
"our space" at times, but we want it in the context of knowing that
someone out there cares about us. Belonging to a family, a network
of friends, a group of colleagues, or a social, community, sport, or
political organization helps each of us define our identity further.

When we feel valued or needed by other people, we feel worthy.
This feeling readily translates into a feeling of confidence that
enables us to take charge, take initiative, and take risks. Relationships also help us solve problems. We have people to turn to for
advice or just to be heard. The more connected we are to a network
of supportive people, the more resources for information we have.
Even when we aren't actively soliciting help, valuable information
may sift through the network to us—information we can use in our
work and in our personal lives.

Often, the busier we are at work, the more we need the support of others. Recent research in the medical profession even suggests that individuals who maintain healthy relationships will actually live longer than those who are loners. Survival skills include forging relationships with colleagues and friends, establishing emotional ties with others, and maintaining relationships with people whom we can ask for assistance and advice. The practitioner must continually ask:

- Am I making time for the important relationships in my life?
- Am I expanding my own personal support group?
- When was the last time I spent some noninterrupted time with good friends? With family?

NOURISHMENT: SATISFYING OUR PHYSICAL, EMOTIONAL, AND SPIRITUAL NEEDS

We nourish ourselves when we set aside time to relax, regroup, and recoup. We experience further nourishment by trying out new things or by taking time to develop interests other than work. We can accomplish nourishment in various ways. One way is by "tuning out"—reading a novel, taking a nap, or watching television. Another way is by "tuning in"—getting in touch with our spiritual selves by practicing meditation, for example. Still, a third way to nourish ourselves is by venting tensions through such activities as sports and hobbies. This "toning up" is done by physically and mentally exerting ourselves in ways that are different from the activities we engage in at work. Many organizations have recognized this need by building up their company "campus" to include gyms and workout rooms. Some even have jogging paths, swimming pools, and even volleyball courts! These companies find, interestingly enough, that these facilities do pay for themselves. Employees have somewhere to go for a much-needed break, and the proximity of these physical spaces enables the employee to be less interruptive of his or her day.

It is so easy to forget that overwork can lessen our effectiveness. When we're involved in large-scale organizational projects, we may not see that there's a point beyond which performance starts to fade. People who don't take the time to nourish themselves may show physical and emotional signs of stress. Practitioners should continually ask:

- Am I rejuvenating myself outside of work?
- Am I giving myself permission to take a time-out?
- Am I taking care of myself the way I admonish others to take care of themselves?

ENJOYMENT: THE COMMON DENOMINATOR

Enjoyment is the thread that runs through and connects all aspects of balance. When we enjoy our work, our relationships, and our free time—and feel positive about our futures—we experience true balance. If we don't have enjoyment, then employment, commitment, development, and nourishment seem like so many demands we have to handle—if we could only find the time.

Balance isn't better time management; it's better boundary management. We *can* have it all, just not all at once. Balance means making choices and enjoying those choices.

Certainly, it is true that organizations cannot be overresponsible for assuring balance in the lives of each employee. However, because balance is an issue that so dramatically impacts employee performance, the organization can assess what it might be doing that discourages or even prevents it.

- Does the organization uphold a value system that promotes obsessive workaholism?
- Are families considered in decisions on relocation?
- Are benefits made available for childcare?
- Does promotional competition discourage personal and team morale and relationships?
- Is use of vacations and personal counseling encouraged?
- Do meetings start early in the morning or go well into the evening?
- Are employees expected to travel on weekends?

The challenge of balance is the dual responsibility of organizations and individuals. When individuals and organizations understand and act on the need for balancing the four elements, they are moving together toward a holistic workplace, one that recognizes a range of employee needs, the interconnectedness of those needs, and the relationship of such needs with achieving organizational goals. Career development efforts in the future will address more and more of these last two elements. Practitioners, in the ideal, should seek this balance in their own lives, and model it for others.

|9|

Postscript

One of the strongest messages for the new millennium is the one of self-accountability for one's own career. The entitlement age is rapidly disappearing, and the guarantees of the past are nothing more than a memory in many of the more progressive organizations. Corporations are responding to the wake-up call of constant and demanding changing economic conditions that are forcing companies to reevaluate their human resource requirements and commitments. Likewise, employees are being forced to take stock and redefine their job and career satisfaction in light of the new world of work.

Corporations are developing new attitudes and strategies to encourage employees to take the leadership role for developing their own career. These companies believe that their competitive advantage in the future depends on their capacity to create a development culture that promotes individual ability, not individual advancement; career resiliency, not company reliance; and career empowerment, not company entitlement.

More and more companies are espousing a philosophy that builds on strong performance management groundwork and provides a guided process for career growth and job satisfaction for every employee. These companies intend to benefit employees whether they stay or choose to seek opportunities elsewhere that more closely match their talents and aspirations.

The framework for this last chapter revolves around five basic recurring questions that plague the practitioner. Each will be explored briefly, each requires further refinement by the practitioner or leader. Each may help the practitioner who, after reading this book, still needs to sell the effort.

What Is Career Development Anyway?

Excellent companies today are committed to developing a process that benefits the organization as it strives to sustain a high-performing, competitive workforce ready to provide quality services and products to its global customer base. At the same time, they strive to provide every individual they employ with the opportunity to contribute to the company's success for as long as that is possible. When there is no longer a job/career fit, the company realizes that the employee is responsible for pursuing other options.

For these organizations, career development is not a program, but a process that integrates and supports ongoing activities, maximizing the value of on-the-job experience with training and development opportunities. Career development expands career options through challenging job assignments combined with education and training. It is a business decision-making process that fully involves its people by getting input from them on their career interests and expectations. This helps to strategically place them in positions that maximize their contribution to the success of the business and enables the organization and the individual to reach their maximum potential.

What Is the Business Need?

Simple: Career development makes good business sense. Fewer vacancies limit traditional opportunities for promotion, advancement, and upward mobility. Because of increased competition and technological advancements, our business environment is continually changing. To perform successfully in today's business world, all employees need to continue to improve their skills, whether they are technical, administrative, or managerial. Organizations recognize that their future prosperity depends on employees taking full advantage of their available human resources.

A well-developed career development process can enable an organization to tap its wealth of in-house talent for staffing, promotion, and development opportunities by matching the skills, experience, and aspirations of individual employees to the existing and future needs of the organization. In this way, an effective career development process contributes to the realization of core organization values and principles—most notably, the principles of employee development and communication. Through career development, organizations actively demonstrate their belief that it is indeed *people* who truly make the difference.

Who Are the Stakeholders?

In designing a system supportive of a development culture, a central theme of partnership must be developed. It is essential that career development be viewed as a shared responsibility between the employee, the leader or manager, and the organization. Each stakeholder has a specific and important role to play to assure an effective career development process.

THE INDIVIDUAL

Individual career planning can be compared to business planning. Business planning is essential for management to know where the organization is now, where it should be headed, and what strategies will get it there. Just as business plans are the vehicles used to maximize profits, so career and development plans are the vehicles available to employees to help them maximize job satisfaction and effectiveness.

Career development provides a framework to move employees from inertia to initiative, from seeing problems to seeing possibilities, from being critical of the organization to taking control of their own future. This awakening leads employees to develop a portfolio that includes transferable skills and competencies, realities about options, and ideas for concrete action planning. This empowers employees to be their own "talent agent," to be better able to sell themselves when the organization has a "casting call" for new projects and opportunities. Being ready and able to articulate their career aspirations and expectations not only helps employees but also benefits the organization who can identify those who are prepared to meet the future and the challenges it brings. Those who choose to ignore the "writing on the wall" will be ignored, and they will have difficulty finding job/career satisfaction from any organization.

THE TEAM LEADER/MANAGER

While the individual has primary responsibility for directing his or her own career, the manager or team leader needs to be the career advocate. Just like the athlete who uses the assistance of a "coach" to improve his or her game, the employee needs a "career coach." The manager must use a variety of familiar management skills and apply them to the career context. Frequent discussions with employees about what they do best and what they want to do should be routine, not a reluctant part of the manager's responsibilities. The manager should provide candid feedback about the employees' strengths and weaknesses, offer advice when needed regarding realistic career expectations in the organization, link the employees formally and informally to the available resources, and offer support for the development plan. This type of ongoing dialogue enhances productivity and results in a partnership that aids the employee match with positions or projects that maximize their talents.

THE ORGANIZATION

The organization supports the process by developing and maintaining systems and structures that provide needed information, offer development opportunities, and establish evaluation and reward systems that encourage managers to develop people, and employees to develop themselves. A shared responsibility with the individual and manager leads developmentally minded organizations to these core beliefs:

- Employees are empowered to learn and grow in their careers.
- People have the opportunity and tools to develop their knowledge and skills to the fullest potential.
- Career development is a process that enables people to make cross-functional and cross-divisional moves where they have a strong interest, and where there is value to the organization is essential.
- Career development is integrated with performance management, team building, compensation, individual business needs, and recruitment systems.
- Employees take responsibility for their career development.
- Career development through management and specialist paths is equally valued and fully supported.

What Happens to Career Development During Downsizing?

The significance of a career development effort is particularly paradoxical in light of many company downsizing and restructuring activities. Developing a talent pool in the midst of downsizing seems, at first, contradictory. However, this is a reality that many companies are forced to deal with in corporate America. Those that respond quickly and effectively to the new corporate agenda of strategically developing human resource talent while simultaneously experiencing growth or no-growth pains will gain a competitive edge in the marketplace and become a model of success for others to follow.

The "new employment contract" requires individuals to shift paradigms from an employment mentality to an employability mind-set. Downsizing is likely to continue to be a reality in many corporations. The key is resiliency for employers and employees. It may be called restructuring, rightsizing, or realignment, but the truth is, the employer must flex with the economic conditions. For employees, the employment continuum requires that they always be prepared and that they alone determine if they're headed for opportunity or obsolescence. If employees are laid off, having a career plan allows them to be more responsive and seize opportunities that match their experience, needs, and desires. If an individual is spared by one downsizing, instead of relaxing, this person must realize that he or she could become a target the next time economic conditions force the company's hand. Again, the "career-ready" employee realizes it is not good enough to just survive; it is important to "thrive" in a constantly changing business environment that continues to shift, redesign work process, and adapt to a team-oriented mode.

What Is the Bottom Line?

For some individuals career planning may come naturally and instinctively. They know how to evaluate their strengths, they know what they want to do, and they develop strategies to achieve their goals. However, for employees who have developed a co-dependency with the organization there needs to be a more proactive and structured approach to self-development. When we view career development as a strategic imperative and design systems that create a development culture, we prepare our employees for the business challenges of the new millennium. And instead of being the "parent" to employees we become learning partners with them. Everyone benefits when we create a development culture for employees who can add value and make a contribution to an organization's goals and objectives. When individuals have the opportunity to determine their professional and personal goals they are more likely and willing to be independent instead of codependent, to learn instead of lament, to produce and perform instead of procrastinate, to be empowered instead of demanding entitlements.

References

Barnes, Kim. *Exercising Influence and Getting Results.* Berkeley, Calif.: Barnes and Conti, 1994.

Bernstein, Beverly. *The Feedback Wheel.* Scranton, Pa.: Career Systems International, 1991.

Bernstein, Beverly, and Kaye, Beverly. *Connections: A Networking Map.* Scranton, Pa.: Career Systems International, 1990.

Bernstein, Beverly, and Kaye, Beverly. *Mentworking™: Building Relationships for the 21st Century.* Scranton, Pa.: Career Systems International, 1996.

"Career Leverage Inventory." Scranton, Pa.: Career Systems International, 1994.

Farren, Caela. *Who's Running Your Career?: Creating Work Stability in Unstable Times.* Austin, Tex.: Bard-Stephen Press, 1996.

Gutteridge, Thomas, Leibowitz, Zandy, and Shore, Jane. *Organizational Career Development: Benchmarks for Building a World-Class Workforce.* San Francisco: Jossey-Bass, 1993.

Hackman, Richard, and Suttle, Lloyd. "Work Design." In *Improving Life at Work.* Santa Monica, Calif.: Goodyear, 1977.

Jacobson, Betsy, and Kaye, Beverly. "Balancing Act." *Training & Development Journal,* February 1993.

Kaye, Beverly. "Advisory Group on the Seven C's." *Training & Development Journal,* January 1992.

Kaye, Beverly, and Jacobson, Betsy. "Mentoring: A Group Guide." *Training & Development Journal,* April 1995.

Kaye, Beverly, and Jacobson, Beverly. "Reframing Mentoring." *Training & Development Journal,* August 1996.

Kaye, Beverly, and Leibowitz, Zandy. "Career Development, Don't Let It Fizzle." *HR Magazine,* September 1994.

Kirkpatrick, Donald L. *How to Manage Change Effectively.* San Francisco: Jossey-Bass, 1985.

Lombardo, Michael, and Eichinger, Robert. *Eighty-Eight Assignments for Development in Place: Enhancing the Development Challenge of Existing Jobs.* Greensboro, N.C.: Center for Creative Leadership, 1989.

McKee, Kathryn, and Kaye, Beverly. *New Compensation Strategies for New Career Patterns.* American Society for Personnel Administration, 1989.

McMahon, John E., and Yeager, Joseph. "Manpower and Career Planning." In Robert Craig (ed.), *Training and Development Handbook*, 2nd ed. New York: McGraw-Hill, 1976.

Naisbitt, John. *Megatrends Asia: Eight Megatrends That Are Reshaping Our World*. New York: Simon & Schuster, 1996.

Rohrlich, Jay. *Work and Love: The Crucial Balance*. New York: Harmony Books, 1980.

Schön, Donald. *Beyond the Stable State*. New York: W.W. Norton, 1971.

Thomas, Roosevelt. *Beyond Race and Gender: Unleashing the Power of Your Total Workforce by Managing Diversity*. New York: AMACOM, 1991.

Vaill, Peter. *Learning as a Way of Being: Strategies for Survival in a World of Permanent White Water*. San Francisco: Jossey-Bass, 1996.

Waterman, R. H., Waterman, J. A., and Collard, B. A. "Toward a Career Resilient Workforce." *Harvard Business Review*, 1994.

Resources

Suggested career planning books available from your local library or bookstore.

The Age of Paradox. Charles Handy. Harvard Business School Press, 1995. In this book, one of the brilliant and engaging thinkers of our day helps to search for order in a time of numbingly rapid change. The content ranges widely over business, family, education, citizenship, money, relationships, and myriad other subjects that touch the very core of our search for meaning and argues that although the paradoxes of modern times cannot be solved, they can be managed.

The Age of Unreason. Charles Handy. Harvard Business School Press, 1990.
The future world of work looks mighty different from the way it looks now. Catch a glimpse of it before it bowls you over.

Altered Ambitions: What's Next in Your Life? Betsy Jaffe. Fine, 1991. When Jaffe asks women if their lives are different from what they expected at age 25, 40, or even 60, she hears a resounding "Yes." Designed to help women be more flexible, savvy, and open to the changes they face in the 1990s and beyond, it shows how to reshape one's career, relationships, and health by tapping into strengths and overcoming weaknesses.

Beyond Workplace 2000. Joseph H. Boyett with Jimmie T. Boyett. Nal-Dutton, 1995.
Using examples from many actual companies, this extraordinary and insightful book provides not only a blueprint for the company of tomorrow, but a survival manual for working Americans who find themselves at the corner of all this change.

The Career Is Dead; Long Live the Career. Douglas T. Hall. Jossey-Bass, 1996.
This book shows that a "new career contract"—under which people adapt quickly, learn continuously, and change their work identities over time—is indeed alive and well in the best-managed organizations.

The Career Trap. Jeffrey G. Allen. AMACON, 1995.
Most people hit a wall after ten years in a career. This book demonstrates how to vault that wall by assessing your skills, identifying potential opportunities, and landing a better job with a raise in pay.

The Challenge of Change in Organizations. Nancy J. Barger and Linda K. Kirby. Davies-Black, 1995.
This book shows how to provide people with the kind of information and support they need to deal positively with the impact of change on their work lives. It focuses on what people as individuals need in times of change and transition.

Changing Course, A Positive Approach to a New Job or Lifestyle. Maggie Smith. Pfeiffer, 1994.
This book shows how to manage major changes in our lives, both professional and personal, and turn them into paths for new, energizing growth.

Competing for the Future. Gary Hamel and C. K. Prahalad. Harvard Business School Press, 1994.
This volume offers a blueprint for what your company must be doing today if it is to occupy the competitive high ground of the future. It is both a handbook for industry revolutions and a guide to creating the markets of tomorrow.

Danger in the Comfort Zone. Judith Bardwick. AMACOM, 1991.
This book examines the phenomenon of the entitlement mentality in the American workforce and people's preoccupation with their rewards rather than their responsibilities.

Designing Career Development Systems. Zandy Leibowitz, Caela Farren, and Beverly Kaye. Jossey-Bass, 1986.
Offering a fundamental look at introducing a systems approach to career development and management in an organization, this is a primer for any human resource professional or manager considering a revamp or re-creation of career development.

Excelerate. Nuala Beck. HarperCollins, 1995.
Beck's much noted theory of the New Economy is all about transformation. It's about moving away from old established industries. Replacing them are high-knowledge industries and other sectors that revitalize themselves by adapting new technology and taking on new markets.

The Changing Nature of Work. Ann Howard. Jossey-Bass, 1995.
This book envisions the future of work, its effect on workers and organizations, and the expanded knowledge that will be needed to optimize its returns. It examines critical postindustrial transformations in work, workers, and the experience of working and assesses the implications of those changes.

The Fourth Wave. Herman Maynard and Sue Mehrtens. Berrett-Koehler, 1993.
The Fourth Wave examines the ways business has changed in the Second and Third Waves and describes ways it must continue to change in the Fourth. The changes concern the basics—how an institution is organized, how it defines wealth, how it relates to surrounding communities, how it responds to environmental needs, and how it takes part in the political process.

From Chaos to Confidence. Susan M. Campbell. Simon & Schuster, 1995.
This book may be used as a self-study course on how to embrace the change process, beginning with helping one recognize how to resist change and explore how to grow beyond this resistance at one's own pace. Through Campbell's six-step approach, managers, and workers as well, can come to view chaos and conflict as opportunity.

From Downsizing to Recovery. Richard L Knowdell, Elizabeth Branstead, and Milan Moravec. Davies-Black, 1994.

Herein are options for downsizing that promote corporate health while maintaining humanity in dealing with employees. This book looks at outplacement from three perspectives: the long-range business perspective of the downsizing organization, the immediate crisis perspective of the terminating manager, and the traumatic perspective of the employee affected by the downsizing.

Healing the Wounds: Overcoming the Trauma of Layoffs and Revitalizing Downsized Organizations. David M. Noer. Jossey-Bass, 1993.

This volume provides human resource and other corporate professionals with a model and guidelines for revitalizing an organization hit by change. While it speaks rather specifically to needs arising from downsizing, the strategies are applicable to all organizational change initiatives. There are comprehensive sections that explore the irrevocable shift in the psychological contract between employee and organization, as well as specific pragmatic coping mechanisms for both partners.

JobShift: How to Prosper in a Workplace Without Jobs. William Bridges. Addison-Wesley, 1994.

This book has an individual, or employee, perspective. It describes how our vision of a job that we grew up with is vanishing and shows how we can thrive in this de-jobbed future. It suggests that we change the way we think about work and workers.

The Learning Edge. Calhoun W. Wick and Lu Stanton Leon. McGraw-Hill, 1993.

Responding to a crucial new market reality, this book offers a dynamic, concrete approach all managers and executives can use to create the capabilities needed for success. It presents a compelling examination of how individuals and organizations use intentional learning as the activator and accelerator for success.

Life Launch: A Passionate Guide to the Rest of Your Life. Frederick M. Hudson and Pamela D. McLean. Hudson Institute, 1994.

This unique book provides the tools for productively approaching change during the adult years with confidence, vigor, and excitement.

Life Skills: Taking Charge of Your Personal and Professional Growth. Richard J. Leider. Pfeiffer, 1993.

Written for working professionals, this thought-provoking book teaches you how to align your career objective, talents, and deepest values. This book leads you through a personal discovery of the vision, vitality, and meaning in your life.

The Lifetime Career Manager: New Strategies for a New Era. James C. Cahrera and Charles F. Albrecht, Jr. Adams Publishing, 1995.

This book shows how to plan a comprehensive career strategy based on your goals, not those of the organization you work for. It helps you recognize danger signals, avoid career crises, and make the best decisions, including how best to attain your goals in your next job if you decide it's time to leave.

Managing the Future. Robert B. Tucker. Berkeley Books, 1991.
This is a guide for business leaders of the current decade. The author recounts great corporate triumphs and disasters of the last several decades—and shows what it takes to keep business far ahead of the pack.

Networking: How to Enrich Your Life and Get Things Done. Donald R. Woods and Shirley D. Ormerod. Pfeiffer, 1993.
This step-by-step workbook defines what networking really is, introduces the process of "bridging" from one network to another, and helps you recognize and reinforce your networking strengths.

Organization Career Development: Benchmarks for Building a World-Class Workforce. Thomas Gutteridge, Zandy Leibowitz, and Jane Shore. Jossey-Bass, 1994.
Organization career development has evolved over the last several decades as a key business strategy for improving workforce effectiveness. This book gives benchmarking data for human resource professionals that provide global insight into the same practice.

Rekindling Commitment. Dennis T. Jaffe, Cynthia D. Scott, and Glenn R. Tobo. Jossey-Bass, 1994.
This book is a road map to becoming the CEO of your own job and a leader for organizational change. It shows how you can secure your own future and the future of your organization by responding actively, creatively, and effectively to the demands of the organization in flux.

Repacking Your Bags. Richard Leider and David Shapiro. Berrett-Koehler, 1995.
This book is written for those who are midway on their journey through life, but it would undoubtedly be useful for people on an earlier portion of the trip. "Living passionately for today and purposefully for tomorrow."

Shifting Gears: Thriving in the New Economy. Nuala Beck. HarperCollins, 1992.
This volume discusses how the new world differs from the old, comfortable one. Beck's research indicates four growth sectors in the new economy: (1) Computers and semiconductors; (2) Health and medical; (3) Communications and telecommunications; (4) Instrumentation.

What Color Is Your Parachute? Richard Nelson Bolles. Ten Speed Press, 1995.
This guide for job seekers has been a perennial on the best-seller list of the *New York Times* since its publication in 1972.

Working Without a Net. Morris Schechtman. Prentice-Hall, 1994.
In response to the fundamental changes sweeping corporate America, this book presents a cutting-edge management philosophy that challenges unrealistic, outdated approaches. The author teaches the essential skills for adapting to a rapidly expanding corporate culture—or to any organization or situation where structure and vision are needed.

About the Author

Beverly Kaye, Ph.D., is president of Career Systems International in Scranton, Pennsylvania. A prolific writer, sought-after lecturer, and leading management consultant, she has been recognized as a leader in the field of career development for more than twenty years.

Kaye has devoted her career to researching corporate strategies for retaining knowledge workers and the significance of attitudes to organizations and individual careers. With her Career Systems associates, she has been able to apply her expertise to the design and delivery of effective career development and talent management systems in organizations worldwide. She has created training programs and strategies to link development and retention to other human resource and business initiatives in organizations.

Kaye's cutting-edge management and career development programs are used by such leading corporations as American Express, Amgen, Compaq, Lucent, United Airlines, Chrysler, Nortel, and Sears. Kaye has received many honors and awards for her work in this field including the prestigious Best Practice Award from the American Society for Training and Development for her work with corporate clients Dow Corning, Bechtel, Chevron, and First USA.

A prolific writer, Kaye is coauthor of *Love 'Em or Lose 'Em: Getting Good People to Stay* (Berrett-Koehler, 1999), a best-seller that shares her latest research on management strategies for developing and retaining today's knowledge workers. She has also published more than forty articles in professional publications including *Training & Development, Workforce,* and *HR Magazine.* She is frequently called upon by the news media to comment on career development and retention topics. Recent interviews appeared in the *New York Times,* the *Los Angeles Times,* the *Chicago Tribune, Time, Fortune,* the *Washington Post,* and *USA Today.*

Career Systems International offers Kaye's vast portfolio of training tools to companies worldwide. Focusing on career development, talent retention, and formal mentoring programs, these tools are available in various formats to satisfy a variety of business needs. For a catalog of products or more information, call Career Systems International at (800) 577-6916, fax at (570) 346-8606, or write to 900 James Avenue, Scranton, PA 18510. You can also visit Kaye's corporate web site at www.careersystemsintl.com or her retention site at www.keepem.com.

Index

Organizational planning, 145–147
Organizational politics, 163–165
  approaches to thinking in, 165
Organizational profile, 176, 177
Organizations
  as marketplace for individual development, 181–182
  payoffs for, 17
  shared responsibility for career development, 274–275
  support groups within, 212–213
  value systems of, 176–178
Orientation programs, 232
Outplacement counseling, 44, 193
  typical objectives of, 194
Outplacement services, 36, 52, 128, 129
Outputs, 58–59
Overspecialization, preventing, 123

Participation, in career development, 7–8
Performance, 24
  developing criteria, 60–61
  improved, 59, 253
  standards of, 98
Performance Appraisal Training for Both Managers and Employees (case), 100
Performance appraisals, 35, 40, 99, 230–231
  annual, 52
  evaluating, 41
  past, 76
  programs, 26
Performance management systems, 5
Personal skills, evaluation of, 10
Personal styles, 92
Personality tests, 52
Person-to-organization mismatch, 128
Pilot program, 56
Plan development, 187–188. *See also* Career development; Development
  actions, 189
  deadlines, 190–191
  determining needs and desires, 188–189
  resources available, 190
  specifying actions, 189
Planning, 9. *See also* Preparing Stage
  as essential component of Preparing Stage, 58–73
  risks, 70
Planning teams, as communication technique, 233
Political trends, 23
Politics, in organizations, 163–165

Power, 32
Practitioners, 8, 21
  addressing future trends, 22
  broadening the traditional definition of development, 266–270
  dealing with resistance to change, 27
  developing relationships with others, 265–266
  participating, 263–270
  payoffs for, 19
  responsibilities, 223–224
  role in Strategizing Stage, 195–196
  roles of, 68–69, 105
  skills acquired through participation, 264–266
  visibility gained by, 266
Preparing Stage, 9–10, 21–73
  analysis, 21
  planning process, 58–73
Preretirement counseling, 44
Preretirement services, 36
Priority-setting, 82
Problem solving, 27, 89, 211
  networking and, 166
Problems
  associated with change, 27
  human resource, 60
Process mechanisms, 64
Productivity, 4
  increasing, 59
  low, 5, 176
  maintaining, 4
Profession categories, 109
Profiling Stage, 10–11, 75–106
  components, 75–77
  identification phase of, 77–84
  influence during, 161–162
  performance appraisals during, 99
  responsibilities, 105
  value of, 76
Profitability, 24
Program participants, success indicators for, 63
Projects, assigning temporary 211–212
Promote-from-within training program, 126
Promoting Downshifting: A Matter of Choice (case), 125
Publications, as valuable indicators of future directions, 140
Publicity, necessity of, 260
Public-speaking groups, 218

Quality, 4
Quality initiatives, 231
Questioning, 53
Questionnaire method of self-reporting, 247–248

If you find the mini-cases sprinkled throughout this book to be helpful in sparking your own creativity, we would like to invite you to participate in a learning network to continue this kind of sharing. Career Systems International in Scranton will publish a newsletter of practitioner cases several times a year; we'd love to help others gain the benefit of your experience.

To keep it simple, just give us your ideas (a paragraph or two will do) within any of the following parts of the book:

Preparing: Ideas for process start-up, for example, advisory groups, surveys, focus groups, and data collection

Profiling: Ideas for self-assessment or reality-testing activities (workshop, self-directed, computer-driven, or online activities); ideas for systems that support this process

Targeting: Ideas for delivering information related to changes in the business world; ideas for stimulating goal setting, option-thinking, etc.

Strategizing: Ideas for planning tools, of any kind, or for organization support mechanisms

Implementing: Ideas for linking training, education, or assignments to the career development plan; ideas for monitoring, assessing, and storing this information

Sustaining: Ideas for keeping the process alive, for rewards, or any ideas for organization sustaining structures

Please send all ideas to:

Career Systems International
900 James Avenue
Scranton, PA 18510
1-800-577-6916
Fax 717-346-8606